T0289801

SHAREWORTHY

ROBIN LANDA
& GREG BRAUN

SHARE
WORTHY

Advertising That Creates
Powerful Connections
Through Storytelling

Columbia Business School
Publishing

Columbia University Press

Publishers Since 1893

New York   Chichester, West Sussex

cup.columbia.edu

Copyright © 2024 Greg Braun and Robin Landa

All rights reserved

Library of Congress Cataloging-in-Publication Data

Names: Braun, Greg (Writer of Shareworthy), author. | Landa, Robin, author.

Title: Shareworthy : advertising that creates powerful connections
   through storytelling / Greg Braun and Robin Landa.

Description: New York : Columbia University Press, [2024] | Includes index.

Identifiers: LCCN 2023053890 | ISBN 9780231208260 (hardback) |
   ISBN 9780231557344 (ebook)

Subjects: LCSH: Brand name products. | Branding (Marketing) |
   Advertising. | Storytelling.

Classification: LCC HD69.B7 B739 2024 | DDC 659.1—dc23/eng/20240131

LC record available at https://lccn.loc.gov/2023053890

Printed in the United States of America

Cover design: Ana Carolina Mitchell

To my wife Kris and my daughter Kaia, I dedicate this book to you.

—Greg Braun

For my husband, Harry, and my daughter, Hayley. I love you more than you'll ever know.

—Robin Landa

CONTENTS

FOREWORD

I t's estimated that 150,000 new videos are uploaded to YouTube every minute, equating to thirty thousand hours of new content per hour.

And in our industry alone, it's estimated people are exposed to anywhere from four thousand to ten thousand ad messages per day.

Which is to say, people are inundated, smothered, and overwhelmed with messages. So many messages, in fact, that most get lost in the ether. Add to this ad-blocking technology, which gives people the power to avoid anything they don't want to see, and we find ourselves faced with an existential question:

Going forward, how do we achieve the simple act of connecting with people?

The answer is simple yet challenging:

By creating work people voluntarily seek out rather than deflect.
By creating work that gets buzz and becomes part of the zeitgeist.
By creating work that breathes fresh air into the culture rather than pollutes it.
By creating work that means something beyond just the product being sold.
What kind of work is this?

Simply put, brilliant and purposeful storytelling. Stories are how humankind has always learned and understood things.

"Sometimes reality is too complex; stories give it form."—Jean-Luc Godard
"Those who tell stories rule the world."—Hopi proverb
"Some stories may be unjustly forgotten; no stories are unjustly remembered."—W.H. Auden

Robin and Greg have written a book that will help you understand how to tell stories that mean something to people in today's climate. Stories that demonstrate purpose and heart. Stories that combine selling with ethics to create something different.

They have an important story to tell, read on.

David Lubars
Chief Creative Officer
BBDO Worldwide

ACKNOWLEDGMENTS

Many of our industry's most talented and accomplished leaders were willing to take time away from their professional responsibilities and busy lives to share their expertise to contribute to this book. So many that we are unable to list them all here. We are not just grateful to each of them for their generous support, a tribute to the collaborative culture of the advertising industry, but humbled, encouraged, and awed by all that they do.

In that spirit, we want to offer deep thanks to our friends and colleagues, Dr. Stylés Akira, Cristiana Boccassini, Mike Bokman, Lucy Burton, Luciana Cani, Will Chau, Dong Chen, Valerie Cheng Madon, Brett Colliver, Erin Evon, Sophie Gold, Pancho González, Melissa Grady Dias, Greg Hahn, Evan Horowitz, Ben Howard, Harsh Kapadia, Kevin Koller, Owen Lee, Eoin McLaughlin, David Mesfin, Dawit N. M., Ivo Purvis, Jaime Robinson, Luiz Sanches, Derek Sherman, Jo Shoesmith, Guan Hin Tay, Simon Usifo, Ellis Verdi, Thea Von Engelbrechten, Ben Wagner, Alex White, Susan Young, and so many other brilliant creators who shape the media landscape with their extraordinary brand stories. We extend a very special thanks to David Lubars for so eloquently writing the foreword to this book. To all of them, old friends and new ones, we are happily in your debt.

We value the true partnership and standards of excellence exemplified by Myles Thompson, publisher and founder of Columbia Business School Publishing, and Brian C. Smith, associate editor at Columbia University Press. Working with you has been a privilege in every sense of the word.

For their insights and support, we thank Steven Au, Dr. Jill Bellinson, Rafael Bracero, Deborah Ceballos, Isabella Cecconi, Meaghan Dee, Diane Gibbs, Gary Goldsmith, Rose Gonnella, Dr. William Rowmanowski, Gerald Schoenhoff, and Neil Teixeira.

At Kean University, Robin is grateful to Dr. Lamont Repollet, president; Dr. David Birdsell, provost and senior vice president of academic affairs; Dr. Laura Baecher, associate provost for faculty development; David Mohney, dean, Michael Graves College; Rose Gonnella, associate dean, Michael Graves College; Reenat Munshi and the Office of Research and Sponsored Programs; and all of Robin's Michael Graves College colleagues. Great thanks to art director, Ana Carolina Mitchell who designed the *Shareworthy* book cover and to the student design team who worked with us—Elena Pejovska, Patrycja Sliwowska, and Michael Scarpelli.

As for Greg, any success he's managed in his life, he owes to the loving and unwavering support of his family, who continue to be his inspiration. As for Robin, she is deeply grateful for her husband's, daughter's, and friends' steadfast support and excellent feedback.

SHAREWORTHY

INTRODUCTION

WHAT PEOPLE WANT

On a summer afternoon in August, Joe was playing stickball on a street in Chicago. Even though the sun was pouring down on him, Joe always kept his eye on the ball. The only thing that could distract Joe was the sound of the Good Humor ice cream truck's tune. That little song meant he soon would have a frozen treat, one that he and his buddies waited for each day.

For one hundred years, Good Humor has been serving its ice cream from trucks. And their jingle was a beloved cue to children. Until recently.

The brand was about to celebrate its centennial when a nationwide reckoning on social injustice in the United States thrust the ice cream brand's jingle into a cultural conversation. When the origins of the song "Turkey in the Straw" were made known and went viral on social media, Good Humor could have responded differently. However, Good Humor "listened to the tone of the country, and set out to change the tune," according to their communications firm, Edelman.[1] Although Good Humor had sold its fleet of vehicles to ice cream distributors and individuals in 1976 to focus on selling their brand in grocery stores, the brand responded, "It had been ages since Good Humor made a splash in the cultural conversation, so on its 100-year anniversary, the brand wanted to use the moment to raise its profile in culture and become top of mind for consumers."[2]

Good Humor turned to RZA—rapper, composer, and founder of Wu-Tang Clan—to compose a new ice cream truck jingle to represent all communities, and they made it available to any ice cream truck vendor. A new jingle, composed by a successful Black artist, replaced notes from a two-hundred-year-old racist anthem. Across the news media and social media platforms, people showed deep appreciation for Good Humor's actions.

All shareworthy stories have use-value, how they satisfy a social need or audience's want as afforded by their attributes, whether that's entertainment, information, or inspiration.

WHAT THIS BOOK OFFERS YOU

You might be born to art direct or write. Or born to lead a business or agency. You might know what advertising does and why. But this book offers an actionable roadmap for generating the kind of creative advertising that people willingly share within their own social circles. Case studies and interviews with eminent creative professionals worldwide provide an exclusive look into the thinking behind award-winning campaigns from across the globe. This book provides thought-provoking content to enhance your knowledge and further your success.

As the retired dep. global chief creative officer of Commonwealth/McCann, Greg Braun brings his vast industry experience to this book. He's worked on such brands as Chevrolet, Toyota, Starbucks, United Airlines, Citibank, and Hyundai and has created work for the Super Bowl, the Oscars, and the FIFA World Cup. Braun's work has been recognized by the major awards shows, including Cannes, the One Show, the Clios, and Effies, and he's been a judge for the One Show, Clios, NY Festivals, London Internationals, and the Emmy Awards.

Robin Landa is a bestselling author, creativity expert, and legendary university professor who brings her ability to break down complex information into accessible content. Together, Landa and Braun offer great insights into shareworthy inclusive advertising that recognizes the diversity of people's views across media. Revealing the significance and creation of engaging advertising from creative to business to ethics, this book also provides ways for readers to harness its power to produce responsible, inclusive, and resonant advertising.

This book includes perspectives from diverse and global communities; we present award-winning case studies to help readers understand complex ideas and the methodologies employed by successful brands. As the peer reviewers noted, we make a case for why an inclusive approach to advertising storytelling will lead to more successful outcomes and elevate equity, and we emphasize the responsibility involved when creating pop culture artifacts. The chapters provide very clear content for reflection and implementation. The unique features of this content will transform your thinking in order to do the following:

- Conceive and craft responsible, relevant, and resonant brand stories for advertising that people engage with and find worth sharing.
- Embrace diversity, equity, inclusion, brand activism, and eschew tropes, stereotypes, and negative messaging.
- Employ corporate social responsibility, purpose-driven ideas, sustainability, authenticity, and the brand's promise.
- Find and utilize insights into the audience to craft unique "ownable" shareworthy advertising.
- Build relationships with people—authentically empowered audiences are engaged audiences, enabling brand experiences that can then become shareworthy.
- Understand the process of creating groundbreaking ad campaigns through insights from case studies and expert practitioners themselves that are validated by tangible success metrics.
- Activate the power of earned media as the public, "co-owners" now, willingly share the brand story across their own channels and within their own reference groups.
- Harness strategic creativity.
- Tell new shareworthy stories in unique ways.
- Realize the next great advertising story may look nothing like advertising.

AUDIENCES AND USES

This book is a roadmap to identifying and crystallizing shareworthy advertising with examples from across the globe. Although appropriate for almost anyone interested in advertising, branding, or marketing, it will be especially helpful to five types of audiences:

Faculty in advertising, marketing, branding, and design will find this content valuable in supporting their curricula in brand storytelling, ideation, art direction, copywriting, strategy, media planning, account management, and any related course. Unlike existing titles, this book offers an inclusive approach with insights from esteemed creative professionals worldwide.

University undergraduate and graduate students will find this content accessible and actionable; it will inform their work for the long term. We know because we have taught thousands of university students who have gone on to rewarding careers. Alumni tell us that this content helps them secure the careers they desire, stay ahead of their peers on the job, and advance quickly.

Aspiring, novice, midlevel, and experienced creative practitioners will find that this content enhances their strategic creativity, illuminates inclusive thinking, augments their skillset, and provides a unique take on what makes advertising resonate, ultimately shareworthy, and efficacious. Some professionals, even those with a wealth of experience, may be stuck in a position where they feel stagnant, are not flourishing, and that is not authentic to who they truly are. This book will show readers how to broaden their thinking and construct appealing, relevant stories that move a brand forward to gain the recognition and success they deserve.

Marketers and business professionals who want career enhancement and a better understanding of the creative process will find this book valuable in helping them find insights, employ North Star concepts, think creatively and more strategically, build brand constructs, think without a playbook, and learn what diverse audiences find relevant and engaging. With the insights into the creative process found here, readers will become the business pros the creative teams will respect most and listen to—which will set them apart from their peers.

Executive leadership, team leaders, managers, and project managers will find this book a valuable resource for guiding their employees, teams, and enhancing their team's performance across the board. In most cases, a team's work reflects the team leader's performance. They can also use the chapter on diversity, equity, and inclusion (DEI) to improve their workplaces.

CHAPTER 1

WHY SHOULD A BRAND TELL A STORY?

Marta vividly recalled her mother's advice regarding college parties, especially cautioning against excessive drinking. As a college junior capable of looking after herself, she believed she could navigate them unscathed. Drinking alcohol never held much appeal for her—a penchant more aligned with her roommate, Susan. Stepping into the off-campus party, the overpowering scent of beer and sweat greeted them, accompanied by a lone bowl of chips amid an array of alcoholic beverages.

After a couple of hours, Marta felt the pang of hunger and attempted to coax Susan to leave. However, Susan, egged on by her boyfriend, persisted in downing shots on an empty stomach, reaching a worrying count of drinks. Marta noticed Susan appearing unwell. The next instant, Marta found herself dialing 911.[1]

STORIES WORTH SHARING

How do you get not only college students to stop binge drinking but others as well? People think college kids are the only ones engaging in binge drinking, but that is not the case—one in six U.S. adults binge drink.[2] Most alcoholic beverage companies urge people to "drink responsibly," but few do little more than post that message with their advertising. AB InBev tried a different tactic.

The Beer Cap Project, an initiative from the AB InBev brewer and agency MullenLowe Group, encourages other brands, such as Uber, Cabify, KFC, Papa John's, and others, to put their own branded caps on bottles of Colombia's Aguila Beer.[3] All involved are food, water, or transportation brands.

"Each year, the beer industry spends billions of dollars to promote responsible drinking, but binge drinking is still a huge problem around the world," said Carlos

Andrés Rodríguez, MullenLowe SSP3's chief creative officer behind this campaign. "Experts have found that consuming water while out, eating and going home earlier are all ways to drink responsibly, so we wanted to do something that has never been done before and remove Aguila's logo from the caps and give this space to other brands."[4]

Why join with food, water, and transportation brands? Featuring discounts from the brands on the caps encourages drinkers to mitigate the effects of alcohol with food and drink and elect to ride home with Uber or Cabify rather than drive buzzed or drunk.

By taking a proactive tactic and offering practical mitigation, InBev told a worthwhile story, turning their brand into a good citizen. Here, the call to action benefits the individual as well as society.

Stories people find worth sharing vary from individual to individual and audience to audience; however, they possess some common characteristics.

They land in culture and have the following functions:

- The media finds them newsworthy (Good Humor's jingle by RZA).
- They start conversations or amplify current conversations (Nike's "Dream Crazy").
- They change conversations (Dove's "Real Beauty").
- They are authentic to the brand's values and mission (Ben & Jerry's).
- People participate with them (Wendy's in *Fortnite* or on X).
- People find them entertaining (Midea's 90 *Minutes of Air Conditioning* movie).
- They inspire people (the Ad Council's "Love Has No Labels").
- They do something worthwhile for people or the planet (DDB Chicago created "Chillboards," an activation for Molson Coors, that cooled down the rooftops of homes in Miami).
- They inform people about important issues (Canadian Women's Foundation, "Violence at Home #SignalforHelp").
- They offer worthwhile practical benefits (InBev's the Beer Cap Project).
- Purpose-driven marketing is authentic to a company's values, not performative (Patagonia).

WHY STORIES?

When our friends get together over coffee, they ask, "What are you reading? Which plays or films do you recommend?" Many people enjoy being transported by a well-told story. Whether it is around a campfire or in the form of the written word, people value stories that function to entertain or educate; one only has to peruse scripted entertainment programming, fiction best-seller lists, song lyrics, epic poems, theater offerings, and religious or cultural traditions. Storytelling is universal, ancient, and contemporary.

What's fascinating about the relationship between people and stories is that many don't seem to mind engaging with the stories that brands tell. In fact, enough people happily participate with them to keep brand storytelling alive and well (depending upon your point of view).

Advertising has set its own rules for storytelling. Brands have backstories; spokesperson's stories sit in for brands; brands tell consumers' stories; and, of course, brands tell fictional stories that can be contrived, interesting, outright annoying, manipulative, or worth sharing. It's likely people have enough wits or awareness to distinguish between a fictional brand story and reality or perhaps between an ethical story and a damaging one. It would be a challenge for advertisers to keep reminding people that some of the stories are imaginary—stories told to promote goods and services. Advertising stories are games of make believe that people either want to engage with or not. But it is imperative that advertisers tell ethical stories and not damaging ones because that distinction is tentative. All stories can affect people's thinking and feelings.

In a recent study in *Nature Communications*, the researchers explain why the presence of good storytellers fosters increased social cooperation as well as benefiting the storytellers themselves, improving their chances among reproductive partners and receiving community support.[5]

Without Nike's brand story, activism, and ubiquitous swoosh, it would be nothing more than a generic corporation—factories, goods, people sitting in boardrooms and behind desks. A brand is nothing more than a faceless product, service, company, or organization that has a proprietary name unless the brand has socially responsible values, a mission, communicates its values and mission through a cohesive North Star narrative, and provides use-value that benefits individuals or society.

Why tell a brand story? Because the stakes are high, worldwide competition is brutal, and stories are how modern consumers best relate to and remember brands. According to research by Jennifer Aaker, professor at the Stanford Graduate School of Business, "Stories are up to twenty-two times more memorable than facts or figures alone." Furthermore, "Stories persuade.

Story can move people to action. You can persuade others by taking them on an engaging journey."[6]

In a glutted global marketplace, any brand's story helps to differentiate it—make it memorable and perhaps unforgettable. Nearly forty years later, Judge Raymond Dearie, acting as the third-party reviewer of the seized Mar-a-Lago documents, resurrected the 1984 Wendy's catchphrase, "Where's the beef?"

"Where's the beef? I need some beef," Dearie said during a half-hour conference call with the attorneys from both sides.[7]

We appreciate brand stories that embody good citizenship and ethics, aligning with a company's values and mission. They should influence positive conversations, addressing relevant topics for their audience while leaving room for exploration and delivering value to people or the planet, rather than focusing solely on profit-driven manipulation. These advertising narratives need to be thought-provoking enough for people to want to share them. Moving from mere noticeability to being shareable involves a significant leap because when a story becomes share-worthy, it resonates with individuals on a personal level.

INTERVIEW: GREG HAHN, CHIEF CREATIVE OFFICER AND COFOUNDER, MISCHIEF, THE 2022 AD AGE AGENCY OF THE YEAR

Greg Hahn

Greg Hahn founded Mischief in 2020. "I wanted to create a place where people—both employees and clients—could come and do the best work of their lives, with less layers, pretense, and other unnecessary complications," he says.[8] In 2022, less than two years into its existence, Mischief was named Agency of the Year by *Adage* magazine, Agency of the Year by *Campaign US*, and the second most innovative agency by *Fast Company*. Greg was formerly the CCO of BBDO New York. During that time, BBDO was recognized as the most-awarded agency in the world by the *Gunn Report*. It was also named Agency of the Year at the One Show/ADC Awards and at the Webbys multiple times. Greg is the winner of two Emmy Awards and multiple Cannes Grand Prix Awards.

What is the danger of complacency in a communication field such as advertising?

For agencies, I think complacency is the road to irrelevance. Advertising feeds on *what's next*, and *what's new*, and *what's happening*. If you become too comfortable with the way things have always been done, then you're suddenly far behind everybody else. Advertising can be such a chaotic environment at times, so when you find something that's comfortable, it's easy to settle there. But when you do, you've got to make sure you're never comfortable with that comfortable feeling. You should always feel like you're progressing and pushing yourself.

Growth comes from doing the stuff that you're not really initially great at. Especially when you're starting out as a creative in advertising, there's a lot you don't know. Don't be afraid to say so because you're there to grow and to learn. So, if you're in a place where you feel like you're not getting pushed or you're not getting challenged, then I think you're at the wrong place.

What role does courage play in brand storytelling, and what would you say to encourage bravery from other marketers or brands?

People always ask, "How did you get that approved or how did you sell that idea to the client," and a few things come into play here. One is that we don't really "sell it," we talk them through it, and it all starts with collaboration.

We bring them into the process early to say, "Here's what we're thinking, and here's the strategy behind it." We never just bring our client an idea and say, "This would be really cool and it will blow up." We always have a strategy, and we walk them through how we got from this particular strategy to this particular execution so it all makes perfect sense. By the end, it's almost like math, where you're able to look at the solution and say, "Of course."

The other thing we have to instill in our clients and in ourselves is that the *riskiest thing to do is put something out there that nobody notices* because then you risk blowing your whole ad budget. I've had conversations with clients in pitches and have said to them, "You don't have the budget to be boring." You need us to do something that people will notice and that gets a share of attention that's even beyond your budget (figure 1.1).

Fundamentally, what makes any campaign worthy of sharing?

Well, for me, it's always my mark of a great idea or even a brilliant one, when it seems completely obvious after someone else does it. It's kind of like, *holy shit*, that felt so right, and that's exactly it, but I didn't get there. So, when that happens, that's usually what you want to share. I think people share things for a

1.1 "Chillollipops"; Agency: Mischief @ No Fixed Address New York; Client: Coors Light.

couple of reasons. One is because it says something about themselves, so if you appreciate the consumer's intelligence, then when they get it, they want to share that with other people, and it's just sparked some sort of emotional reaction. Depending on what the topic is, some initiatives have that built into it, and if you execute it right, it's going to go viral, such as the "Sandy Hook Promise" campaign, for example. But more often in advertising, you're tasked with consumer-packaged goods that don't inherently have that tension built into it, so you have to find the tension, and that tension is what gets people emotionally involved. We always like to find an enemy or tension to work against—whether it's cultural or it's baked into the product itself.

It may be helpful for me to give an example. One of the first things we did at Mischief was the project for OkCupid to promote voting (figure 1.2) and this voting badge that they offered on their site. So, they gave us the stat, which showed that "registered voters are 85 percent more likely to get a message and 63 percent more likely to get a match" than those that didn't. That's a pretty interesting stat but kind of dry, so we just built tension into it by creating the sticker that said *VILF*, which is *"Voter I'd Like to F***."* We then just leaned into it by making it something a little more hooky or a little more catchy that we could then throw the tension into.

As modern consumers expect more from the brands they engage with, how is Mischief able to connect with them so effectively?

I think they expect more from them as a service within society and what they are doing and how they sit in the world. I think values have become really important to people. You won't buy a brand if you don't align with their values.

1.2 "Cockblocker"; Agency: Mischief @ No Fixed Address New York; Client: OkCupid.

As far as the engagement goes, I think that's actually more on advertising agencies and clients than consumers. I don't know that consumers wake up wanting to interact with brands, and I think that's not a bad thing because it puts the onus on us to make something worth interacting with.

Mischief work always seems to assume the consumer is smart, clever, capable, and opinionated—something ad agencies haven't historically given the customer credit for. How is that part of Mischief's approach to brand engagement?

There's 100 percent a thread of that throughout our work. Respecting your audience and appreciating their intelligence is, for one thing, too rare with advertisers. And another thing is that it's just a way to really connect with somebody. It's a way to say we feel you, we see you, and we get you, and when you do that, they're more likely to share what you're putting out there because it reflects upon them. It becomes a badge, as in, "This really interesting, entertaining thing was out there, and now I'm going to share it because it shows I'm the kind of person who gets this kind of entertaining thing."

Is respect for the consumer's intelligence something that you have to deliberately inject into the Mischief operating culture, or is that just something every employee innately knows?

The people we like to hire have that built into them, and the more work we put out, the more it becomes obvious what kind of philosophy we have. That said, we don't ever want to have just one tone or one sort of trick to our work, but we do want it to always have a certain level of intelligence, or fun, or quality to it that says, "Okay, I don't know why, but that feels like Mischief-level work."

There seems to be a corporate social responsibility (CSR) component to so much of your work. Why is that important to your company and the brands you collaborate with?

The Kim Jong-Un campaign was for RepresentUs, which is social responsibility at its core because it's for voter rights; and while not all of our work does that, I think clients who have those kinds of programs do like to come to us because we can take tricky, difficult, knotty problems and make them seem linear and simplified. I think that's one of our gifts at Mischief is that we like hard problems, and we're able to kind of unknot the knot.

What are the dynamics of Mischief agency culture that continually inspire breakthrough unconventional creative solutions?

We have really good planners, and I'll say that is our secret weapon, and that's been different from any other agency that I've worked at.

Creatives and planners here work as one. They work on strategy; they work on some of the creative—it's very collaborative, and that's helped us so much just because we have planners that know what's going to help the idea and then creatives that know how to build insights into their work. It almost feels like cheating in some ways because once we walk out of the briefing sessions, there are often already ten great ideas floating around.

As technology has radically changed content consumption and creation, what are constants of great brand storytelling that you feel have remained unchanged?

I think everything we do always has to come back to human insight, no matter what method you use to put it out there. The tools are the tools, and you have to learn them, but if they don't connect to anything human, then it just becomes fodder, and nobody will care.

Someone had a great quote, and we use it a lot now as we're talking to some of our clients, and it's, "Just because it's easier than ever to make something, it's not easier to make something good." So everyone can have these tools, and everyone can create something, but it has to have an idea behind it.

And the idea is everything to us. Then the technology to put it out there can help shape it, but it all has to come back to the center of the idea. I think that while technology gives you a lot more things to play with, they are still just expressions of the idea and not the idea itself.

A good example of that is the Kim Jong-Un campaign for RepresentUs (figure 1.3). A lot of people call it the deepfake idea but, honestly, it was just about how do we best execute this thought, and the thought was that America is so divided, and we're doing a nonpartisan political campaign just to get everyone to vote and to care about the 2020 elections.

The human insight was—nothing will unite us as Americans more than a common enemy. So who would benefit from us not voting? That, of course, would be foreign dictators. They're happy because we're doing their job for them by bringing down our own democracy, so let's put that in the spotlight. Now, within the execution of the ad, how do we get dictators to literally tell us not to vote. Then that just led to labels of deepfake, but it wasn't like we started with, "How do we digitally do a deepfake?" That's backwards because we started with the core idea.

Does Mischief have a philosophy about how consumer brand affinity is achieved through authenticity?

I think the biggest thing that keeps coming up for us is just humanity. The work shouldn't feel like a corporate message or that a thousand people had to approve this idea. We tell our clients, "It should feel like you guys maybe didn't

1.3 "Dictators"; Agency: Mischief @ No Fixed Address New York; Client: RepresentUs.

send us through the chain." It's like we just did it, you know? And that'll be fresh because clients tend to iron out the interesting wrinkles, and we like keeping some of that in there. Just things that make it feel like, "Oh wow, how did they get that through?"

It's funny but, yeah, having also worked in the big holding companies, I also think a lot of agencies are their own worst clients in that respect—they're so afraid of having a bad meeting or showing something that they think is not going to go over well with the client, that they over censor themselves. You just want to create an environment where that doesn't happen.

Is there anything we haven't asked you that you would like to share with our readers?

I wish I would have known this a long time ago, and it's easy for me to say now, but to enjoy the ride. I was so freaked out about where my next portfolio piece was coming from, or what my next move was, or where my next job would be, and there's so much of advertising that's out of your control. Sometimes you feel your fate is in the hands of a client that can give a thumbs-up or thumbs-down to your future because if they approve something, in my head, it was like *this is the one that's going to win the Super Bowl*, and if they don't approve something *you've got nothing*.

So that drove me nuts. What I would tell people is to just focus on what you have at hand and also that it's a long game. You will produce stuff you like, but enjoy the process because sometimes you look back on it and think to yourself, that process should have been really fun, and I was too stressed out about it, and 90 percent of what we do *is* the process. Very little of it is the awards versus the actual making of it, so always enjoy the process.

CHAPTER 2

IT'S NOT ABOUT THE BRAND—
IT'S ABOUT THE AUDIENCE

BUILDING THE BRAND BEGINS WITH THE AUDIENCE

The scene opens on a lonely tower with a single window that rises above a vast forest. As the camera zooms in, we see a forlorn young woman perched in the window. She's wearing a flowing white dress and has uncommonly long hair (figure 2.1). The voiceover says, "Once upon a time, there was a princess with really long hair who was waiting for a prince to come save her." It's a familiar story that suddenly takes a refreshingly unfamiliar turn. The voiceover continues with a chuckle and says, "Not really . . . who has time for that?"[1]

Instead of being stereotypically white and blonde, in this telling, the self-reliant princess is Black. The princess orders a ladder from Amazon Prime one-day delivery and promptly proceeds to liberate herself, becoming the hero of her own story. She goes on to found Rapunzel's— a hairdressing empire that's "killing it." All of this is revealed to the beat of "Feeling Myself" by Nicki Minaj. The voiceover concludes with the parting thought, "And the prince? Well, who cares?"[2] It's an example of the brand storytelling power of a simple insight, that charting our own course in work, leisure, or life often starts with a single step. The modern fairy tale ends with the super (tagline superimposed over the imagery) that reads, "Prime changes everything."[3]

Jo Shoesmith, global chief creative officer at Amazon, elaborated, "Rapunzel's story would have ended quite differently with the delivery of a single ladder, and that's a really nice, simple idea. Then that's when the craft steps in and we think, 'Ok, we can just tell that story, or we could put that story on steroids and think about what's going on in culture right now.' She doesn't just get out of the tower, but if she's a young woman now, she might actually run

2.1 "Rapunzel Doesn't Need a Prince"; Company: Amazon; Client: Amazon Prime.

her own business and be quite entrepreneurial. So, as you start to just layer-up, that happened very naturally."[4]

The Holy Grail/Marketing Gold: An Insight

> The task is . . . not so much to see what no one has yet seen; but to think what nobody has yet thought, about that which everybody sees.
>
> —Erwin Schrödinger (1933 Nobel Prize in Physics)

A consumer *insight* is a revelation (an eye-opener) or realization (awareness) about the target audience's need or belief, or the true nature of how they think, feel, or behave—a truth or finding no one has yet noticed brought to light. That insight or truth ultimately should warrant responsiveness—a change in the way you look at a behavior, situation, branded product, or service—and it should be the catalyst for idea generation and storytelling.

Insights into the audience are vital to breakthrough shareworthy storytelling. What does the audience need? Desire? Why does the audience do what they do? On which media platforms do they spend their time? Which causes do they care deeply about? Will they align themselves with your brand's values?

How do you find an insight? Research and observation are the keys. You might find an insight at an *intersection* of factors, such as technology, demographics, trends, the economy, social movements, pop culture, and so on. You can find an insight via an intervention—go onsite—visit a supermarket, for example, to see how people select consumer-packaged goods or how people behave. Listen to what people are saying and not saying on social media platforms. Examine what they are saying about the competition.

In this chapter, we're going to examine examples of successful insights derived from consumer needs, pain points, misconceptions, or even the act of listening to people's issues when others ignore them. All these insights are consistent in one key way—they all come from a rigorous examination of the audience.

AUDIENCE RESEARCH MEANS HARNESSING THE DISCOVERIES

Laying a foundation for understanding your audience means conducting research. Consumer research takes many forms, and any or all of the following may be harnessed by a brand. Primary quantitative research is original data often collected via polls or surveys; primary qualitative research is original data often collected from focus groups or observational research; secondary academic research is collected from preexisting scholarly sources, such as peer-reviewed academic journals presenting experiment findings. Secondary nonacademic research often utilizes preexisting coverage in the media such as newspapers and news coverage, and sentiment analysis determines the positive, negative, or neutral opinions of an audience, often as expressed through social media posts and comments.

Based on McKinsey & Company research, 72 percent of contemporary consumers actually expect brands to understand their preferences and interests as individuals, and 76 percent are frustrated when that is not delivered.[5] Assisting brand practitioners in communicating to audiences more impactfully is demographic and psychographic research data that may be gained through primary quantitative research or primary qualitative research (focus groups, observational research), as well as other methods. Research is a process of discovery, and discoveries are the insights that, when harnessed, can elevate the power of brand storytelling.

There are other uses for a product other than the stated or intended purpose. There are other people who might be interested in consuming a product other than those that have been targeted by the brand. So, a brand that is forward thinking can take advantage of this notion and locate unintended consumers that haven't been addressed by the brand or who have made use cases for the product, which the brand did not intend. We call this process

"Audience Discovery," and it's like finding gold on land you already own. [6]

—Stylés Akira, PhD, founder & chief creative officer, The Annie Agency; Lecturer, USC
Annenberg School for Communication & Journalism

One such discovery affected the business of a well-known whisky brand. Canadian Club found itself confronted with a problem. It was once the number-one whisky brand in America in the 1960s and 1970s.[7] But over time, the prominent brand occupied a position that was not high on the consideration list of drinkers under the age of forty-five. The company determined it needed to appeal to drinkers aged thirty to forty if it was going to alleviate seventeen consecutive years of quarterly losses.[8] Audience research revealed an unexpected discovery. It wasn't that young male drinkers didn't like the taste or quality of the product but rather that young males identified Canadian Club as a "dad drink," and like many young adults, they felt that their dads were decidedly *uncool*.[9]

Derek Sherman and Jason Standfield were the creative directors at Energy/BBDO developing the campaign, and Sherman said:

At the time of this campaign, nobody was drinking whiskey. The trend was martinis for guys, cosmos for women. Maybe you remember those swingin' days. This was before *Mad Men* made this era cool. Your dad wasn't Don Draper then, he was a pot-bellied guy with a mustache and possibly a Speedo.

Canadian Club was in its seventeenth straight year of sales declines. Many bartenders said they had not heard of it, when there was a bottle on the bottom shelf behind them. It was a pitch, and the client-to-agency brief was "It's Cool to be Canadian." But when my partner Jason Standfield and I went out to bars and spoke with drinkers directly, they told us a different story: They avoided this brand like the plague because it was what their dads drank with their buddies in 1.75-liter bottles. The last thing a young drinker wanted to be seen as at a bar was their dad. (Things have changed since then, but this was a barrier nobody could surmount.) We decided to use this barrier as the solution. Before we could make the brand cool, we needed to make your dad cool.[10]

This key discovery manifested itself in a new campaign from Canadian Club and its ad agency Energy/BBDO that flipped the script, reminding young adult whiskey consumers that, long before they came along, their dads were actually cool. In fact, in the pointed words of one of the ad's body copy, "Your Dad Was Actually Kind of Bad-Ass." One magazine ad featured a newly married couple posing for the camera, shot in a retro photographic style. The headline read, "Your Grandma Didn't Approve of Your Dad"—humorously but emphatically dispelling any associations the audience may have held between their fathers and nerdiness.[11] Another featured a retro image of a sharp young man performing onstage with guitar jamming, accompanied by a headline young adults wouldn't typically associate with dads: "Your Dad Had Groupies" (figure 2.2).[12]

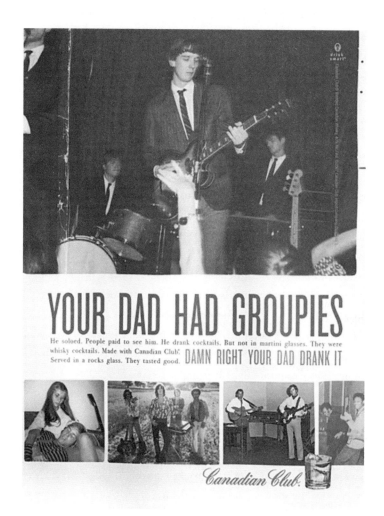

2.2 "Groupies"; Agency: Energy/BBDO Chicago; Client: Canadian Club.

Every ad signed off with the tagline that represented not only a distillation of the audience research discovery but the effective repositioning of the state of *dad-ness*. The new Canadian Club tagline brazenly read, "Damn Right Your Dad Drank It." In the span of just four months, and with no changes in pricing, product offerings, or distribution, the new campaign succeeded in reversing Canadian Club's sales decline.[13] Annual sales increased for the first time in sixteen years, and the campaign was awarded an international Gold Effie Award, which honors outstanding market effectiveness.[14] It was a storytelling success that was only enabled by audience research, which then led to the discovery audiences found memorable, impactful, and compelling. And as a fitting endnote, one of the Canadian Club campaign's creative directors, Derek Sherman, said, "*Mad Men* started later that same year, at first having the characters drink Jack Daniels—but they switched to Canadian Club, for free."[15]

Insight Based on People's Pain Points

Recognizing the gap that exists in a given brand category means identifying the particular pain points in the consumer experience that are not being addressed. Those pain points may be related to the rational functional benefits of a brand's product, but often, the benefit sought is an emotional one.

Consider that many children develop strong emotional attachments to plush toys (as well as attributing mental lives to them).[16] Misplacing or losing a cherished stuffed animal is often upsetting for kids, especially younger ones, which makes it a *pain point*—a persistent issue that frequently inconveniences or annoys people, users, or customers—for their caregivers.

What many caregivers don't realize is not only can a plush toy be a source of a child's comfort and safety, but it also might be one of the biggest germ collectors in one's home. Lysol Laundry Sanitizer to the rescue.

> Lysol had earned its way into households with a promise to kill 99.9 percent of germs. But today, with new, natural category entrants, moms thought Lysol was too harsh. So how were we going to convince moms we were gentle enough for even their kids' clothes as we launched into the entirely new category of laundry? By showing moms that the items their kids love the most are actually the germiest, we increased sales of Lysol Laundry Sanitizer by 58.3 percent and proved to moms that they could trust Lysol—everyday.[17]

For two weeks, Lysol (a U.S. cleaning and disinfecting brand owned by Reckitt Benckiser) ran a hospital for stuffed animals. Reckitt Benckiser identified that 80 percent of children's toys are "covered in bacteria" and often in need of repair. To raise awareness among parents of its product, Lysol Laundry Sanitizer, Lysol, with McCann New York, invited kids across the United States to submit their stuffed animals for Teddy Repair, a program to help fix and disinfect kids' stuffed animals.

With their parents, children applied to the Teddy Repair website, uploaded a photo of their beloved toy, and let Lysol know what needed repair. Lysol selected five hundred toys that were most "loved to pieces," which were then repaired and sanitized. Although the target audience was mothers, here's a clever bit to address a pain point for the adjacent primary target audience—a RFID (radio-frequency identification) bracelet so that the child could track their toy during the repair process using their parent's smartphone. Why is this a solution to a pain point?

According to Dr. Naveed Saleh, "During the course of a young child's lifetime, typically only one toy (or blanket) will become an attachment *object* . . . an object that soothes a sleeping child when Mommy is not around . . . an object this child cherishes and possesses . . . an object that evokes distress in this child when it's away for a wash."[18] This time, the toy was away for a wash and a repair.

The tracking bracelet alerted the owner to each stage of the repair process and progress made; kids received a photo and personalized update. Once repaired, Lysol mailed the plush toys back to their owners. For the children whose plush toys weren't selected, Lysol partnered with DIY expert Mandi Gubler to offer tips so that parents could fix and sanitize the cherished toys at home.

Contagious, a creative and strategic intelligence service, points to the efficacy of the insight into understanding that children "humanize" their toys as well as anthropomorphize them, attributing mental lives to them, as noted earlier. Therefore, admitting the plush toys into the "hospital" and allowing the children to track their progress eases separation and makes sense in the minds of the children.[19]

"Cleaning products are often viewed as a low-interest category, but through a combination of a clever insight, an abundance of hard work and a lot of attention to detail, Lysol is creating a wealth of shareable content about the power of its laundry detergent with this campaign," explains Contagious.

Contagious continues, "Each story has a ripple-on effect as users share them, each toy represents a new potential customer, and the submissions process doubles as a stylish form of data collection, creating a ready-made audience for Lysol Laundry Sanitizer."[20]

The Teddy Repair story hero medium was TV, with supporting interactive/online, packaging, PR, product design, social media, influencers, and experiential.

Like Lysol's teddy spa, effective campaigns address contemporary audience needs in a way that's culturally relevant. In 2021, Facebook CEO Mark Zuckerberg introduced the metaverse as an immersive virtual space. While welcomed by many, it can also be interpreted by some as a symptom of an increasingly disorienting and isolating ascension of digital socialization at the expense of human interaction.[21] Virtual reality (VR) gaming shares many of the same properties as the metaverse, including real-time immersive 3D environments and customizable avatars. It is, therefore, potentially relevant that a VR gaming addiction study reported in the *American Journal of Play* indicated significant increases in the conditions of loneliness, anxiety, depression, and social fears as a result.[22] As this cultural conversation continues to evolve, effective brand stories reflect it in relevant ways.

The Icelandic Tourism Board dovetailed perfectly with Mark Zuckerberg's metaverse announcement video with an announcement video of their own titled "Visit Iceland: Welcome to the Icelandverse." This good-natured comedic spoof offered a different kind of utopian future, with the natural wonders of Iceland as a real-world antidote to the disconnection and disassociation that modern audiences are experiencing in a post-pandemic world of remote working, Zoom meetings, and virtual happy hours. The Iceland tourism chief visionary officer Zack Mossbergsson, who bears an unmistakable resemblance to Zuckerberg, explains to the audience, "Enhanced actual reality without silly looking headsets. In our open world experience everything is real, and has been for millions of years. It's completely immersive, with water that's wet, and with humans to connect with," at which point Mossbergsson turns to the swimmer next to him in an Icelandic natural hot spring and asks with comedic irony, "You're human, right?"[23]

Ten days after launch, "Introducing the Icelandverse" achieved 6 billion impressions, more than one thousand press pickups, and $11.5 million in media value. All with 100 percent positive press sentiment that was realized for less than $50k in production costs.[24]

Sigridur Dogg Gudmundsdottir, the head of Visit Iceland, elaborated on the pain points of modern audiences when she said, "What can you experience out in the real world? We were all locked inside, and that's part of the message with the Icelandverse of course. You can come to Iceland and touch water that's wet, and see things with your eyeballs. . . . We want more meaningful experiences out in the real world."[25]

Both Lysol's teddy spa and Inspired by Iceland's "Visit Iceland: Welcome to the Icelandverse" represent not just brand stories but ones that first fulfilled a practical need (germ reduction or vacation experience) on the way to fulfilling a much more important emotional one (trust and comfort for Lysol and spiritual grounding in a technological world for Inspired by Iceland). In the process of finding an insight into the physical needs of consumers, which ultimately became emotional solutions, the impact of those communications is enhanced due to the fact that emotional stories are proven to drive attention and memorability, particularly over the long term.[26] For example, WARC's 2020 *Health of Creativity* report analyzed the most award-winning global ad campaigns from 2015 to 2018 and discovered that over half of them strategically focused on emotion. Furthermore, the WARC study determined that emotion is particularly effective in terms of implementing behavioral change and improving brand health.[27] This finding is consistent with the 2019 analysis of Australian Effie Award–winning ad campaigns that concluded that long-term market share growth is achieved more effectively through the use of emotional advertising.[28] All of this equates to increased engagement, as evidenced by both the Lysol and the Iceland Tourism Board success metrics.[29] Authentically and empathetically addressing audience pain points embodies the principles of shareworthiness.

Finally, as Lenny Stern, cofounder of SS+K, said, "Finding that way of being funny, without being mean, is not always easy, but it's very true to the brand of Iceland." Perhaps as evidence of that dynamic, Mark Zuckerberg himself responded to The Icelandverse video on Facebook, posting, "Amazing. I need to make a trip to the Icelandverse soon. Glad you're wearing sunscreen too," he said, in reference to Mossbergsson's exaggerated sunscreen scene.[30]

An Insight Based on People's Misconceptions

Procter & Gamble (P&G) announced a "comprehensive Climate Transition Action Plan–Net Zero 2040–to accelerate action related to climate change. We set a new ambition to achieve net zero greenhouse gas emissions across our operations and supply chain by 2040, with interim 2030 goals to ensure meaningful progress this decade."[31]

This ambition proves challenging without consumer compliance. For example, Tide (a P&G brand) cut emissions at its factories 75 percent in the past decade; however, some studies suggest that more than two-thirds of emissions happen at the consumer-use part of the "laundry lifecycle."[32] That's because heating hot water drains energy and your wallet. "You can lower your water heating costs by using and wasting less hot water in your home. Water heating is the second largest energy expense in your home, accounting for about 18 percent of your utility bill."[33]

Tide and agency Saatchi & Saatchi's campaign #TurnToCold is based on a misconception—people think they need to wash their laundry in hot water to get it completely clean—which became their insight. The campaign asked people to "Turn to Cold with Tide." Tide brand communication stated, "Watch out, the Cold Callers are here! Tide has brought two of the coldest icons in pop culture, Ice-T and 'Stone Cold' Steve Austin on board to convince everyone to #TurnTo-Cold. Did you know that washing in cold water can reduce your energy use by 90 percent?* If not, you can be sure they'll tell you. Join the Cold Callers in their mission for a better future!"[34]

(Tide's caveat: *on average, when switching from hot to cold water)

And while many companies have made commitments to sustainability, such programs can't be fully executed without consumer compliance. In light of this, Tide leveraged its relationship with the NFL, and its reach of 80 million viewers, to keep the #TurnToCold campaign going. Not only its scale but the fact that the sports league possesses large numbers of both men and women (47 percent of NFL fans are now female) made the NFL an ideal partner. Fans even had a chance to win a Tide Cold Washer, a talking washing machine featuring the voices of 10 NFL players urging customers to wash in cold water, and TV advertising included Atlanta Falcons quarterback Matt "Matty Ice" Ryan."[35]

Actively identifying and then addressing a brand or product misconception can often dispel a myth in the mind of the consumer and, in the process, open the door to creating a brand-new positive dialogue with the audience. It's a form of insight that was leveraged to great effect for Tide's #TurnToCold.

AUDIENCES WANT THE TRUTH

It's been said that audiences have never been more savvy to marketing messaging. Another way of describing the dynamic would be as one of outright suspicion and distrust of advertising, with research from Brand Keys stating only 13 percent of Americans have a great deal of trust in the medium.[36] Advertising distrust appears to be in decline worldwide according to research from Ford and Harris Insights, indicating 77 percent of global consumers believe it is now harder to trust brands. This is especially relevant considering modern consumers are predisposed to punishing brands they regard as insincere, with 67 percent agreeing that once a brand loses their trust, there's no way it can be restored.[37] For these reasons, it's never been more important for brands to tell stories that are consistently authentic as a requisite for shareworthiness.

Consider the plight of Italy in the midst of the COVID-19 pandemic, where 95 percent of all companies are composed of fewer than ten employees and small businesses are especially vulnerable.[38] The once vibrant Italian bar industry was hit especially hard, with the FIPE trade association estimating 8.3 billion euros in missed revenues for bars and restaurants there.[39] It was against this backdrop that Heineken launched an unprecedented campaign on their behalf.

The campaign created for Heineken by the ad agency Publicis Italy/Milan, titled "Shutter Ads," was appropriately embodied in social media with the hashtag #backthebars. In this campaign, the media money that Heineken traditionally dedicated to prominent high-traffic billboards was instead redirected to an innovative new media space—the pervasive shuttered doors of local bars themselves (figure 2.3). In fact, local bars received 10 percent of Heineken's global media budget, representing a new and crucial cash infusion for them, with the purpose of keeping them from going out of business.[40]

Cristiana Boccassini, chief executive officer and chief creative officer of Publicis Italy/Le Pub network was a key leader on Heineken's "Shutter Ads" and explained the project:

When the Covid crisis hit, bars were forced to go into lockdown, closing their shutters and losing almost 70 percent of revenues. With the on-trade [on location proprietor] being an essential partner to the Heineken company, it was important to make sure bars would survive and to offer them support in any way possible.

Heineken shifted the way they used to program media buying, redirecting the existing media budget from outdoors to the shutters of hundreds of bars across the world, supporting them directly and concretely. The ads showcased messages like "*See this ad today, enjoy this bar tomorrow,*" or "*This bar is not*

2.3 "Shutter Ads"; Agency: Publicis Italy, Milan; Client: Heineken.

closed, it's gathering strength," displayed on both the bars that had closed 24/7 as well as on the shutters of those closed during the day, reassuring consumers that their favorite and loved bars would soon be back in business. [41]

There are several ways in which Heineken's "Shutter Ads" campaign demonstrated authenticity through activation. (1) Heineken had long-standing relationships with independent bar establishments throughout the country; (2) as a beer brand, Heineken was a legitimate stakeholder in the health and well-being of the local bar industry; (3) Heineken was activating a ubiquitous yet underutilized fixture of urban Italian bars; and (4) the brand's direct financial contribution to the bars in need was a specifically stated figure of 7.5 million euros that was shared with the public in a demonstration of transparency. Due to Heineken's authentic approach to a real-world problem, the brand story was shared to such an extent that the campaign delivered 40 percent more media value than traditional OOH (out-of-home). And most validating of all, 100 percent of the bars in the initiative were able to successfully reopen.[42]

Boccassini encapsulated the philosophy behind Heineken's "Shutter Ads" initiative, saying, "By acting transparently, pragmatically, and responsibly, the campaign turned into an igniter that showed how purpose and authenticity are key components to be culturally relevant and enhance consumer perception."[43]

There are several devices that help audiences perceive truthfulness in brand storytelling—voice, tone, demonstration, consistency, and transparency.

Voice: The voice should avoid excessive hyperbole and exhibit clear intent in its messaging. For example, written in plain language, one of Heineken's "Shutter Ads" had the headline, "See this ad today, enjoy this bar tomorrow," accompanied by the tagline, "Heineken is paying this bar directly for the ad space, to help them open again. #backthebars."[44]

Tone: The tone should match the message. In the case of Heineken's "Shutter Ads," the tone reflected a reverence for the future of the local bars as opposed to an overt celebration of the brand itself.

Demonstration: Audiences need to see evidence of the brand's intent. Heineken's "Shutter Ads" innovative new media buy physically appeared on the bars that patrons actually frequented.[45]

Consistency: Authenticity in the mind of the consumer is associated with trust; consistency in a brand's messaging can communicate that an initiative is more than a one-off and instead represents a program reflecting its mission or brand's values.

Transparency: Authenticity in the mind of the consumer is also tied to transparency. For example, Heineken's "Shutter Ads" campaign not only supported local bars during the pandemic, but the brand was specific about precisely how much money (7.5 million euros) was redirected toward their cause.[46]

AUDIENCES DESERVE RESPECT

Respect starts with a brand's sincere assumption that the consumer is intelligent, discerning, has values they adhere to, and has opinions that are worthwhile. It's a powerful principle in engaging audiences, and it's a simple one: the concept of respect for the consumer. The *New York Times* deployed this strategy of audience respect against a climate of unprecedented disrespect for the free press with striking results.

Then President Trump's term in office was marked by his animosity for the press, with dangerous implications. On Twitter, Trump used the term *fake news* 273 times in 2019, which was a 50 percent increase over 2018. In addition, he accused the *New York Times* of treason and pronounced that reporters from the *Washington Post* "shouldn't be allowed on the grounds of the White House." The daily White House press briefing, which has long been considered a function of the president's accountability to the American people, declined from one hundred formal briefings in 2017 to approximately fifty in 2018.[47] This is in the context of Trump describing the press as "the opposition party" and "the enemy of the people" twenty-one times on Twitter in 2019.[48]

Within this environment, violence and intimidation became potential threats to journalists worldwide. In response to a White House discussion with Trump, the publisher of the *New York Times*, A. G. Sulzberger, said the former president's language was "not just divisive but increasingly dangerous."[49] The executive director of the Committee to Protect Journalists, Joel Simon, pointed out that a minimum of thirty journalists had been imprisoned in 2019 for the charge of reporting fake news. Simon stated, "We'd view that as governments around the world taking advantage of Trump's 'fake news' framing and using that as a pretext for imprisoning journalists."[50]

In light of these attacks, the *New York Times'* business future was facing threats on multiple other fronts as well, including declining newspaper daily print circulation and a growing expectation among consumers for free digital news. Of course, the trend is not unique to the *New York Times* and affected the newspaper industry as a whole. While the combined circulation of all daily weekday newspapers enjoyed a peak of 62.82 million copies in 1987, that number had steadily declined to just 24.29 million daily copies in 2020.[51]

Further challenging the *New York Times'* marketing efforts were the developing trends regarding public trust in the media. When asked to indicate their level of trust in the mass media to report the news fully, accurately, and fairly, 12 percent of U.S. adults indicated "none at all" in the year 2000. By the year 2022, that "none at all" lack of trust percentage had risen to 38 percent of all U.S. adult respondents. Meanwhile, the share of U.S. American adults who express trust in the national news to report the truth has declined from 76 percent in 2016 to 61 percent in 2022.[52]

Facing continuing inflammatory rhetoric from then President Trump, growing mistrust of the media, declining daily print circulation, and the migration of news consumption to digital platforms, the *New York Times* launched a multiyear campaign that was fundamentally based on respect for the intelligence, judgment, and values of the consumer. The *New York Times* defined this target audience as "The Curious Reader." Psychographically, this target audience was seen as those who consistently valued the truth over sensationalistic content and who would see their paid subscriptions as an essential expression of support for both the courageous journalists and the organization that was committed to bringing it to them.[53] In essence, the success of the *New York Times'* campaign initiative hinged on a belief in the integrity of their audience.

That multiyear initiative was known as the *New York Times* "Truth" campaign and launched with the tagline "The Truth Is More Important Than Ever," which debuted as a TV commercial that aired during the 2017 Oscars, with additional support appearing in print, out-of-home billboards, and digital.[54] The commercial that appeared during the 2017 Academy Awards opened with polarizing perceptions of truth that appeared as stark black titles animating onto a white screen. Each title opened with the consistent presentation of "The truth is . . ." and included statements such as, "The truth is our nation is more divided than ever," "The truth is alternative facts are lies," and "The truth is the media is dishonest." What then followed was a flurry of rapid and deeply polarizing titles that included the likes of "The truth is the Supreme Court seat was stolen"; "The truth is 600,000 immigrants will be let in"; "The truth is there is no evidence of voter fraud"; and, "The truth is we need to police the police." Each of these controversial statements was encapsulated by the delivery of an arresting and sobering conclusion that illustrated the need for the facts. All delivered in the form of consecutive titles that read, "The truth is hard to find," "The truth is hard to know," and finally, "The truth is more important than ever," before slowly transitioning to the iconic *New York Times* masthead logo.[55] Print, digital, and high-impact out-of-home echoed this sentiment, sparking a nationwide conversation about the truth." The campaign then evolved to substantiate the *New York Times'* unwavering commitment to delivering that truth as demonstrated by the incredible risks endured by their journalists in their pursuit in a series titled "Dedicated Reporters." Here, audiences saw video content, print, and social media that utilized never-before-seen photos of journalists doing their jobs in the midst of pandemic outbreaks, the refugee crisis, Iraqi counter-terrorism, and other volatile environments requiring exemplary dedication.[56]

The *New York Times* multiyear "Truth" campaign, which first launched in 2017 with "The Truth Is Worth It" campaign, achieved results that were an impressive validation of its efficacy.[57] Three key goal categories were identified by the organization in order to evaluate success: communication objectives, marketing objectives, and commercial objectives.[58]

In terms of the *New York Times'* communication objectives, the goal was to achieve a significant number of earned impressions, media coverage, engagement, and positive sentiment. The "Truth" campaign generated over 5.12 billion earned impressions, with an earned media value of $16.8 million. The campaign also generated 59 percent more positive sentiment than all other *New York Times* conversations in the previous year, and the *New York Times* became the most searched-for and most talked-about brand during the Oscars.[59]

Considering marketing objectives, the goal was to shift the perception of the *New York Times'* global on-the-ground reporting to being seen as a resource worth paying for. The campaign resulted in a 28 percent increase in "is worth paying for" sentiment, a 35 percent increase in "understands my needs as a reader" sentiment, as well as a 10.7 percent increase in purchase intent.[60]

Finally, regarding commercial objectives, just twenty-four hours after launching, the campaign delivered a 100 percent increase in its subscriber base versus the previous six weeks.[61] In addition, Q1 2017 became the best quarter for subscriber growth in the organization's history, and in Q2 2017, the *New York Times* advertising revenue grew for the first time since Q3 2014.[62]

The *New York Times'* "Truth" campaign engaged their target audience, the "curious reader," in a way that was characterized by a deep respect for their values, intelligence, and judgment—fundamental principles that brands ignore at their own risk. For that very reason, when an audience recognizes that they are truly and sincerely valued, their engagement with a brand can become magnified in powerfully positive ways.

AUDIENCE EMPOWERMENT EQUALS AUDIENCE ENGAGEMENT

> The way the world is heading is voluntary engagement.
>
> –David Lubars, president of Cannes Film & Press Juries[63]

Traditional media platforms, such as network television, assign a passive role of viewer to the audience. That shifted during the digital age as new tech platforms enabled interactivity. Beyond basic interactivity lies consumer empowerment, where advertisers actively grant audiences the ability to amplify their behavior in connection with the brands they engage with. This can take the form of building, creating, celebrating, or championing; when empowered in meaningful ways, consumers reciprocate with increased engagement.

The Educational Theatre Association conducted a survey that revealed 85 percent of schools canceled 2020 performances as a result of the pandemic. One of those was the Thurman White Academy of the Performing Arts Middle School, so Cox Communications, their ad agency 180LA, and Nexus Studios created an empowering solution. Working with Oscar-winning animation director Patrick Osborne, each young performer acted out their parts remotely over Zoom, and then, using Animoji technology, their performances were converted into fully animated versions of themselves (figure 2.4). Each student's character

2.4 "Drawn Closer"; Agency: 180LA Los Angeles; Client: Cox Communications.

was seamlessly edited together within a fully rendered animated environment complete with sound effects, musical score, and title design for a complete animated short.[64]

Mike Bokman, the 180LA ad agency executive creative director on Cox Communication's "Drawn Closer" campaign, shared:

> For middle schoolers, being social is everything. And yet, a year into the pandemic, distance learning was still going strong and extra-curricular activities remained canceled, robbing many kids of the one place where they find their sense of belonging. This was especially true for theater students, so we reimagined the school play as an animated short, performed by students from the safety of their own homes. After a year of missing out, it was a pleasure to give these kids the chance to reconnect and express themselves, at a time when they needed it the most. [65]

In the instance of "Drawn Closer," Cox Communications enabled a middle-school drama department to reenvision a school play as an animated film, empowering them in ways they didn't think were possible in the midst of COVID-19.[66]

Another demonstration of empowering the consumer for increased engagement also implemented a technological solution but for a radically different audience. Modern hard-core gamers frequently don't take breaks to eat, and in gamer vernacular, it's been said that when in the thick of gaming action, "If you bite, you die."[67] In fact, gamers dedicate approximately eight hours and twenty-seven minutes weekly, and distracting one's gameplay for food can frequently compromise success.[68]

As a brand inherently associated with food, Heinz partnered with Activision to identify in-game sanctuaries where modern gamers, in the heat of highly intense titles such as *Call of Duty*, could actually snack in safety. Maps of these coveted locations were shared with consumers and expanded organically by the gamer community themselves.[69] Heinz and Activision's "Hidden Spots" campaign, created by the ad agency GUT in São Paulo, empowered the audience in a way that was profoundly relevant to the quality of their experience—and that engagement had meaningful results. The "Hidden Spots" campaign resulted in the mapping of over 150 Heinz Hidden Spots, over 29,000 interactions, and more than 550 million global impressions across thirteen countries.[70]

In an interview with the information hub Chief Marketer, Heinz brand director Ashleigh Gibson explained, "You have to be authentic and you can't just speak at them. We need to provide actual value in regards to gameplay, understand who they are, understand why they're there, and maybe what some of the pain points are in regards to gameplay. . . . Identifying a real-world insight around the challenge in eating while playing games was really important to us. And once we unlocked that, we were able to partner with Activision to execute it."[71]

The Cox Communications "Drawn Closer" and the Heinz + Activision "Hidden Spots" campaigns are dramatically different in terms of their audiences but remarkably similar in their deployment of a fundamentally simple principle. Authentically empowered audiences are engaged audiences, enabling brand experiences that can then become shareworthy.

QUESTIONS TO ASK WHEN LOOKING TO EMPOWER AN AUDIENCE

Is the audience a witness or a participant?

A *witness* is passive and a *participant*, in this context, is a consumer who's been empowered to interact with the brand and affect their experience with the brand. In advertising industry vernacular, it's the difference between utilizing a lean-back medium, such as traditional broadcast television, and a lean-in medium, such as mobile or experiential, that allows for active audience involvement.

Is the audience's brand experience customized?

An empowering brand grants the audience the ability to affect their experience in a way that's customizable or personalized in some way. In other words, treating the consumer as an individual as opposed to imposing a one-size-fits-all relationship is a form of empowerment.

Is the audience's voice amplified?

Brands that create devices to amplify the accomplishments, preferences, or communities of their audiences serve to empower them. This can take the form of a brand sharing, showcasing, or celebrating the interactions of their consumers in the heightened ways that they're unable to as individuals.

ÜBER-FAN AUDIENCES: MEET THE SUPER FAN

There are some product categories that are known in the advertising industry as low-investment categories. Often, these products also fall into the category described as impulse buys. Chewing gum, within the confectionary product category, would match both these criteria despite the fact that it represents a highly competitive market that also demands shareworthy advertising stories in order to effectively impact audiences. But there's another audience that differs entirely in its emphatic, sometimes bordering on religious, attachment to their brands. These are the über-fan audiences, who live and breathe a property, sometimes for generations, and that can never be engaged in the typical ways. Think European football fans, San Diego Comic-Con attendees, *Game of Thrones* devotees ("Thronies"), and even pet owners. These über-fan audiences are incredibly discerning, and in order to reach them, brands need to demonstrate that they are respected, empowered, and heard. Only then will those audiences become the brand ambassadors that indoctrinate others through sharing.

As a speaker at the annual Advertising Week, New York, event, "The Many Shades of Super Fan Loyalty," author Greg Braun stated, "When we look at super fans as a marketer, what we're thinking about is that it's someone that inherently is not satisfied with just being a witness. It's someone who wants to be a participant. Then we as advertisers have to give them those opportunities." Braun went on to emphasize the utmost importance that an über audience places on genuine communication and genuine content, saying, "If we're not authentic to that property, then they will tear a brand apart."[72]

Consider, for example, international soccer (or fútbol). To put things in perspective, the 2021 Super Bowl had a global audience of 140 million viewers, while the 2018 FIFA World Cup (it occurs every four years) had a global audience of 517 million.[73] Regarding the sport, Liverpool legend Bill Shankly summarized this audience's sentiment nicely when he said, "Some people believe football is a matter of life and death, I am very disappointed with that attitude. I can assure you it is much, much more important than that."[74] Any brand looking to resonate with this international football audience, which included the likes of Hyundai, Chevrolet, Adidas, and others, had to first acknowledge that audience's extreme passion.

As an example of executing for an über-fan audience, let us investigate another wildly different, yet equally rabidly passionate audience that often can be found at Comic Cons throughout the United States—Hyundai's branded partnership with *The Walking Dead* series on AMC. By its fifth season, this TV show became the most watched cable television drama series of all time.[75] What started as product placement in the series became unsustainable long-term from a content perspective out of the brand's respect for the program's storyline. Automotive companies naturally showcase their newest models each year, and that's not possible during a zombie apocalypse where the entire industrialized world has ground to a frightening halt per the *Walking Dead* narrative. So, instead of emphasizing product placement, Hyundai offered fans of the show an opportunity to participate based on one of the program's predominant themes—survival.[76] An app was launched where consumers could radically customize a Hyundai Veloster or Santa Fe to become a zombie survival machine, complete with armored siding and spiked wheels. The site's graphics, customizability, and interface were state-of-the-art, but there was only one problem. As Braun shared with the audience at Advertising Week, New York, "Die-hard *Walking Dead* fans called bullshit. They said that the vehicle didn't have enough clearance to get over skulls, and the low-profile tires would slip on the guts. So, we (Hyundai's ad agency Innocean/USA) said, 'If you think you can do better, then here are the tools to do it with.' We then crowd-sourced all the survival machine weapons, which resulted in crazy innovations like the cow-catcher, doom-whistle, and flamethrower."[77] Once the agency recognized, embraced, and empowered the über-fan, the app realized unprecedented success, resulting in 150,000 builds, increasing traffic to Hyundai.com by 150 percent and making the Hyundai Walking Dead Chop-Shop the #1 Automotive Lifestyle app in the iTunes store.[78] The winning fan design was fully constructed and physically appeared at the New York Comic-Con for an in-person attendee audience of 130,000.[79]

We've examined many aspects of audiences in this chapter; however, as diverse as the examples included here are, they're typically unified by several recurring themes. When a brand listens to its audience and then authentically understands their needs, values, and desires, demonstrating that through action, the audience is then recognized, respected, and empowered in all the ways that result in a meaningful engagement that is shareworthy.

INTERVIEW: JO SHOESMITH, GLOBAL CHIEF CREATIVE OFFICER, AMAZON

Jo Shoesmith.

Jo Shoesmith is the global chief creative officer at Amazon.[80] She leads brand creative, design, production, social, and brand identity functions, as well as agency partnerships, in the largest fixed-marketing portfolio investment at Amazon. This includes retail, cultural events, Prime, Alexa, and Amazon brand. Under her leadership, teams created the 2021 award-winning Michael B. Jordan "Alexa's Body" Super Bowl campaign, launched Amazon cofounded Climate Pledge, created the "Prime Changes Everything" and "A Voice Is All You Need" campaigns, and made some of the world's most loved and shared Holiday ads. Prior to Amazon, Jo was the chief creative officer at IPG agency Campbell Ewald and, before that, a creative leader at Leo Burnett Chicago, Melbourne, and Clemenger BBDO Australia.

Why is it particularly important for big brands with big voices to tell human stories?

When you are a big brand, your voice has the potential to be very loud. It's important to remember that with every story we tell. I want people to relate to it AND see themselves in it.

In spite of its scale, it's interesting to consider that Amazon is actually a relatively new brand in comparison to others. How does the relative youth of Amazon influence the stories it's sharing?

Our youth makes us nimble and, therefore, always relevant. We're able to quickly say, "Okay, we're going to do this now because it makes more sense and it's the right thing to do." That flexibility that comes with our relative youth means we haven't created all this rigidity that can exist in companies. It also allows us to always be building things, and that's really exciting.

Over the last several years, Amazon has always been known as a brand but not always known as a brand storyteller in the advertising space. That's changed noticeably in recent years with Amazon "Mind Reader" on the Super Bowl, Amazon Prime "Rapunzel," and so many more. Can you tell us about the evolution of the way Amazon shares its stories?

Being a people-focused company and being so close to our customers, we have always had great stories to tell. You just have to look through our customer

2.5 "Woman's World"; Company: Amazon.

reviews to get a window into that. Over the last few years, we've continued to sharpen how we tell those stories in new and culturally relevant ways.

Amazon "Woman's World" aired on Mother's Day and told the empowering story of a team of all-women delivery drivers in India (figure 2.5). Can you talk about why this story was especially important for Amazon to share?

It was one of the first stories I heard when I came to Amazon. The female drivers are powerful and confident, and we wanted to depict that. They also all talked about their children being the motivation for why they were doing it. They didn't see themselves as change agents; they saw themselves as mothers first and foremost. And so, we ended up telling it as a Mother's Day story because, at its heart, this was a story about women providing for their families.

Amazon Prime "Rapunzel" is such an engaging and memorable story about the capability of the service, but it was also powerful in terms of societal messaging. In the commercial, we open on a lonely princess trapped in a mythic tower, but utilizing Amazon Prime, she doesn't wait for a prince and instead escapes to chart a bold path of her own. Would you talk about that aspect of this commercial or others?

I think everything we make is an opportunity to bring a different perspective. In the early stages of the development of the Rapunzel spot (see figure 2.1), we knew we had a great take on the original story. But we also knew we had to find a great way to tell it. That's why I love the process of making things because that's when we get to go, "Okay, how are we going to make sure that this is memorable, relevant, and unexpected." In this series of commercials, that was a big part of our focus. We gave Medusa a girls' night out, thanks to a new pair of sunglasses purchased on Prime, and Napoleon realized that he wanted a different career path after watching *Mrs. Mazel*.

2.6 "Cleopatra Has a Change of Heart"; Client: Amazon Prime; Company: Amazon.

There seems to be a purposeful note of DEI (diversity, equity & inclusion) in much of the stories Amazon is telling. From Amazon Holiday's "Kindness, the Greatest Gift," to Amazon Alexa's "Cowboy," and Amazon Prime's "Cleopatra" (figure 2.6). Is it important for brand storytellers to create content with a purpose-driven mindset?

Absolutely, it's very important. We hire amazing, diverse talent; we scrutinize our work to make sure that we're not missing an opportunity to do better from a DEI perspective.

We actually did something a couple of years ago for Christmas—a casting decision—that inspired my favorite letter from a customer. It was written by a mother whose daughter is a little person. Our holiday ad that year had a party scene, and in that scene, we cast a little person. She was all glammed up, looking fantastic, with all of her friends, enjoying her night out. And this mother sent us a letter, and she started with, "Thank you for not casting a little person as an elf in a Christmas ad." She was thrilled that her daughter got to see someone like her in a moment like this. That's important to me.

Alexa's commercial "Mind Reader," which aired on the Super Bowl, received a great deal of positive response from audiences for its charm, wit, and especially its candor. Of course, Alexa can't read minds, but in this commercial, the couple Scarlett Johansson and Colin Jost give us a fun look at what life would be like if it could [see figure 2.7]. Can you talk about the thought process behind its creation?

I think the Super Bowl is a particularly interesting example. Imagining how a mind-reading Alexa could wreck a relationship by revealing unfiltered thoughts

2.7 "Mind Reader"; Client: Amazon Alexa; Company: Amazon.

was a super funny premise from our Agency Lucky Generals and a continuation of the self-deprecating humor we've become famous for on the Super Bowl. The most important part of the process was finding a couple who had a good sense of humor about themselves and didn't take themselves too seriously—Scarlett Johansson & Colin Jost were perfect. I think, ultimately, people could relate to it because it's such a true couple story as well. Everyone I knew who reached out to me said, "Oh, my God, if Alexa was reading my mind I'd be divorced." I think there's something really disarming about being honest like that and saying, "We know you're saying this, so we're going to have fun with it."

Is there an insight about brand storytelling that you would like to share?

I truly believe "creativity is a team sport." More names on the entry list for an award is a good thing because it shows that you play well with others. You also shouldn't limit your idea to how you imagine it when you put it down on paper. You have to be open enough to say, "Everyone who touches this, I trust, and they will make it better," which includes the director, the agency, the client, everyone. My best pieces of work have been the result of groups of people coming together to make something great.

CHAPTER 3

WELL, IT IS ABOUT THE BRAND, TOO

I f we asked you to think of an ice cream brand that is flavor-packed, has clever flavor names, and seems as if the founders emerged from a 1960s hippie commune with a robust social conscience, which brand would you think of?

"With a $5 correspondence course in ice-cream making from Penn State and a $12,000 investment ($4,000 of it borrowed), Ben and Jerry open[ed] their first ice cream scoop shop in a renovated gas station in Burlington, Vermont."[1]

Ben Cohen and Jerry Greenfield successfully built a brand world with consistent values and actions. They competed against monster-size companies' brands (Häagen-Dazs made by Pillsbury, Sealtest and Breyers made by Dart & Kraft, Borden's, and Good Humor [now owned by Unilever]) to capture people's taste buds and hearts.[2]

BRAND CONSTRUCT

Cohen and Greenfield built a brand construct, which means they built an imaginary world, just as great novelists and filmmakers do. A brand construct is a theoretical assembly of three main points: what people want and might need in the near future; how the brand fits into what people want and anticipates what they might appreciate; and most importantly, how the brand's attributes stand out as distinctive in a crowded commercial arena. By creating a construct, the brand or entity stakes a claim—it seeks to "own" a position in the consumer's mind, preempting the competition. ("Own" is in scare quotes here because most brands do not literally own attributes unless they hold a patent.) People think of that brand as related to a claimed attribute or construct. For example, in their market categories, Ben & Jerry's owns interesting-tasting ice creams, Disney owns family fun, Jeep owns rugged, go-anywhere vehicles, and Apple owns creativity. That construct fills a gap in how the brand is positioned in the marketplace.

A brand construct provides an armature for its overarching North Star story, focusing strategy to form a unique, differentiating, ownable, and ideally extraordinary brand position intended to persuade people to think of it in a certain way. With the goal to deliver on the brand promise, a strategic guiding construct stresses the value promised to people and is put to the test over time. The brand promise captures the unique point of view (POV), offerings, and benefits promised to the consumer, which help to define its position in the market and in the consumer's mind.

Burberry brand's heritage infuses its construct with a pioneering spirit yet suggests twenty-first-century culture. Thomas Burberry created innovative weatherproof outerwear so that people could explore new spaces in the outdoors. "This spirit is embodied by a quote from Thomas Burberry that continues to inspire and imbue the brand's collections today: 'Inherent in every Burberry garment is freedom.' "[3]

In a spot titled "Open Spaces," created by Riff Raff Films and Megaforce, we see four weightless young people moving through the sky, gracefully exploring the outdoors as they jump and move, navigating the obstacles of the open spaces. Eventually, they come together as one unit, interconnected with nature and each other.

Directors at Megaforce told *Little Black Book*, "We had so much fun working on this campaign—as much as it looks! For this film, we had the idea to celebrate the joy of being free, the love for nature, and the strength of the collective. These are familiar themes to Burberry's vocabulary as well as its heritage of exploring the outdoors. We wanted to communicate these notions and it's such a nice feeling when something out of our imagination becomes a reality."[4]

The year before, when Burberry needed a Christmas film, they turned to Riff Raff Films as both a creative agency and production company. Riff Raff collaborated with directing quartet Megaforce and dance collective (La)Horde for the choreography. The Burberry creative brief's goal was "to capture what Burberry stands for today." The creatives wanted to create something "playful, unique and to also capture a sense of friendship and togetherness through the dancers."[5]

"We found the idea for this film [while] digging through Burberry's history. The founder, Thomas Burberry, created innovative weatherproof clothing that was used by polar explorers, which gave us this idea of a story that saw its characters braving the elements," Megaforce told *Creative Review UK*. To show friends navigating their way together through harsh weather conditions, through adversity, made sense given Burberry's history, goal, and construct—what the world was going through during the pandemic.[6] This Burberry film is a contemporary nod to the "Singin' in the Rain" sequence from the titular 1950s classic film. The dancers, dressed in Burberry apparel, gracefully circumvent the hailstorm; the contemporary choreography and creative direction make Burberry feel of-the-moment, culturally relevant.

BRAND MANIFESTO

A brand manifesto is a creative, aspirational declaration of intent. Transcending the corporate mission but aligning with its values and principles, it is a motivational statement that positions the brand on an emotional plane. When a clear point of view emerges, a brand essence, and a raison d'etre beyond profit, a manifesto conveys not only authenticity but also aspirations and possibilities of transformation.

Avis's advertising manifesto is an example of a clever under-the-radar way to tout customer service throughout a campaign: "No.2ism. The Avis Manifesto." The vast majority of brand manifestos started as internal documents to guide and motivate internally facing audiences. Then manifestos gained so much momentum that clients pushed for them to become consumer-facing.

One main goal is to provoke a relevant emotional response from the audience. Considerations include:

- Contributing to individuals, society, and the planet
- Declaring and demonstrating the brand's social values
- Delineating the benefit the brand offers to people
- Conveying the "why" behind the brand
- Communicating the brand essence/personality/spirit
- Articulating the brand's higher purpose
- Turning people into believers who will become brand sirens or take up the cause

The manifesto could be thought of as the primary (emotionally appealing) story in the larger brand narrative. It is an invitation to share the brand's purpose and how the brand benefits people—an opportunity to connect with people on a shared aspirational journey. It can take any form: film, typographic design, spoken or written text, or even an object; for example, Lululemon's manifesto is printed on its reusable shopping bags.

Benetton Group's *Clothes for Humans—Manifesto* is a short film reflecting the United Colors of Benetton's "brand new design philosophy" created by creative agency 180 Amsterdam. Excerpt: "Humans. Some are happy. Some are sad. Some are both. That's what we make clothes for—humans."[7]

Lululemon's website notes about theirs: "Our manifesto is one way we share our culture with the community. It's an evolving collection of bold thoughts that allow for some real conversations to take place. Get to know our manifesto and learn more about what lights our fire."[8] Their manifesto's visual design is by Pentagram.[9]

For their international tourism campaign for Colombia, ProColombia, the government entity in charge of promoting international tourism, launched a new brand manifesto for the South American country. Their new tagline, supported by extensive research about the essence of Colombians, "The most welcoming place on Earth," is inspired by the (generalized) spirit of the Colombian people. They will leverage this manifesto message to inspire future campaigns.[10] "Warmth and kindness were apparent and clear proof points that allowed us to design and validate the manifesto," according to a spokesperson [for ProColombia]. "It also comes at a time when the foreign promotion of Colombia has become more important than ever before," reports Tanya Gazdik in MediaPost.[11]

When Cadillac's global chief marketing officer, Melissa Grady Dias, wasn't satisfied with its manifesto, she invested creative energy into the rewrite with the main goal of "widening their target audience from traditional luxury buyers to the self-made luxury buyers of the future."[12] The theme is "Make Your Way," which speaks to people who "achieved greatness through guts, grit and determination."[13]

When we asked Grady Dias what role a brand manifesto plays, she said:

Brand manifestos are longitudinal and foundational to the brand and serve as its voice and North Star. At Cadillac, our brand strategy informs everything we do, from the way we write briefs, create content, and find partners.

Moreover, it permeates into other functions like design, sales, engineering, and customer experience. Our partners in those divisions have told me that the words empower them to ensure they are delivering the right Cadillac experience in their day-to-day decision making. It serves as an inspiration to us and others who surround or love the brand.

When we develop campaign manifestos, they are rooted in the brand work but also anchored in a moment in time. Usually, they have some type of more tactical objective, such as a launch, reveal, or the opening of orders for a specific vehicle. They are more external-oriented, focusing on an emotion we are trying to elicit or an action we are trying to drive, whereas the brand manifesto transcends everything.

Grady Dias also explained the role of audience insight when crafting a manifesto:

The audience plays an incredibly critical role. A lot of developing a manifesto is about who you are and what you stand for, but it is critical that the customer is at the center of that, and we know who our potential customers are, what motivates and inspires them, and what is important in their lives. When we first developed our "Make Your Way" manifesto, we conducted an analysis of our owner base and realized they shared our pioneering and entrepreneurial spirit. Compared to other luxury brands, a disproportionate number of our customers are self-made people who set off on their own to pursue their dreams. They are mavericks. That is also core to the Cadillac DNA—it's apparent in the story of our founder, Henry Leland, and the numerous innovative firsts we brought to the automotive industry, such as the first use of interchangeable parts, the first electric starter, the first airbags, and all the way up to the world's first true hands-free driver-assistance technology for compatible roads, Super Cruise. There is a boldness and optimism that is innate to both sides and which we celebrate in our customers. Our brand purpose is "We Exist to Champion Big Dreams and Bold Ambition," which is just as much about our audience as it is about us.[14]

Mozilla's manifesto addendum is titled "Pledge for a Healthy Internet," and it includes ten principles. Part of the manifesto addendum reads:

The open, global internet is the most powerful communication and collaboration resource we have ever seen. It embodies some of our deepest hopes for human progress. It enables new opportunities for learning, building a sense of shared humanity, and solving the pressing problems facing people everywhere.

The manifesto continues to say Mozilla has seen this promise fulfilled in many ways over the last decade:

We have also seen the power of the internet used to magnify divisiveness, incite violence, promote hatred, and intentionally manipulate fact and reality. We have learned that we should more explicitly set out our aspirations for the human experience of the internet.[15]

WORLDBUILDING

Brand worldbuilding establishes the groundwork for storytelling. It involves crafting a values-driven brand, shaping the actions, voice, and tone of the stories, determining key messaging themes, and choosing visual and written elements that make the brand desirable. This process sets the stage for all creative solutions, ensuring authenticity and maintaining appropriate consistency throughout.

Building a world might ensure sufficient brand awareness so that people can recall your brand's identifier (i.e., the brand's name and logo [usually the most recognizable brand identifier besides the name], visual style, signature color, or tagline) from a category and recall the need that your brand fulfills. "Brand awareness is the likelihood that a person retrieves a brand identifier and a product category or category need from memory across brand-relevant situations."[16]

If you were to ask most people who consume media to explain Dove's construct and world of beauty, they'd probably be able to explain it. Since 2004, Dove has built its construct and brand world around the Campaign for Real Beauty, with its groundbreaking discard of flawless professional models replaced by "real women." "Dove's sales skyrocketed, and its ads continued to build a fantasy world of aspirational 'realness,' a you-go-girl pink-ribboning of any fleshy norm that bred insecurity, from fat stigma to racism to ageism."[17] For instance, Dove hopped on a cultural moment about ageism when one of Canada's largest media companies fired Lisa LaFlamme, fifty-eight, a popular female television anchor, who had allowed her hair to go gray (though the media company executives do not state that as the reason for termination). A national uproar accusing the media company of ageism ensued. Other global brands, such as Wendy's, joined in the discussion—Wendy's temporarily changed their brand character's red-colored hair to gray.

Dove has stuck to its "real beauty" construct in an attempt to contribute to a more positive conversation about beauty standards for women and girls. They faced scrutiny and backlash for some missteps. *Toxic Influence*, a recent Dove film (from their Dove Self Esteem series), shows different pairs of mothers and their daughters watching the toxic misconceptions that young women influencers profess online and then discussing it. Dove's message in the film is that the greatest influence on a girl should be her parents and that Dove will provide some of the tools to help families navigate the pestilent propaganda online. About *Toxic Influence*, wrote Mireille Silcoff for the *New York Times*,

> Dove has found a way to align itself with virtue and outrage while keeping its own beauty tips unspoken. Nobody is on the side of nightmare YouTubers telling teenagers to file down their teeth; to attack such people is shooting fish in a barrel. But as marketing, it's almost genius: adopting a righteous tone while remaining as broadly inoffensive as any megabrand desires.[18]

To continue tackling the issue of "real beauty" standards in the digital age, Dove highlighted "research claiming that by the age of thirteen, 80 percent of girls distort the way they look online."[19] Dove's *Reverse Selfie*, a 60-second film (created in partnership between Ogilvy and Mindshare, 2021), is told in reverse, a sequel to *Evolution*, a film Dove created in 2006, which pointed out, very effectively, the beauty ideals foisted on women by the beauty industry, fashion world, and perpetuated by the media. *Reverse Selfie*, aimed at parents with "Have #TheSelfieTalk," punctuates the potentially damaging effect of young women heavily editing their selfies to maintain what they believe to be a desired beauty standard. In *Reverse Selfie*, we see a tween girl manipulate her appearance to transform herself to meet an ideal she has bought into. "The reverse journey ends with her staring at the mirror, obviously discontent with the way she looks."[20] The ad reads: "The pressure of social media is harming our girls' self-esteem. Let's reverse the damage."

In the fashion category, Eileen Fisher established an early differentiating core brand value.

In an industry in which, by some measures, a truckload of clothes is burned or buried in a landfill every second, she was an early pioneer of environmentalism as a core brand value. . . . A decade ahead of many of her competitors, Ms. Fisher started her Renew line in 2009, which sells secondhand garments, while the Waste No More initiative takes damaged garments and makes them into fabric. Patagonia was also early to embrace organic materials, has a long history of political activism and once ran an ad telling people not to buy its products.[21]

Fisher was unconventional yet successful at the start, both in her minimalist fashion design and her business model focusing on reuse and sustainability.[22] Women responded enthusiastically.

When Carrie Battan interviewed Fisher for *The New Yorker*, Battan asked about communicating the fact that their clothing actually is environmentally sustainable. Fisher replied:

It's a huge challenge to communicate, and it's a challenge to stay true to what we say, and to really walk our talk. It's not simple to say, "We took all these plastic bottles and made shoes!" There's a lot to try to communicate to the customer. . . .

There's too much stuff in the world, so how do we make sense of creating a good and meaningful business, and, at the same time, reckon with overproduction? How do we make more of the good stuff and less of the wrong stuff? . . . There's just too much of the wrong stuff.[23]

The Eileen Fisher brand partnered with T Brand Studio and animation director Katy Wang to create "Circular By Design," the story of their circular system. "It starts by creating clothes that work together effortlessly, made with the highest quality and sustainable materials we can find. We take back and collect gently used Eileen Fisher garments through our Eileen Fisher Renew program.

Anything that we cannot restore or is damaged beyond repair then goes through our Waste No More team to be transformed into something new."[24]

BUILDING THE BRAND CONSTRUCT AND WORLD

A well-articulated North Star concept clarifies brand essence, purpose, and values providing an armature for story-building. It must be authentic, true, outline the transformational goals for its customers, focus on reducing confusion as to its "why"—its purpose—and, of course, follow through on its brand promise and values through its actions.

Consider:

- The *brand's self-identity* (character) is how the business wants to be perceived by their audience.
- A *brand archetype* is a paradigm for presenting a brand—its symbology, values, behaviors, and messages—as a persona, thus making it more recognizable and relatable to top-priority audiences by feeding into the human experience and allowing consumers to identify narratives and symbolism quickly and effectively. (Please see chapter 5 for more about archetypes.)
- A *brand personality* is a set of human characteristics and/or personality traits attributed to a brand.
- A *brand image* is the audience's actual perception of the brand.
- A *brand narrative* is the story a brand tells as a means of defining itself to its internal and external stakeholders in order to provide a context for its past activity, a rationale for its current activity, and a direction for its future activity. (Please see chapter 5 for more about brand narratives.)

Brand construct —> Brand archetype —> Brand personality —> Brand narrative

For the advertising creative team, a brand construct helps them determine if an individual ad idea is on-brand (in step with the brand's core story and promise) or off-brand (not in step with the brand's core story and promise). Advertising that is off-brand confuses people and dilutes the brand's greater story.

ADVERTISING IDEA AND ON-BRAND ALIGNMENT

An on-brand idea conforms to what the brand signifies as well as to what the client hopes will influence the desired perception of the brand by consumers.

We're measuring the brand against the ad idea for each metric. On a scale of 1 to 5, where do the brand and your idea fall? They should very nearly match up.

The **brand** ranges from (1) Mainstream to (5) Unconventional

1	2	3	4	5

The **advertising idea** ranges from (1) Mainstream to (5) Unconventional

1	2	3	4	5

The brand ranges from (1) Profit-driven to (5) Triple-bottom-line-driven: People, Planet, Profit

1	2	3	4	5

The advertising idea ranges from (1) Profit-driven to (5) Triple-bottom-line-driven: People, Planet, Profit

1	2	3	4	5

The brand ranges from (1) Purpose-led to (5) Sell, sell, sell

1	2	3	4	5

The advertising idea ranges from (1) Purpose-led to (5) Sell, sell, sell

1	2	3	4	5

The brand ranges from (1) Having a sense of humor to (5) Humorless

1	2	3	4	5

The advertising idea ranges from (1) Having a sense of humor to (5) Humorless

1	2	3	4	5

The brand ranges from (1) Disruptive thinking to (5) Same-old

1	2	3	4	5

The advertising idea ranges from (1) Disruptive thinking to (5) Same-old

1	2	3	4	5

The brand ranges from (1) Individuals to (5) Family-oriented

1	2	3	4	5

(continued on next page)

(continued from previous page)

The advertising idea ranges from (1) Individuals to (5) Family-oriented

1	2	3	4	5

The brand ranges from (1) Plays hard to (5) Works hard

1	2	3	4	5

The advertising idea ranges from (1) Plays hard to (5) Works hard

1	2	3	4	5

The brand ranges from (1) Aspirational to (5) Grind

1	2	3	4	5

The advertising idea ranges from (1) Aspirational to (5) Grind

1	2	3	4	5

BRAND NARRATIVE TOOL

Here's a fill-in the blank tool to help work out the brand narrative:

The entity thinks the brand signifies:_____.
The target audience thinks the brand signifies:_____.

Now, the brand's core emotion is:_____.
The brand's core emotion should be:_____.
The core ad campaign emotion is: _____ because: _____.

The North Star ad idea signifies or signals:_____.
The two top competing brands signify: _____and _____.
Our brand signifies: _____ and is differentiated by _____.

To align all, we need to communicate the following message to the audience: _____ and compel them to take the following action:
_____.

AUTHENTICITY

For an advertisement to capture and engage the top-priority audience, it must be authentic to the audience, recognizing what they desire and want; authentic to the brand or entity—consistent with the brand's or entity's values; authentic to the company's or brand's purpose and ideally committed to a cause; authentic to the zeitgeist or a culture moment; and finally, authentic in its creation and production—conceived, created, and produced by people who are from the target audience, worthy of the people who support the brand or entity.

For any advertiser, storytelling builds brand affinity and can be a call to action—a force for turning brands into heroes, for people's desires and needs to be made realized/achievable/reachable, and to meeting objectives.

Genuine authenticity can't be imitated; it transcends a trend or a tactic. It's an essential core that brands must communicate through transparency, ethical steadfastness, and their corporate initiatives.

Gen Z acts and feels differently than previous groups—they're all about authenticity, according to market research firm GWI's Zeitgeist report (Base: 9,223 social media users aged sixteen to sixty-four across seven markets).[25] Even within the limited scope of social media, Gen Z seeks authentic human connection.

"Authenticity involves empathy, understanding, and representation," according to Sitecore's mid-April 2022 survey, which asked 1,174 U.S. consumers about their views. People want brand messaging and actions that illustrate that. Eight out of ten people reported they want brands to:

- "Illustrate empathy for their in-the-moment needs
- Provide insightful recommendations
- Actively demonstrate brand values through action
- Remember actions already taken"[26]

In addition, consumers expect to see themselves reflected in brand messaging. "The vast majority of those surveyed (81 percent) say brands should try to ensure that customers feel represented in the organization's marketing and communications. Plus, 85 percent indicate they want brands to reflect 'real life' versus 'perfect life' experiences—an obvious appeal for authenticity."[27]

Of interest for this same group surveyed, Sitecore reported that 59 percent said they prefer that brands remain neutral or do not comment on social issues. Additionally, they want full transparency about political party affiliations or social issues that brands support financially.[28]

Authentic to the Audience

The story idea *validates* what the audience desires and their aspirations and needs, whether practical benefits or problem solving, and addresses how the brand *fulfills* their desires and needs. This holds for even very young audiences. A case in point is the LEGO activation in Harlem, New York.

The LEGO Group and agency Amplify teamed up with artist Hebru Brantly for an activation—to turn children's wishes and ideas into a Lego playground in West Harlem, New York City.

> *Fly Away Isles* is inspired by the playful, optimistic imaginations of local children from non-profit youth development organization, The Brotherhood Sister Sol (BroSis). Together with Hebru, the LEGO Group invited the children to use the ultimate creative medium, LEGO bricks, to build and share their ideas for how they would help their community play more. The installation follows new research from the LEGO Group, which found that a third of parents (29 percent) in the U.S. say they don't play enough as a family, with 82 percent of children living in New York wishing for more play.[29]

The brand's playground and accompanying mural are part of LEGO's "Rebuild the World" campaign centered on children's vast imaginations. It opened on LEGO's ninetieth anniversary, celebrating with its first World Play Day.

For adults, Corona beer's Corona Island is a paradise in the middle of the Caribbean, where architecture blends in with the natural landscape, and people can connect with nature. To ensure Corona Island operates with a minimal environmental footprint, they partnered with nonprofit Oceanic Global. "Corona Island has achieved Oceanic Global's three-star plastic-free Blue Seal for eliminating single-use plastic and adopting sustainable operating best practices at scale. From construction to energy production, food sourcing and guest experiences on-site, sustainability is at the center of every decision and touchpoint of Corona Island."[30]

As social media evolves, brand-builders must leverage media platforms during the times they play potent roles in consumers' lives. Platform popularity will shift, some will expand, and others will fade into obsolescence, however impactful ideas will consistently connect with and resonate with audiences. "Consumers' desire for authenticity is going to the next level, and BeReal is a reflection of that. Brands who understand this and follow the trend will be more effective—both on BeReal and on the mainstream social platforms," notes the ad agency Movers + Shakers' website.[31] The digital landscape will continue to evolve, with some platforms expanding and some ultimately fading into obsolescence. What will remain consistent however are the big ideas that connect with audiences by speaking to them in relevant and meaningful ways.

e.l.f. brand cosmetics was an early adopter of TikTok and now BeReal. "We know Gen Z is playing on this; we know our consumers are on this platform. [So we asked] 'How [can we, as a] brand, authentically lead and lean in?' This is a new frontier, and we've always conquered new frontiers. This is an opportunity for us," said Laurie Lam, e.l.f.'s chief brand officer.[32]

SP☀TLIGHT

e.l.f.: The First Beauty Brand on BeReal/Movers+Shakers

About e.l.f./Insights from Movers+Shakers:

e.l.f. Beauty is known for being an early adopter of emerging platforms popular among its Gen Z consumers. Over the summer of 2022, e.l.f. made waves as the first beauty or skincare brand on BeReal, a photo-sharing app popular among millennials and Gen Z. The early adoption of BeReal continued e.l.f.'s leadership in emerging social platforms, including their record-setting #eyeslipsface TikTok campaign in 2019, and their *Billboard* chart-topping launch onto Triller in 2020.

BeReal exploded in popularity because it offered people a truly authentic look into each others' lives. e.l.f. recognized this as an opportunity to build deeper connections with its fans. The e.l.f. team conducted the launch with its

(continued on next page)

(*continued from previous page*)

creative agency, Movers+Shakers, whose Culture Squad had been following BeReal's rapid growth (figure 3.1).

After soft-launching with its own content feed, e.l.f. held a launch event on August 5, 2022. They gave away a promo code to the first 150 people who became friends on the app. The promo code gave fans a free Hydrated Ever After Skincare Mini Kit, a kit full of the brand's bestselling skincare products.

3.1 "e.l.f. Beauty"; CMO: Kory Marchisotto; Chief brand officer: Laurie Lam; Director, brand marketing: Brooklyn Boston; *Movers+Shakers*: CEO & cofounder: Evan Horowitz; Chief creative officer & cofounder: Geoffrey Goldberg; Creative content producer: Kevin Sullivan; Senior strategist: Melis Cifcili; Account manager: Amelia del Campo.

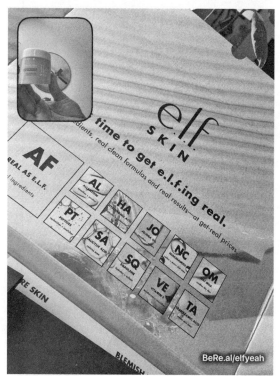

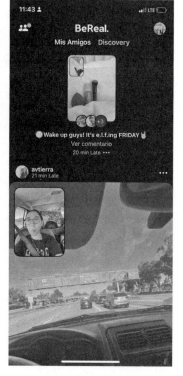

3.1 (*continued*)

(*continued on next page*)

3.1 *(continued)*

Once "friends" with the brand on BeReal, fans could look forward to exclusive behind-the-scenes insights into e.l.f.'s team members, from new product innovation to team happy hours. The @elfyeah channel shared an unfiltered and in-the-moment look at what life at e.l.f. is really like. "At e.l.f., we celebrate originality and 'e.l.f. expression.' So it made perfect sense to join BeReal and get real with our fans," said Kory Marchisotto, CMO, e.l.f. Beauty.

e.l.f.'s move drove 27 million press impressions in the first few weeks. Media from *Fast Company* to WWD [*Women's Wear Daily*] to *AdWeek* took another look at the nascent social platform, suddenly of interest to brand marketers. For months after the launch, the press continued to discuss e.l.f.'s work in articles about BeReal.—Movers+Shakers

Authentic to the Brand

The story idea and core message must be consistent with the brand's values.

Traditionally associated with rock musicians such as The Sex Pistols and iconic actors such as James Dean, Converse has long been linked to creative mindsets, counter-culture rebels, and even fashionistas, from Elvis Presley to Rhianna to Sarah Jessica Parker. Gen Z demands authenticity; Converse is garnering their attention by staying true to their brand promise through digital campaigns, such as Bitmoji styles on Snapchat, sneaker collaborations, and music artist collabs—for example, musician/actor Miley Cyrus has collaborated with Converse. Cyrus's collection featured wild paisley patterns and platform sneakers.[33]

Converse All Stars, a global network connecting creatives, providing digital and physical experiences, commissioned work, and mentorship opportunities, is "rooted in creativity," according to Sejal Shah Miller, Converse's chief marketing officer. Shah Miller described this initiative of 2,300 people worldwide as a "grassroots micro-influencer community." "We ultimately are a brand of creativity and self-expression, and our vision is tied to unleashing the creative power of youth," Shah Miller told *AdAge*.[34]

For the LGBTQIA+ community, the Converse All Stars Pride campaign focused on "Found Family" (people purposely bound together, not necessarily by blood). In their gallery experience, Converse notes, you view "unfiltered stories of the LGBTQIA+ community, spotlighting how their found families allow them to continue to break barriers and be their most authentic selves. The goal is to show individuals across the various intersections of the LGBTQIA+ community [so] that they are seen, heard and that there are many individuals who are ready to embrace them as family on their journey to Pride."[35]

Converse also found people's support in how they reacted to a tragedy, the mass shooting on May 24, 2022, in Uvalde, Texas, where a gunman massacred nineteen children and two teachers at an elementary school. A pair of green Converse shoes was one of the heartbreaking artifacts of one victim, ten-year-old Maite Rodriguez, who often wore her favorite green high-top Converse shoes with a heart drawn in marker over her right toes.

When actor Matthew McConaughey was in Washington, DC, to address lawmakers, beseeching them to act on gun control, Camila Alves McConaughey held a pair of green Converse shoes during her husband's news conference.[36] Converse reacted to a viral social media outpouring to rename the style to honor

Rodriquez. Instead of renaming the style after Rodriquez, Converse made charitable donations, including $250,000 to the Uvalde Strong Fund.[37]

Timberland, another footwear brand, is earning Gen Z's notice by staying true to its brand values; its website states, "From the start, we used our products to solve problems. This dedication grew to solving problems for our communities. That dedication has stayed constant and grown into tackling bigger issues like climate injustice and responsible manufacturing."[38] Timberland is another brand that has a take-back program, the Timberland Loop Circular Design Platform, a commitment to circularity. The program encourages customers to return their Timberland-branded used clothing and footwear, apparel, and accessories to reduce landfill waste.

To meet a cultural moment, Timberland is in the metaverse. Offering a blended physical and virtual experiences, in partnership with Epic Games' Unreal Engine and CONCEPTKICKS, Timberland invites players to reimagine product design, centered on Timberland's CONSTRUCT: 10061 program: "The partnership invites players and footwear aficionados from around the world to enter the universe of design, creation and innovation—highlighted by an immersive playable experience in Fortnite."[39]

In the "Moldy Whopper" video, we see Burger King's signature sandwich, the Whopper, rotting in time-lapse footage to the sound of Dinah Washington singing "What a Difference a Day Makes."

On YouTube, a viewer commented, "Someone's either about to be fired or about to be promoted."

Why show your signature product rotting? Burger King reports, "The beauty of real food is that it gets ugly. That's why we are rolling out a WHOPPER that is free from artificial preservatives. Isn't it beautiful? #NoArtificialPreservatives."[40] (Agencies: INGO/Stockholm; DAVID/Miami; Publicis/Bucharest; Mayflower/New York).

About the Moldy Whopper, Fernando Machado, the former CMO of Restaurant Brands International (Burger King, Popeyes, and Tim Hortons), told *Muse by Clio*,

> We understand that the biggest risk is to do something people are not going to notice or care about. We took a leap of faith and pushed the boundaries further than we normally do for BK—but for a good cause. We've been working on removing preservatives from artificial sources from our

products for many years now, and we've started to reach some of the key milestones where we're comfortable talking about the changes publicly. So, we needed something special. When we saw "Moldy Whopper," it was love at first sight.[41]

Machado's concern—doing something people aren't going to notice—is well founded. In their research on boredom in interpersonal encounters, social psychologist Mark Leary and his three colleagues found that people can bore others either by *what* they have to say or *how* they say it: both content and style matter.[42] Being noticed works, but being provocative enough to encourage participation and sharing is even more impactful.

Consider Volvo's E.V.A. initiative, created by agency Forsman & Bodenfors, Gothenburg. Did you know that many automakers produce cars based on data from male crash-test dummies? Volvo believes men and women should be equally represented in testing. With the E.V.A. initiative, they are sharing the results of more than forty years of research. "By letting everyone download this, they hope to make every car safer. Because at Volvo, we will always put people first."[43]

Authentic to the Purpose

Patagonia is a classic example of a company that practices marketing with a mission, where the idea is true to the brand's purpose and ideally acts for a cause beyond its own profits. In all of Patagonia's advertising stories, the company's dedication to their mission is evident, and they are enlisting the audience to join their mission. For example, think of the now-classic full-page ad Patagonia ran in the *New York Times* in 2011, "Don't Buy This Jacket." The ad explained to readers why they shouldn't buy the Patagonia jacket featured in the ad on Black Friday. The ad provided facts and explained the effect of manufacturing a jacket on the environment. The purpose behind Patagonia's strategy was to raise consciousness about consumption—to dissuade people from buying what they don't need—to only buy when they need something.

"When we're making decisions that are driven by our beliefs but very counterintuitive, that's where we're having a lot of success," said Joy Howard, former VP of global marketing at Patagonia. "Like trying to grow a wetsuit—because neoprene is such a dirty industry you can't even manufacture it in the U.S.—and giving the IP [intellectual property] away to encourage other surf companies to use it. We've been giving away IP almost as fast as we can develop it. It's not something that seems to make business sense but when we think about who we are and what we're trying to achieve it makes total sense."[44]

Yvon Chouinard, Patagonia's founder, wrote on their website that rather than "go public," they are "going purpose":

> Instead of extracting value from nature and transforming it into wealth for investors, we'll use the wealth Patagonia creates to protect the source of all wealth.
>
> Here's how it works: 100 percent of the company's voting stock transfers to the Patagonia Purpose Trust, created to protect the company's values; and 100 percent of the nonvoting stock had been given to the Holdfast Collective, a nonprofit dedicated to fighting the environment crisis and defending nature.
>
> . . . Each year, the money we make after reinvesting in the business will be distributed as a dividend to help fight the crisis.[45]

Patagonia has always practiced the People, Planet, Profit formulation. In 1978, Freer Spreckley coined the term *social enterprise* and first articulated the triple bottom line in a book entitled *Social Audit—A Management Tool for Co-Operative Working* in 1981. John Elkington said he coined the phrase "triple bottom line" in 1994 to urge business leaders to reconsider capitalism. This framework advocates for a transition in business priorities, moving away from solely pursuing profits towards embracing a holistic approach that prioritizes the well-being of people, the planet, and all its inhabitants.[46]

When companies make decisions and send out messaging that is driven by their beliefs, it often resonates. Patagonia focuses on purpose and sticks to its values.[47] Patagonia founder Yvon Chouinard and his nuclear family "have transferred their ownership of Patagonia, valued at about $3 billion, to a specially designed trust and a nonprofit organization . . . created to preserve the company's independence and ensure that all of its profits—some $100 million a year—are used to combat climate change and protect undeveloped land around the globe."[48]

Aerie, building on the brand's values of body positivity and its commitment to self-acceptance, inclusivity, no retouching, and a redefined beauty standard, is flipping social media messaging to the positive as well. Amplifying its mission, Aerie is partnering with influential positivity-spreading social media voices, such as Alisha Boe, and previous partners, such as Aly Raisman.

"As we build on the strength of Aerie, we are committed to helping our community find their happy and prioritize positivity," Jennifer Foyle, president and executive creative director, AE [American Eagle] & Aerie, told Bloomberg. "We know that social media can have a negative impact, which is why we are creating a safe and happy space that fosters healthy conversations and cultivates a positive social scroll for our Aerie community."[49]

Their initiative on TikTok and Instagram features tips to combat negativity on social media, such as how to take a break from social media and using positive affirmations to combat the din on the internet.

Authentic in Creation and Production

The team conceiving, creating, and starring in the story should be as diverse as the audience; for instance, if it's a story aimed at a BIPOC (Black, Indigenous, people of color) audience, the creators in front of the camera and behind the camera should largely be BIPOC.

To support and fuel small businesses, PayPal partnered with Tongal and its international community of independent creatives to produce a holiday campaign. "Make it One to Remember" is the campaign's hero video, directed by Kelsey Taylor, who oversaw forty-seven creators across six countries to develop the concept and digital content, including shorter content for localized versions for different markets.[50]

Don't spend your budget on panels discussing the lack of diversity in the industry. That's performative allyship. Spend your budget hiring BIPOC talent behind the camera as well as in front of the camera. If you want to have BIPOC directors or companies do your work, it's just as simple as giving them your work.

—Sophie Gold, founder and executive producer, Eleanor

SP☀️TLIGHT

Pure Leaf's *The No Grants* Film

Women often pay a financial, emotional, or career cost when they say "no" at work. In partnership with Edelman's data and intelligence arm, DXI, Pure Leaf Tea conducted a study examining the consequences of saying "no" at work.

"The study revealed that every time a woman says 'no' to things like working late or overtime or taking on additional shifts at work, she stands to lose over $1,000 in future earning potential, and the underrepresented minority workforce stands to lose almost 40 percent more.... By the end of 2022, 100 women received *'No' Grants*, and Pure Leaf committed $1M over the next three years to expand the program."[51]

Pure Leaf teamed up with Olympian track and field athlete Allyson Felix, who said no by walking away from a major sponsor, taking a stand on fair maternity leave and postpartum rights (figure 3.2). To support women, Pure Leaf created *No Grants*. Teaming up with Felix created a greater connection to the no narrative.

"Each grant provides women with $1,406—the maximum amount Pure Leaf's study uncovered is what a woman loses each time she says no at work.... In addition to financial support, applying to the *No Grants* automatically gives

3.2 *"The No Grants"*; Agency: Edelman; Production company: Eleanor; Executive producer: Sophie Gold; Director: Dawit N. M.; Client: Pepsico—PureLeaf; Images courtesy of Dawit N.M. with permission of Pepsico.

3.2 (continued)

(continued on next page)

(*continued from previous page*)

3.2 (*continued*)

any applicant access to an emotional support community through SeekHer's Community Care Program."[52]

Created in partnership with Edelman, the campaign features a powerful hero film narrated by Felix and produced by the only AICP (Association of Independent Commercial Producers) production company owned by a Black woman, Sophie Gold, Eleanor, and directed by Dawit N. M. (born in Addis Ababa, Ethiopia, and now based in Brooklyn, New York) for Eleanor.

Dawit N. M. spoke to us about Pure Leaf's *The No Grants* film.

At first, the initial budget was small, and it only allowed us to film Allyson and use stock footage for the vignettes of the other women. While researching

Allyson's story about her pregnancy and her sponsors, I was really over-whelmed with emotions and how it closely tied to my mom's story of when she had me.

After reading the treatment, the creatives at Edelman and PepsiCo were so in love with the treatment that they ended up increasing the budget to allow us to shoot the other scenes that were needed for the film.

What sold them and won them over was the idea of life. The main element that carried the film wasn't Allyson but a heartbeat. That heartbeat repre-sented Allyson's child, the future generation. It also represented the anxiety that people face when they say "no." And lastly, the heartbeat was a natural rhythm that everyone is familiar with. And so that heartbeat ended up giving life to this entire project and to everyone involved.[53]

Authentic to the Zeitgeist or Cultural Moment

The story idea should be relevant to the times, to culture or a cultural moment, and to the context in which the story is told.

"We have to remember that culture is a powerful homonym. It is both the world of art and human creations that surrounds us, but it is also our identity, the ideas, behaviors, customs, origins that define who we are. We need to ask our-selves what part of culture we want to play a part in, and what role we want our brand to play. In this way culture becomes our compass—not a line we cross, but an arrow that points us in the right direction," explains Kate Nettleton, group strategy director, VCCP.[54]

Working with Thea Von Engelbrechten to promote their Lola bag, Burberry created a miniature version of it for a sponcon (sponsored content) star turn in Von Engelbrechten's popular Sylvanian drama (@Sylvaniandrama)—creative miniature soap operas using animal figurines on TikTok. Although it was spon-con, Von Engelbrechten didn't alter the story for Burberry. Burberry and Von Engelbrechten organically wove the Lola bag into the story.

The episodes, which come out about once a week, regularly get over a million likes apiece, and the account counts Joe Jonas among its recent followers. Each TikTok follows emotionally static animal figurines caught in sensa-tional situations, juxtaposed against throwback pop songs, slang-heavy mis-spelled captions, and on-the-nose emoji usage. (Think: a broken heart emoji, the caption "my marriage is falling apart," and The Killers' "Mr. Brightside" playing in the background.) Videos with the hashtag #sylvaniandrama, where people post their own Sylvanian scenes, have more than 10 million views.[55]

About the featured sponcon for Burberry, Maggie Griswold, contributing fashion editor for *Cosmopolitan*, wrote,

I get it. We're all susceptible to ads. It's kind of the whole *point*. But a luxury brand teaming up with a TikTok account that uses children's toys as props to create adult dramas? It's such an unexpected pairing that I have to respect it. And even more than that, it makes me want to purchase the product being advertised. (!) Frankly, it's the only sponcon that has ever mattered—or will continue to matter. Designers and brands, take note. *This* is what the people want![56]

SP TLIGHT

EE Hope United Women's Euros Campaign Title: "Not Her Problem" case study from Saatchi & Saatchi

As a technology leader, EE is committed to making life online safer and happier for people in the UK.

In 2021, BT (a then-home nations football sponsor and EE's sister company) founded Hope United, a campaign platform and team of football ambassadors, to tackle online hate during the Men's Euros. EE inherited the Home Nations football sponsorship from BT for 2022 and wanted to use the moment of the Women's Euros to bring Hope United to the fore, tackling online hate once more.

But online hate in the context of the women's game brings the added layer of gender and sensitivity to how women's lived experiences differ from men's. Globally, women are twenty-seven times more likely than men to receive online hate.[57] While sexist words might seem surface-level, they build a culture of misogyny that impacts women's experiences in the real world. This can range from chipping away at the confidence women need to reach their full potential to robbing them of a sense of safety as they stay mindful of the threat of male violence.

Our research found that 67 percent of the UK believes that if men stopped aiming hate and criticism at women online, the level of online sexist abuse would greatly reduce.[58] Sexist hate often starts with a man on a phone or behind a keyboard. Men have the power and responsibility to step up and help stop it.

This led us to a very simple campaign insight. **Tackling sexist hate is not women's problem to solve. It's men's.**

How could we get men to help tackle sexist hate online? How could we deburden women of this problem?

Working in close partnership with Professor Matthew Williams—a hate crime expert at the University of Cardiff and founder of HateLab, a global hub for data and insight into hate speech and crime—we found that guilting and shaming men would only shut them down and not reap the engagement and action our campaign needed.

We needed a campaign with attitude. Something that would inspire men to take more of the burden and help tackle the issue without painting women as helpless victims.

Enter Hope United 2.0 (figure 3.3). A team of inspiring home nations football ambassadors, including Rio Ferdinand, Lucy Bronze, Demi Stokes, and Jordan Henderson, assembled to make sexist hate Not Her Problem.

Our hero "Problems" TVC [television commercial] explores the many problems women face in everyday life, with the conclusion that sexist hate should never be one of them. The film unapologetically heroes our female Hope United ambassadors and is based on their real experiences of being both women and professional athletes at the top of their game.

The script was built on and expanded as we spoke to more and more female players. The goalie's teeth and knuckles came directly from an ex-Lioness; ten days before filming Demi Stokes's partner gave birth, and we rewrote her newborn baby scene with her; and the period scene, in particular, was mentioned time and time again in conversation with pro and ex-pro players as a problem they faced whilst training.

Supporting OOH [out-of-home] and social helps bring our "Not Her Problem" message to life in all channels. And a suite of digital skills—"Hope Drills"— delivered by our Hope United ambassadors. Each Hope Drill manifests as a short-form video to show men (and, in fact, the nation at large) how to challenge and report sexist hate online and women how to protect themselves from hate in digital spaces.—Saatchi & Saatchi

(continued on next page)

(continued from previous page)

3.3 Full squad with logo; Client: EE; Agency: Saatchi & Saatchi; CCO: Guillermo Vega; Executive creative director: Will John; Creative directors: Will Brookwell, Nathan Crawford; Copywriters: Sarah Heavens, Alex Kosterman; Creatives: Olly Fernandez, Martin Headon; Art director: Nathan Crawford; Designers: Sergio Ortiz, Hetty Blair; Motion designers: Devin Arden, Mario Muslera; Animator: Benkee Chang; Production company: Academy; Director: Sasha Rainbow; Producer: Jacob Swan Hyam; Photographer: Shamil Tanna; Photoshoot producer: Sarah Knight; Social shoot producer: Will Breeden; D/OOH producer: Adrian Reilly; Production: Mill Experience; Executive creative director: Stephan Bischof; Design director: Will McNeil; Executive producer: Ben Young; Senior producer: Sinead Catney & Samira Abdelmalek; Technical director: Mark Dooney; Developer: Seph Li; Designer: Annie Keogh; Designer (C4D / HOUDINI): Vladislav Solovev and Daphne Westelyncpk; UX director: Katerina Lillywhite.

Creative and Client Team Interview

Speech and quotes taken from Saatchi's "ThinkBox TV Creativity Awards Interview"[59]

Respondents:

- **Alice Tendler**, group head of brand marketing, BT Group
- **Will John**, executive creative director, Saatchi & Saatchi
- **Sarah Heavens**, senior creative, Saatchi & Saatchi

What role does TV play for the brand, and why?

ALICE: TV plays a crucial storytelling role for us. As a technology leader, EE is committed to driving positive change in our digital lives—which involves tackling complex issues like online sexist hate. As a medium, TV gives us space to highlight the issue at hand in a way that feels properly emotive but also entertaining.

WILL: Exactly that. TV is the place to make people sit up and engage with totally new ideas and perspectives, because we have that wiggle room to get our message across on a mass level.

What was the brief for this TV ad?

SARAH: The brief was super simple because we had a clear insight. Anecdotally, the vast majority of our Home Nations female footballers have received online sexist hate. And according to the UN, globally, women are twenty-seven times more likely than men to have received sexist hate online. But women aren't sending hate to themselves so they shouldn't be the ones to tackle it… it's not their problem! Instead, men should be the ones to step in as allies and help solve it.

WILL: We wanted to raise awareness of online sexist hate as an issue without making women seem like victims and get men to be part of the solution without making them seem like male saviors. Women in football and beyond face loads of problems in their everyday lives—but online sexist hate should never be one of them. So we briefed our teams to bring this insight to life in a defiant and empowering way.

How did the winning idea arise?

SARAH: We'd already been talking to our female Hope United athletes to get them involved in the campaign, and during this process collected loads of insights around the daily problems they face. Stuff like leg injuries, sleepless nights from childcare, the potential threat of your younger, quicker opponents, and even coming on your period while training and being miles from a usable loo.

WILL: Getting all of this color from our athletes led to our "problems" script—where we bring all of our athletes' problems to life and then finish on the rug pull that online sexist hate shouldn't be one of them.

ALICE: The script was just so simple and inspiring, it felt like the answer had been staring at us the whole time. I love that it celebrates the experiences of our athletes as well as the experiences of all women. At no point does any woman come across as a victim.

Why did you choose the director?

ALICE: We were all aligned that we needed a female director to do our problems script justice. Someone who would really understand it through a lens of lived experience.

SARAH: When we first spoke to Sasha (Rainbow, our director) we knew she was the one. Not only is she award-winning, she's just a great human.

WILL: Sasha has so much energy and empathy, it's amazing. She's worked across multiple disciplines, including film, art direction, photography, and

(continued on next page)

(*continued from previous page*)

costume, and brought a discerning attention to detail to her craft that really shows in the final film.

How was the creative idea developed from the point of client buying into the idea to the day of the shoot/going into production?

SARAH: The key thing post-sell was to nail the details of the problems. We went back to our female players and really got into the details of the problems they face. So, for example, we chatted with Rachel Brown-Finnis who got her teeth knocked out when she was a goalie! This felt too badass to ignore, so, obviously, we developed a scenario where we shot her in a dentist's chair getting two new front teeth.

WILL: We also chatted with Demi Stokes, whose partner was due to give birth at any moment. We wrote that into our script, and in the film showed Demi awake and rocking her new-born baby to sleep in the early hours… only for her alarm to go off because it's match day. When we filmed Demi, her baby was only ten days old and she had actually played a match the week before on only two hours' sleep!

ALICE: We were also keen to show the truth of women's experiences, not sugarcoat it. Which is why we planned for prosthetics to depict Lucy Bronze's leg being stitched up, and the period shot—not a massive "problem" per se but a very familiar one, and as a big advertiser, we're able to help normalize conversations and experiences you don't always see on screen.

When did the ad launch and how (was it part of a multichannel campaign, etc.)?

ALICE: The ad launched on July 6 to time with England's first game against Austria. It was very much part of a multichannel campaign—we had out of home, outdoor screen takeovers, deck chairs, even beer mats. We also had a suite of social "Hope Drill" assets teaching people how to lean in and help tackle online sexist hate.

SARAH: Plus a number of organic "Shirt Swap" tweets from our male Hope United players who committed to wearing our female players' shirts and tackling any online hate they might receive while they were away representing their country.

WILL: And it doesn't stop there.… Each of our Hope United ambassadors wore a unique shirt design based on the hate they had received online. These shirts feature throughout the campaign and represent the real data our message is founded on. We put so much into the details, it was a lot of heavy lifting!

ALICE: The campaign ran until the end of the tournament, and we rounded it off with some reactive social and OOH [Out-of-Home] that tracked the hate our players received but reframed it with messages of hope. So we did absolutely loads. But our TVC is the jewel in the crown and really drove recognition and impact of the campaign as a whole.

How was it received?

ALICE: The reception was so brilliant. I can't believe how many organic positive mentions we got, not just in industry press but in consumer press, too—from the *Athletic*, to *City AM*, to the *Irish Times*.

SARAH: Also my personal fave… Laura Bates, the founder of Everyday Sexism, congratulated our campaign and posted on Instagram wearing our Hope United shirt.

WILL: It was also great to see how the public engaged with our campaign online. Obviously there were a few trolls, but there was overwhelming positivity and support from women and, most importantly, men, too.

What's your top tip for getting a great idea from script to screen?

WILL: A clear, singular insight. One message, one story.

SARAH: Combined with a serious attention to detail and sensitivity to the lived experiences of whoever you're telling the story about.

ALICE: Plus a great team of people, agency and client-side, with diverse perspectives but who get each other and communicate a lot![60]

INTERVIEW: HARSH KAPADIA, EVP, CHIEF CREATIVE OFFICER, MRM NEW YORK

After globe-trotting across four continents, Harsh Kapadia is the chief creative officer for MRM New York. While he has been an ad guy for over fifteen years, he fell in love with it when he was five years old. According to his folks, mealtime, playtime, or just

Harsh Kapadia; Photo by Dorothy Hong.

about any time came to a standstill when the commercial breaks came on. He was transfixed and has been since. With a career that's spanned across India, Australia, the United Kingdom, and North America, the best agencies, and building the most exciting brands, Harsh continues to be smitten to this day. Maybe that's what drives him so hard to continue creating magic for major brands, such as the United States Postal Service, Motorola, Google, Legoland, New Balance, Diageo, and Ford, to name a few.

Harsh has earned several creative awards from major advertising shows across the globe, including Cannes Lions, D&AD, One Show, Spikes Asia, and many more, while earning personal recognition from former first lady of the United States, Michelle Obama, for his leadership and campaigns. He has had the honor to judge award shows such as Cannes Lions, D&AD, ADC, and New York Festival, to name a few, and also serves on the D&AD Impact Council and has been named as the rising star of Madison Avenue revolutionizing advertising by *Business Insider*.

Harsh has been lucky enough to build and lead teams of some of the most passionate people to help build global brands. Moving around the world, Harsh goes by the philosophy that the mix of cultures and curiosity to learn more always leads to great ideas and believes in the application of technology to ideas and ideas to technology and that a big idea can make far more than a great ad or an experience.

How does a brand embrace purpose?

Purpose must be an extension of the brand's DNA. It cannot simply be added on superficially. It can't be purpose-washing.

Ask, "What is the brand obsessed about?" Purpose can extend naturally from that obsession.

For instance, you might see a brand execute a charitable campaign, but it doesn't sit within the framework of how the company conducts business; it will be a temporary feel-good but won't have impact. Purpose should stem either from the brand's DNA, its core identity, or its actions, aiming to generate a positive influence on a community or the world at large.

What kind of power can storytelling hold in advertising?

People only hear interesting stories. A great story can differentiate and make it more memorable for similar-feeling products and services for consumers.

What's your take on authenticity?

Everyone talks about authenticity. Of course, every brand wants to be authentic.

What is authentic to you, to your brand, is what is crucial. If your brand is quirky, continue to stay quirky. The power is in knowing what or who you are.

How can a brand co-opt pop culture?

Culture always has something new to say.

Purpose must extend organically—from seeing what happens naturally in culture.

For Movember, the leading men's health charity, we created "Non-Fungible Testicles," a campaign aimed at raising awareness of testicular cancer risk among the young male NFT and crypto community. We collaborated with art collective MISHKA NYC to create an exclusive collection of NFTs that were released during April, Testicular Cancer Awareness Month.

Proceeds from the NFT sales will be donated to support testicular cancer research. About our campaign, Dan Cooper, director of innovation at Movember, said: "The dynamic nature of NFTs and blockchain technology allows for new fun and innovative ways to reach men and encourage behavior change."[61]

The following are excerpts from the "Non-Fungible Testicles" video.

"Testicular cancer is the #1 cancer among young guys. Yet 62 percent of those most at risk don't know how to check themselves. To get guys in the habit of regularly checking their balls, we turned blockchain technology into a new way to fight cancer."[62]

"Each NFT will evolve depending on how much you 'check in' on it. Owners will be rewarded for becoming familiar with their Non-Fungible Testicles, in the same way they should check their real testicles. Regular self-checks enable men to get to know what's normal for them, so they can act quickly if something changes."[63]

How do you conceive the cultural context of a story?

It is the cultural context that is important to understand.

Storytelling is not about the product—it is the context in which you put it.

The Moto [Motorola] Razr, an iconic flip phone when it first launched in 2004, left memories of the satisfaction it gave people in hanging up. Fast forward to 2021, and hang-up is one of the most positive terms associated with the Moto Razr brand. So, we took that sentiment to the new Moto Razr and used it to end the toxicity of judgment to nonconformists and hate and decided to #hanguponit.

We took the legendary Motorola RAZR, the most iconic flip-phone ever, to empower individuals facing hate by giving them the ability to #HangUpOnIt. We collaborated with influencers who had experienced hate to create GIFs in a language born from social media. These GIFs were then distributed across various social platforms and messaging channels using Giphy. Each GIF was tagged with over two thousand natural search terms, covering a wide range of topics. We ensured that for every type of hate, there was a corresponding GIF ready to counter it. It even caught fire on TikTok with an original song.

Your creative teams are diverse and inclusive. How does that amplify team creativity?

At MRM, we build on culture. We focus on making sure the agency brings in people from different cultures and backgrounds. Many of the new hires are coming from South America, India, the UK, and elsewhere.

It's the diverse thinking that is going to change the way we work. Because we bring multiple perspectives and cultures to the table, if something can't be done, someone on my team will figure out how to do it.

Please offer advice on creative thinking.

You take an insight you found in one context or culture and look to reapply it to another context.

You've lived and worked in four countries. What is something you have noticed that affects your creative thinking?

What might be taken for granted in India might not be utilized in Australia or the U.S.

If you cross-apply what you know, suddenly, you're thinking differently.

It's a kind of cultural MacGyver-ing.

When you're living in a culture, you take the culture for granted. Someone external to the culture might see many possibilities that you don't realize.

CHAPTER 4

CAN YOU FEEL IT? BRAND AFFINITY

EMOTIONAL STORYTELLING IMPRINTS

Babies, puppies, and celebrities—and sometimes all three at once.

When it comes to Super Bowl commercials, that's what America appears to love most. As a seasoned veteran of the Super Bowl's yearly battle of the brands, Greg Braun shares that staple of industry institutionalized knowledge that cycles through the halls of the biggest ad agencies every football season. But for Super Bowl LII, Hyundai decided to take an entirely different approach to storytelling and created a whole new level of brand affinity as a result.

The men and women of the U.S. armed forces, who were stationed at the U.S. base in Zagan, Poland, were about as far from their families on big game Sunday as one could ever imagine when Hyundai decided to create the only kind of family reunion that would be possible—a multisensory virtual one. As Corporal Trista Strauch entered the sensory immersion screen room, the last thing the young mother expected to encounter on deployment was a greeting from her baby son (figure 4.1).

Hyundai and its ad agency Innocean/USA had many talented members collaborating on its Super Bowl campaign team. One who was key was Innocean/USA creative director David Mesfin, who explained, "We wanted to do something that would celebrate the soldiers and honor them. That is very much reflected—especially as we flipped the narrative. We often see soldiers returning home and surprising their family members. This was an opportunity to reverse that and have the loved ones surprise the soldiers."

"The idea was formed from the Hyundai brand tagline: Better Drives Us. In my opinion, it was the philosophy behind that tagline that was the driving force

4.1 "Operation Better"; Agency: Innocean/USA; Client: Hyundai.

of the project." Mesfin continued, "Rather than developing Operation Better from a tactical perspective, we knew that we wanted to highlight the sentiment of being a relatable and caring brand to their audience. We realized that approach would make it easy for internal stakeholders and clients to embrace it."[1]

Often, it's the emotional stories that imprint in the minds of audiences, and research indicates that the level of emotional vividness directly correlates with its ultimate impact.[2] Sometimes to such an extent that, in this case, it wasn't necessary to show Hyundai's vehicles at all. Mesfin explained, "Sharing the story across any digital platforms is less about what you are selling and more about how you are connecting to the viewers. Brand affinity is captured when you are focused on your audience, your storytelling, and the message you are sending."

A campaign that doesn't feature a product for sale is not a new concept—Budweiser has been doing that effectively for years in commercials that feature a horse, a dog, and some music—without beer featured in those commercials. The same holds true with our project for Hyundai. We didn't need a car in the ad to tell people that Hyundai understands its customer base. The objective here was to reconnect family members with their loved ones currently serving in the military. It was not the right time to be handing out business cards and asking them to buy cars. This was a "thank you" in honor of American soldiers. The sentiment aligns with the perception the brand is seeking to achieve. From the comments we received from all of those involved, people respected that, and it was effective.

To say this story made an impact on consumers is an understatement. Mesfin expounded:

As far as the numbers, according to Unruly's Ad Effectiveness Chart, which uses its new combined metric, EQ score, to rank ads on their likely emotional, social, and business impact, the auto brand's commercial ranked on top. Hyundai finished at the top of the Super Bowl edition of Unruly's Ad Effectiveness Chart with a score of 6.1 out of 10—ahead of Coca-Cola's "It's Beautiful," in second place with 5.9—after 62 percent of viewers reported feeling an intense emotional response to the content.

A third (33 percent) of people who watched the ad also said they would be interested in buying the product, while 40 percent felt intense happiness while watching, and 55 percent had a more favorable view of the brand after watching. Additionally, 88 percent of viewers said the content came across as authentic—the highest of any of the ads tested.[3]

We've just examined the power of emotional storytelling and its ability to generate brand affinity on the largest media stage. The same principles apply whether one is airing on the Super Bowl or launching a regional local ad campaign. When it comes to first assessing and then optimizing the emotional power of your messaging, there are key questions to ask about the story you're about to tell.

EMOTIONAL POWER STORYTELLING CHECKLIST

- Does your story relate to human values over merely business ones? It should relate to things such as family, friendship, kindness, independence, courage, and so on.
- Is your story relatable to the audience's lives? The audience should be able to see themselves reflected in your story in a meaningful way.

(continued on next page)

(continued from previous page)

- Is there an arc to your narrative that draws the audience in? As opposed to simply skipping to the solution, is there a protagonist (person, organization, or brand) that must triumph over a challenge or conflict in order to achieve a goal?
- Is your story fresh and original as opposed to being cliché? Familiarity can lead to complacency on the part of the consumer.
- Is your story bold? Stories that don't have an opinion, perspective, or stand for something lack emotional power.
- Is your story honest/authentic? Stories that are artificial or insincere have no emotional power.
- Would you personally share this story within your own reference group, independent of your professional ties to it? As evidence of the importance of this concept, consider that, historically, the act of storytelling is an adaptive behavior directly related to the survival of an individual within a community. It is within human nature to pass along the stories that teach, inform, or inspire those we care about; therefore, the willingness to pass it along is a measure of a story's power.[4]
- Is your story being told in its own best voice and on the optimum channel/platform to reach your audience? The story of *Succession* was intended for the TV or small screen, not a PowerPoint.
- Is your story harnessing a specific emotion? Love, joy, anger, and sadness all have their role in effective emotional storytelling. Multiple emotions may be present in a single successful story but should never be of equal weight. Be conscious of emphasizing a *primary* emotion that best serves to direct that particular story and best serves that particular audience.

EMOTIONAL STORIES FOSTER SHARING

As the police officer approached the automobile for a potential vehicle registration violation, we all seemingly cringed in unison at the impending writing of a traffic ticket when something unexpected happened.[5] As the officer was holding the driver's license of the apprehensive young woman, he said kindly, "So I am giving you a ticket, but the ticket I am giving you is a second-chance ticket." He then went on to say, "Because you've chosen to become an organ donor and potentially give someone a second chance at life, which is awesome, I'm going to give you a second chance and not give you a citation."[6]

Her response was immediate and choked up with emotion as she answered with a smile, "You don't know what that means to me today."[7] What started as the universally stressful scenario of being pulled over turned into an emotionally positive personal thank you from the state highway patrol.[8]

Donate Life California's initiative was called "Second Chances," and it partnered with law enforcement to spread awareness through the power of real-life emotional stories because, although California has the most licensed drivers of any state in America, only 45 percent of them are registered as organ donors. All while 14,000 Americans desperately await a potentially life-saving donation. The concept of the "Second Chances" campaign was to convey meaningful gratitude on a very personal level to the individuals who never ask for thanks but inherently deserve it.[9]

The emotional story gained momentum as well as tangible results—donation awareness month saw a 19 percent increase in organ donor registrations versus the previous year, realized over three million free media impressions, and additional police programs adopted the Second Chances program internationally. The campaign's premise was a simple one based on emotional storytelling: Thank organ donors with an unexpected second chance because they potentially provide second chances to so many others.[10]

We're all familiar with ancient stories, such as Prometheus stealing fire for humankind or Icarus flying too close to the sun, precisely because they have an emotional element that transcends language, culture, and even centuries. That emotional element is ultimately more universal than even language or nationality, as supported by a study conducted by the University of London comparing the emotional responses of people from dramatically different cultures.[11] Framing our shared human condition in another way, Shazia Ganai, the CEO of Neuro-Insight, described in an analysis of the Cannes Creative Effectiveness Lions winners that "the human brain has evolved to encode memories alongside an associated emotion for our survival, therefore emotion plays a pivotal role in what will drive us to action."[12] A modern example of this dynamic was evidenced by the story of twelve adolescent boys trapped in a remote cave in Thailand amidst a rapidly rising tide. The Thai cave rescue resulted in international attention in a host of different languages and a multitude of media headlines, such as "Why the Thai Cave Rescue Captivated the World" and "The Great Escape: Newspapers Around the World Share Joy of Thai Cave Rescue."[13] The appeal of the story wasn't restricted by the Thai language or Thai culture because so many of the emotions elicited were shared by virtue of our common humanity.

It's one thing to recognize the power of emotion in terms of communication; it's another thing to activate the power of storytelling as the optimal delivery device. In psychological terms, stories are a form of social transmission, and according to a study conducted by Jonah Berger, that transmission is further increased when emotions are evoked.[14] In fact, certain emotions, such as amusement, anger, or fear, are classified as high-arousal emotions, and these are all drivers of increased sharing behavior among audiences. Research data supports two key attributes about how emotional stories foster sharing. First, the very act of presenting facts within the construct of a story increases their persuasive power. When a study was conducted regarding the willingness of participants to get vaccinated for hepatitis B, those who received the information within a story showed markedly greater vaccination intent.[15] In an additional study, an ad campaign soliciting sympathy for people experiencing depression compared a fact-based approach to one that utilized characters, a plot, and all the foundations of strong storytelling. The story-based campaign succeeded in increased levels of sympathy even though it represented the exact same factual information.[16] To make your brand messaging motivating and shareable, tell it within a story, make that story emotional, and then it will then be on its way to becoming shareworthy.

FOCUSING ON SHARED VALUES—HUMANS CRAVE CONNECTION

As human beings, we have a set of shared values that affects the connections we make with other entities, some of which are brands. For example, a brand's story often utilizes a source to communicate it to the receiver. That source may take the shape of a spokesperson, an expert, or even a celebrity.[17] Based on research by James C. McCroskey at the University of Alabama in Birmingham, there are three primary attributes that humans connect to the credibility of those sources. Those characteristics are expertise, trustworthiness, and goodwill. Expertise is the knowledge and competency attached to the communicator.

In terms of brand storytelling, it might take the form of a real-life engineer explaining the design of the stability control features of a high-end sports car. Trustworthiness pertains to assumptions regarding the communicator's integrity and character. Here, an example might be a company founder with a long-standing positive track record outlining the brand's sustainability efforts. The third attribute is goodwill, which is the level of caring the source is credited with by the audience. In an advertising scenario it might involve a celebrity with strong public service credentials promoting a charitable cause for the benefit of individuals in need.[18]

Consider how shared values allowed audiences to connect with Donate Life California's "Second Chances" initiative highlighted earlier in this chapter. Credibility (in addition to authority and social attractiveness) is one of the three most essential communicator attributes, dating all the way back to Aristotle's means of persuasion concept of *ethos*. Let's examine how those core communicator characteristics of expertise, trustworthiness, and goodwill, that form the credibility of a source, are activated here.[19] The credibility source attributes were all in play. In terms of traffic and driving, the police officers could be seen as representing *expertise*. The pulled-over drivers were *trustworthy* as donors by virtue of the pink dot indicators on their licenses. *Goodwill* was exhibited both by the one-to-one personal gratitude expressed by the officers and the selflessness of the donors/drivers themselves. When it comes to the human desire to connect, the relationship between communicators and audiences can be strengthened by recognizing that the appeal of these core credibility characteristics is shared; thereby, incorporating them into our brand stories can enhance shareworthiness.

DRIVERS OF BRAND AFFINITY: HOW TO MAKE STORYTELLING SHAREWORTHY THROUGH EMOTIONAL BRANDING

When examining the drivers of brand affinity, it's instructive to contemplate the people in our lives for whom we have an affinity. Chances are, our strongest relationships are attached to the people who love us, who are truthful, who make us laugh, or who inspire us. Consumers who have an affinity for the specific brands that they choose to engage with can make similar emotional connections.

For example, consider that Nike sneakers are typically a mix of nylon, polyester, foam, leather, and rubber—just like the basic ingredients of almost every other mainstream sneaker.[20] Yet notably, Nike has the highest global footwear sales in the world, with a 21.1 percent market share in the United States, versus its nearest competitor, Adidas, with only a 4.7 percent market share.[21] It's no coincidence that Nike's domination in sales coincides with its dominance in the brand affinity measurements of innovation, fashion/style, and purchase intent, outscoring key competitors Adidas, Under Armour, and Lululemon.[22] In short, the key difference in value here isn't materially physical, it's emotional; effective emotional storytelling can be a driver of brand affinity.

BRAND AFFINITY CHECKLIST FOR MARKETERS

- Are your brand's purpose and brand persona (the specific human characteristics associated with the brand, such as friendly, caring, or daring) both identifiable and articulable by the leadership team, the marketing team, and the ad agency team? For a brand to engender affinity through emotional connection, it can't mean multiple different things to multiple different stakeholders. Using the analogy of human relationships, if one thinks about their closest friends, the qualities that endear them to us are clear and consistent over time.
- Are you presenting your product in the form of a story that consumers can organically connect and engage with? As the CEO of Neuro-Insight, Shazia Ginai, states, "Great storytelling is the foundation stone of what the brain needs to drive any real connection with a brand."[23]
- Does your brand take a stand and reflect the shared values of your consumers? This has the potential to not only increase brand affinity but business goals as well. Chief strategy officer and COO of McCann Worldgroup India, Jitender Dabas, refers to this dynamic as the "return on bravery."[24]
- Are you rewarding the consumer for engaging with your brand? The advertising communication should be entertaining, moving, inspiring, or illuminating in a way that elicits emotional engagement. This philosophy is not about creative indulgence and is instead about sound marketing practice. In the WARC Effective 100 analysis of the most effective global advertising campaigns of the year, the use of emotion was the number one creative strategy utilized.[25]

TAKE A STAND OR DO SOMETHING THAT BENEFITS INDIVIDUALS, SOCIETY, OR THE ENVIRONMENT

When companies take a stand on behalf of a social issue or the planet, some ask if it's what consumers want from the brands they engage with. In actuality, it's not simply what people expect, but it's what they've come to demand. This represents a significant shift in the way consumers, particularly millennials and Gen Z, now engage with brands that practice CSR (corporate social responsibility). That cultural shift is something companies seeking enhanced brand affinity need to capitalize on. For example, young consumers between eighteen and twenty-five have a higher awareness of ethical and responsible advertising when buying products or services than consumers forty-six and older. In addition, at 57 percent, over half of U.S. consumers state that they have increased loyalty to brands committed to addressing social causes.[26] These cultural trends go beyond brand awareness and brand loyalty and directly affect purchase behavior. For example, 23 percent of consumers express the intent to switch to purchasing products from brands that better align with their values; 42 percent have already changed brand consumption based on their values; and 21 percent have advocated for other members of their reference groups to switch brands due to a given company's stance on an important issue.[27] In addition, 76 percent of American consumers stated that they would refuse to shop at a company that supported an issue conflicting with their beliefs, and 88 percent of consumers stated that they would actively boycott a brand that demonstrated unethical practices.[28] Again, the age of the consumer is a notable factor. In terms of the willingness to switch brands based on values alignment, shoppers eighteen to twenty-four are three times more likely than consumers sixty-five and over.[29]

With metrics like these, in addition to meeting the expectations of the modern consumer, good ethics is also good business. There's significant evidence that supports the proposal that companies committed to CSR efforts are more profitable. In fairness, there are some detractors who just aren't ready to concede CSR's efficacy, but that said, there are several high-profile examples in the marketplace with which you're probably familiar. After Nike's "Dream Crazy" campaign featuring Colin Kaepernick aired, there was initially significant fallout, but the brand quickly recovered to see its stock price achieve an all-time high of $85.55, increasing in value by $6 billion from the day of the campaign's debut.

Additionally, Nike's second fiscal quarter revenue rose by $297 million versus the previous year's same quarter.[30] Dove's "Real Beauty" campaign, which recently helped promote the Crown Act that bans discrimination against people based on hairstyle or hair texture, realized an 8 percent sales increase in 2021 versus the industry-wide average of 4.5 percent growth. Finally, Ben & Jerry's sales grew by 9 percent in 2021, coinciding with its stance on refugee rights.[31] This efficacy trend is only a continuation of established patterns. Research from the *Journal of Marketing Services* determined that brands with a demonstrable sustainability commitment grew over 4 percent on average versus just 1 percent growth for those without during the same time period.[32]

Does taking a stand represent risk for a brand? In the case of fashion brand H&M, it did when it publicly raised concerns over alleged forced labor in the Xinjiang Uyghur Autonomous Region (Xinjiang), a large region in Western China. It was a bold statement on the part of H&M, considering the region produces approximately 20 percent of the world's cotton, and the country itself represents its third-largest global market after the United States and Germany. The fallout was swift, as a Chinese boycott resulted in criticism from Beijing, closed storefronts, the removal of H&M from e-commerce sites, and $74 million in lost sales for the quarter.[33]

Taking a stand can be challenging and will inevitably alienate some. In advertising circles, it's been said that if it were that easy, every brand would do it, and at the end of the day, it all comes down to that invaluable element of brand affinity. Consumers expect it, consumers demand it, and consumers will ultimately reward the brands that reflect their values. Case in point: Following initial public Nike sneaker burnings in the wake of the Colin Kaepernick "Dream Crazy" TV campaign, the Nike brand's affinity scores actually increased across all five of the measures of "favorite brand," "favorite apparel," "favorite footwear," and "cool brand"—all while the brand realized a 61 percent increase in year-on-year sold-out products.[34] The majority of consumers had spoken.

BE AUTHENTIC/BE TRUSTWORTHY/WALK THE WALK

When the environmentally conscious apparel brand Patagonia ran its classic "Don't Buy This Jacket" full-page advertisement in the *New York Times*, it shocked many industry insiders with its sheer audacity and brutal honesty. It continued that disruptive tradition again in 2020 with another full-page ad in the *New York Times*, but this time, it took the unexpected form of a poem. It read:

> We're all screwed
> So don't tell us that
> We can imagine a healthy future
> Because the reality is
> It's too late to fix the climate crisis
> And we don't trust anyone who says
> We need to demand a livable planet
> Because we don't have a choice
> (Now read this bottom up)[35]

Resigned pessimism, read backward became not only a resolute call to action but also an example of a brand determined to "walk the walk."[36]

Examples of "Walk the Walk"

The skepticism of American consumers has never been more finely tuned. That is why when it comes to earning brand affinity, walking the walk has never been more important for brands. In fact, there's an even more colloquial term sometimes heard in the ad agency business, and it's called the "whack tax." The whack tax refers to when a brand inauthentically trumpets its CSR efforts when, in reality, those efforts are insincere marketing optics as opposed to meaningful benefits to society. Indignant consumers inevitably then exact a heavy tax in the form of negative sentiment, boycotts, brand switching, negative word of mouth, and outright rejection. It's a whack tax, and it's a price brands cannot afford to pay, which brings us to earnest brand action as a crucial ingredient of brand affinity.

One international brand chose to walk the walk in a way that has the potential to define its entire brand. Founded in Sweden in 1953, IKEA offers an expansive range of furniture and home furnishings at price points designed to be accessible to a broad range of consumers. The company currently has 467 stores in sixty-three markets, including North America, Europe, and Asia, and 225,000 employees.[37] While sometimes disparaged for cheap and disposable products, the brand also has a reputation for tastefully designed, affordable furniture that offers a multitude of choices. In short, it's a brand that enjoys a loyal and dedicated following around the world.

IKEA is also a brand that, at times, has been accused of being a mass producer of short-term, disposable furniture that disproportionately ends up in landfills and contributes to sustainability issues. In fact, in the early 2000s, the brand ran national television commercials denigrating furniture determined to be old and that promoted replacing older items with brand new versions simply because they were easily accessible due to low prices and wide selection.[38] Until very recently, CSR was not inherently part of the company's DNA. The current company, however, purports to now be intrinsically oriented by integrating sustainable practice into its entire business model. Knowing its consumers are discerning, here is how IKEA decided to walk the walk.

The intrinsic model now adopted companywide is called the *circular business*, and it started with a commitment to become climate-positive over the next ten years. Circular business is characterized by the brand as a deliberate shift to company practices that eliminate waste, utilize renewable and recycled materials, and support regenerative ecosystems. IKEA has announced that it will dedicate $221 million towards the initiative.[39] To contribute to this goal, IKEA has phased out all nonrechargeable alkaline batteries and replaced them in retail spaces with rechargeable LADDA model batteries. The company also committed to having 99.5 percent of the wood used in furniture be either recycled or certified by the Forest Stewardship Council as sustainable. In addition, a new LED bulb was introduced in stores that is up to 35 percent more energy efficient; they've committed to phasing out plastic packaging by 2028; and in 2021, 56 percent of all materials sourced were renewable. All of which contributed to a total IKEA climate footprint decrease of 5.8 percent versus FY2016.[40]

Each of these developments is noteworthy and commendable, but to truly generate brand affinity, people prefer a story—one that's both worthy of the brand's values and is infinitely shareable: Introducing the embodiment of IKEA's circular business strategy, #BuyBackFriday. Symbolically launched on Black Friday, a retail date that is historically associated with irresponsible consumption, the company's campaign announced the program to buy back used IKEA furniture, which will then be refurbished, sold at a discount, and integrated into a more sustainable circular business model. The program spans twenty countries worldwide (although the United States is conspicuously not included) and has devised consistent pricing models for used items, rolled out a digital valuation tool, and trained 160,000 employees to accommodate the program, which culminated with dedicated showroom space for preowned furniture.[41] From a media planning perspective, it represents the brand's largest media expenditure to date, as #BuyBackFriday was promoted to consumers through television, social media, OOH (out-of-home), and POP (point of purchase). The campaign utilized informal, unpretentious, inviting language with headlines such as, "Sell us something you don't need. We'll find someone who needs it." And "Climate change is our biggest deal on Black Friday." From a performance metrics perspective, the campaign reported 3.7 billion impressions, 88,600 social engagements, and 96 percent positive to neutral sentiment scores. Possibly most relevant of all, the total number of resold items exceeded 61,000.[42] These metrics indicate that the company's CSR message is successfully resonating with consumers and translating into positive behavioral changes. With #BuyBackFriday, IKEA is walking the walk in a way that addresses their consumer's needs, acknowledges their shopping behavior, lives up to their values, and authentically makes a positive impact.

When it comes to brand credibility in the CSR space, there are six key communication dimensions, as outlined in a study published in the *Journal of Marketing Communications*.[43] Those dimensions are informativeness, third-party endorsement, personal relevance, message tone, consistency, and transparency. IKEA's CSR advertising and marketing communication has successfully touched on all of these to varying degrees, but personal relevance, message tone, and transparency, in particular, merit further detail. Personal relevance refers to messages that connect to people's personal life experiences and interests. In IKEA's #BuyBackFriday initiative, consumers could actively contribute to the brand's sustainability story by repurposing their old furniture and realizing a financial return at the same time.[44] In terms of self-promotional tone, the more self-congratulatory a brand is, the more skeptical consumers tend to become about the company's true motivations.[45] Here, IKEA's #BuyBackFriday campaign can be seen deliberately avoiding grandiose heroic hyperbole in favor of a much more sober and grounded tone that projects sincerity.[46] Finally, the brand promoted transparency by being specific about the specific percentages of its climate footprint reductions, as well as its long-term sustainability goals.[47]

We've just explored the power of cultivating brand affinity, and there's a reason marketers link the attribute closely to a brand's persona. That's because, just like with the personalities occupying our lives, as consumers, we tend to have an affinity for brands that conduct themselves with honesty, sincerity, and transparency. While a brand is typically the manifestation of a business, affinity is enhanced when it's beyond a simple consumer transaction and instead becomes a consumer/brand relationship.

INTERVIEW: DAVID MESFIN, CREATIVE DIRECTOR, INNOCEAN/USA AND COCHAIR OF THE INNCLUSION COUNCIL

David Mesfin; Photo by Ezra Mesfin.

David Mesfin is a creative director with over fifteen years of experience with award-winning integrated campaign background, including Super Bowl, FIFA, NFL, and global launch campaigns. He was born in Ethiopia and migrated to the United States at a young age, where he later received his BFA degree in advertising. David has worked on award-winning campaigns for clients such as Genesis, Hyundai, Discord, Honda, AT&T, Sony, Adidas, Oakley, Toyota, Isuzu, Farmers Insurance, and Neutrogena. He is also a director of the documentary Wade in the Water: A Journey into Black Surfing and Aquatic Culture. David is actively involved in supporting the creative industry through mentoring programs and serving as a judge for various awards. He is also a cochair of Innocean Worldwide diversity council and an associate member of the International Academy of Digital Arts and Sciences. His work has received numerous awards, including Super Bowl Silver: Best of AdMeter Commercials over 25 years, One Show, Cannes, Clio, Webby, EFFIE, *Communication Arts*, and the Anthem Awards.

David Mesfin, a creative director at Hyundai's North American ad agency Innocean/USA and one of several key members of the campaign's team, sheds light on how this advertising story came to life (figure 4.2).[49]

How Hyundai Made the Super Bowl #OperationBetter

For most Americans, the Super Bowl is practically a national holiday, and the soldiers far from home at the U.S. Military Base in Zagan, Poland, felt no differently. It took extensive satellite technology and 360-degree immersive viewing pods to virtually transport these men and women of the American armed forces to the big

4.2 "Operation Better"; Agency: Innocean/USA; Client: Hyundai.

game in Houston. What greeted them there was far more exciting than a front-row seat to the Super Bowl; it was a live virtual reunion with their families.[48]

How does the scale of the Super Bowl affect the considerations a creative must make?

Usually, with a thirty-second spot, there's a written script and actors who perform it. But in our case, this idea was kept a secret from the soldiers in Poland. They were told Hyundai was throwing a party for them, and none of them had any idea that they would be part of the film. The three soldiers who were highlighted in the project had no idea they would be seeing their family members. None of them were actors, and they all thought we were there to document this party. To that end, there were a lot of unknowns in trying to organize the project that involved people who couldn't fully know what was happening.

There was also a complicated technical aspect to it. We had to determine what technologies were available for us and which of those would help us execute the project most effectively. There was a lot of trial and error in the preplanning stage and even right up to and during the event. One perfect example of this was the initial thought of having the three soldiers wear virtual reality (VR) goggles. But at the last minute, we realized that the VR devices would block their reactions and facial expressions to seeing their family members. So, we quickly made a last-minute decision to not use them.

To lessen the number of last-minute hurdles, we did do quite a bit of contingency planning. In the six to eight months before we were even onsite, producers spent a lot of time figuring out what could go wrong and always had a plan B for everything. But, even then, things come up, and you must react quickly to it.

One of the things that happened was we brought the first soldier in, and she was surprised with her family. She was so expressive and obviously excited. She was still talking to her family members when the second soldier came in. When he stepped in, he figured out what was happening after hearing her reaction, so his reaction on the live broadcast wasn't as expressive. It was important to the film to capture that experience and feeling of them seeing their loved ones. So, we had to quickly make sure the two of them were quiet and didn't give anything away when the third soldier walked in (figure 4.3). It was those kinds of small problems that could have a significant impact that we needed to solve on the spot.

How did you use storytelling to rally partners (clients, colleagues, military families, the U.S. Government) to your idea?

The elevator pitch that resonated and helped rally everyone was simple. "We all have seen YouTube videos where soldiers would surprise a kid, wife, parents etc. But we have never seen a family member surprise a soldier." Everyone rallied also around the idea because it reinforced the philosophy of "Better Drives Us." It was a complete thought that was authentic and a relatable story based on truth.

4.3 "Operation Better"; Agency: Innocean/USA; Client: Hyundai.

We put many, many hours into this project, and the pitch deck was amazing. Although the project wasn't scripted, we wrote one to help our potential partners experience what we were going to hear from the individuals prior to even casting them. We wanted to paint that picture. The scriptwriter, Nick Flora, my partner, and I wrote the script that suggested how the soldiers would react, how the family would react, even how the kids involved would react. When he read it to the partners, it was emotional, and it really helped. Those words created a visual for everyone hearing them.

You can't go into these ideas thinking everyone is going to buy into your idea. There will be naysayers. So, we knew we would have to genuinely believe in the story for the project and surround ourselves with people who are willing to take it all the way to the end.

How did the #operationbetter story unfold in real time, and how was that planned for and optimized?

Planning for the project was involved. Legal considerations needed to be worked out throughout the various stages. The Pentagon had to approve the location and the soldiers with whom we would work. There were multiple organizations, companies, and governmental offices that had to approve the project every step of the way.

Typically, companies must send their completed Super Bowl advertisement spot several days in advance to FOX. Obviously, this couldn't happen with our project, as it was being shot during the first half of the Super Bowl and then edited onsite. That footage was then sent to Houston (where the Super Bowl was being held that year) so that the additional family footage could be edited in before it was sent off to FOX to run by the end of the game.

The project was optimized because it was not just another preplanned and executed advertisement. It was unique in that it involved raw reaction, which, yes, can be recorded and rebroadcasted. However, what set this project apart was the true surprise and honor it gave to the soldiers on that military base. They were waiting to see this teaser that they thought was about the behind-the-scenes of the base. All of a sudden, they see themselves on national television. And, of course, it was the surprise for the three soldiers who were afforded the opportunity to watch the game with their families. Based on the feedback we received, they were very appreciative and felt honored.

What stories revealed themselves during the filming of #operationbetter, and how can a marketer be prepared to capitalize on similar content opportunities?

Many times, we, as marketers and brands, look into how we can capitalize on similar opportunities, but we tend to forget our larger responsibility of making sure we respect the talent and soldiers in this case. This was the perfect opportunity to make sure we provided value to the lives of both the soldier and their family members. If we are in it to exploit a specific group, the audience will clearly see it. You may win a few awards and a corner office, but I don't think you bring value to the brand or your personal growth as a creative.

Following the shoot, I spent time talking to the soldiers, who I still stay in touch with always. They were grateful to have us, but most of all, representing them and putting a focus on their mission as soldiers at that moment in time meant everything to them. They felt honored and appreciated. The other thing to keep in mind is that the country was very much divided with social and political unrest at the time. As many believed kneeling down during the national anthem was a sign of dishonoring American soldiers, which was not the case, the soldiers did not believe the narrative. However, they still had concerns about the racial injustice happening back home and whether or not they were still respected in their own country. This project was able to show them how very respected they still are.

As a creative, I was able to understand the complexity of the issue with my position as a Black man in the United States and how the idea could actually resonate well since it is a human story that is relatable. They were able to see that here I was, a Black man showing up to support them. It made them feel more at ease that people were there to celebrate them, regardless of the race. To me, whatever happened with this project, everyone knew it was not a political statement. It was about the soldiers, and the soldiers felt that.

How was a campaign sponsored by a car company that didn't feature any cars ultimately an even more shareworthy story as a result?

Sharing the story across any digital platform is less about what you are selling and more about how you are connecting to the viewers. Brand affinity is captured when you are focused on your audience, your storytelling, and the message you are sending.

CHAPTER 5

BEGINNING, MIDDLE, AND END (OR NOT)

Ben awoke in an army hospital three days after a surprise attack in Afghanistan almost killed him and his troop while they were securing a civilian area. (There were children involved, and Ben wasn't going to take any chances they would be hurt.) He was born on the fourth of July in 2000, whole—at the dawn of a new millennium. Now, nineteen years later, he was reborn, facing the mobility loss of his right hand.

"Do you need assistance?" the nurse asked as she approached Ben's bed, noticing he was staring into space. His food had hardly been touched. The nurse wore blue, Ben's favorite color, and had a nametag with a smiley face.

"Thanks. I'm just not used to eating with my left hand," Ben replied. He was trying to be pleasant, given his new circumstances.

How am I going to adjust to this predicament? he wondered. Trying to think this through calmly, Ben knew it was possible to find employment with one working hand. He had witnessed that, and some of his cohorts from the military had similar circumstances. But how would he enjoy riding his mud bike through the woods? *How will I be able to game?* Conventional gaming controllers are not engineered for someone in his position. He started to ruminate.

Ben will always be a gamer—everyone who knows him knows that when he's got his hoodie and headset combo, he's locked in. That's how he managed to get through his senior year of school without losing his mind—gaming online with friends and with his brother. Ben loved to compete against his older brother, Will. They spent wonderful gaming hours together before Ben went to Afghanistan. Ben loved how gaming transported him, took him to other places, and tested his skills. In fact, once out of the army, Ben intended to apply to college to study game design. Gaming wasn't just a hobby for Ben; it was his passion.

"Hey, bud," Will said as he entered Ben's hospital room. "Going home today."

"Hey, Will. What's in the bag?"

Will pulled out the (Microsoft) adaptive controller, which a bunch of committed people designed primarily to meet the needs of gamers with limited mobility.

"As soon as we get home, we're gonna play. I've sure missed gaming with you, little brother."[1]

CREATIVE OR BUST

Like the motto of the Colorado Gold Rush, "Pike's Peak or Bust," if advertising is not creative, it's a bust. The biggest risk is playing it safe going unnoticed.

In their article, "The Power of Creative Advertising: Creative Ads Impair Recall and Attitudes Toward Other Ads," the researchers found that, in context, the presence of creative ads decreased the recall of "regular ads."

> The effects of repetition upon recall for regular ads decreased by 30 percent when those ads were shown alongside creative ads. When creative (vs. regular) ads were repeated, recall for non-repeated regular ads dropped by 70 percent. Furthermore, the current research found that regular ads were judged less favorably when a list of ads included creative ads. Overall, ad attitudes for the same regular ads were 10 percent lower when shown in the presence of creative ads.[2]

Their conclusion is based on their current research: "Advertisers need to develop creative advertising."[3]

WORTH SHARING

People share brand stories that resonate with them. Most often, it happens because there was an insight into the audience's top-priority that hit or on a relevant cultural moment. An effective insight might rely on a convergence of factors about the audience, the brand, and the brand story itself—psychological factors, motivational and behavioral characteristics of the user, positive or negative affect elicited by campaigns, and levels of consumer involvement, among other factors.[4]

"A brand campaign with real human insight always makes it easier for the viewer to relate and therefore want to act, whether sharing, liking, or buying your product," Wes Phelan, executive creative director at Goodby, Silverstein & Partners San Francisco, explained in an interview.[5]

In keeping with our premise, how do you create an ad story that is not only worth watching yourself but worth sharing? Here, our focus is on the quality and characteristics of brand stories worth sharing.

Make People Care

Effective brand stories often make you care and share. What makes people care? What makes a story shareworthy? Yousuke Ozawa, creative director at UltraSuperNew Tokyo, says:

> It's all about emotional surprises. Just when you think the story is going down a certain path, it makes a quick turn, arriving at an unexpected destination. If it makes sense with the product or brand, there's more chances of people remembering the ad. "How did they do that?" or "I can't believe they really did that," are the reactions you want people to have. But above all, the story structure needs an emotional surprise.
>
> With so much good content to compete with, advertisements now have to one-up Netflix, YouTube, and TikTok to be remembered. People are getting educated and sophisticated, so if the advertisement seems slightly predictable, you're swiped. You're better off being told "terrible" because at least you got a reaction from people, and they won't forget.
>
> Before setting a goal to get people to share, I would start with emotion. How do you want people to feel after seeing this advertisement? Work on developing that, then see if you can get people to feel the opposite emotion. The movie *Parasite* is full of emotional surprises. A comedy/drama/suspense/thriller and horror, all in one. The famous Dove "Beauty Sketch" campaign is suspenseful and a heartwarming drama. The viral video of a guy dancing at a festival starts goofy and funny but ends up quite emotional when everyone comes to join, turning his area into a dance party. So, if you want to make

people laugh, start by coming up with funny ideas, then see if you can make them cry. This will catch people off guard, opening them to remember the advertisement on an emotional and mental level, making it go viral.[6]

At a Future of Storytelling conference session that author Robin Landa facilitated, technologist and designer John Maeda, VP of design and artificial intelligence at Microsoft, explained that great leaders lead with story listening, not storytelling. When brands listen to their audiences, people respond well. Whether it's to fulfill people's desires or align with their values, a story that reflects and gives ear to its audience is key to sharing. This is especially true in purpose-driven advertising (marketing related to a social cause or political stance that aligns with the brand's core values). People, especially Gen Z, won't stand for purpose-washing, where companies or brands appear to back or endorse a social issue or political stance without actively supporting it financially with contributions, creating a foundation, or some other action that defines commitment. Importantly, corporate actions must not conflict with messaging. For example, if a brand creates advertising to jump on Women's Equality Day, then they had better employ women in leadership roles.

We asked David Suarez, associate partner and coexecutive creative director of Goodby Silverstein & Partners New York, "Why do you think purpose-driven ads resonate with people, especially Gen Z?" Suarez replied:

> For the first time in history, brands can't just speak *at* [emphasis added] consumers. The Internet not only gave Gen Z the ability to stay informed on all sorts of issues, but it gave them a platform to express how they feel about them. And brands listen.
>
> Whether or not there's been a true reckoning, brands face pressure to show they care about more than turning a profit.[7]

Partnering with the National Deaf Children's Society, Cadbury's "Sign with Fingers Big and Small" is encouraging people to start learning British Sign Language (BSL): "Let's help more people feel included by learning some British Sign Language."[8] While promoting Cadbury Dairy Milk Fingers, they offer little lessons in BSL. In their short hero film, *Missing Out*, we see a teenager telling the camera in BSL, "When you're deaf, you often feel left out of conversations. . . . But if someone can sign even just a few words, that's really nice."[9] To highlight her message, some of the subtitled words are obstructed by people and objects in the spot to allow us to empathize with her frustration of being excluded from what's being said.

Agency VCCP London devised the strategy with consultant and writer Rebecca A. Withey, who uses British Sign Language, as well as a panel of cocreators from across the deaf community. "At the heart of the push is a powerful short film, which will run on TV and online. Based on the concept of 'Dinner Table Syndrome'—a phenomenon where deaf people are inadvertently left out of shared everyday conversations—the creative highlights the issues faced by the community; a word they can't quite lip-read or a joke they're cut off from."[10]

Shareworthy storytelling can take the form of a documentary or demonstration as well. Lush, a cosmetics brand, created *How It's Made*, a series of videos to demonstrate how they create their ethically sourced products. Lush knows its customer base cares about ethics and ethical sourcing; Lush is showcasing their commitment by bringing us behind the scenes.

On November 26, 2021, Lush said goodbye to advertising on Facebook, Instagram, Snapchat, and TikTok; Lush won't return to those platforms until the platform "can provide a safer environment for their users. The serious effects of social media on mental health are being ignored by these platforms. It's time to stop scrolling and be somewhere else."[11]

As Erin Evon, associate creative director, told us, "It's always important to take a step back and make sure your work is culturally relevant and purpose-driven. When I get any brief, I try to take a moment and think if there's a way to answer it that also makes the world a little bit better. For example, maybe you're on a brief for a laundry machine that can wash even more laundry in each load . . . that could be an opportunity to tap into an idea around sustainability.

"When your work is making a difference, people will naturally want to share it."[12]

The Appeal of Transformation

Imagine your life without YouTube, Instagram, or smartphones and your town without movie theaters, sports stadiums, and most other entertainment venues. Now imagine living in early-nineteenth-century America when a medicine show, a traveling troupe of performers and hucksters, came to town. With origins as far back as fourteenth-century Europe, a medicine show was "structured around entertainers who could be expected to draw a crowd who would listen to, and then undoubtedly purchase the medicines offered by, the 'doctor' who made two or three sales pitches a night."[13] (You might be surprised to learn that Harry Houdini was involved with traveling medicine shows as a spirit medium and performing escape acts. Less surprisingly, P. T. Barnum was a medicine pitchman.)

Most traveling medicine shows featured a "strong man," a weak man who had been transformed by the cure-all medicine being hawked. On stage, the (now transformed) strong man amazed audiences by performing stunts, such as pulling horses with his bare hands, which, of course, he could do with the benefit of the snake oil medicine.

If we examine the strong man's role, we can better understand the appeal of transformation. This brand will make you sexier, younger-looking, stronger, more virile, and on the cutting edge—whatever it is you are seeking. In other words, it will help you become the person you aspire to be.

Do beauty creams work? Are people purchasing hope in a jar? Hope is key.

According to psychologist Abraham Maslow, we have a hierarchy of needs that influences our behavior. Once we meet our basic needs, our focus shifts to self-actualization—to our aspirations. We also need to look at what people need to feel secure for themselves, their families, their friends, and their communities. To keep our place in society and not be excluded, we follow norms. For instance, we maintain our hygiene regimens so that we are not ostracized. Products such as mouthwash, dandruff shampoo, and deodorant all bank on the fact that almost all of us keep to these norms. The transformed customer is the one with fresh breath after using the mouthwash.

In *Ways of Seeing*, critic John Berger writes that publicity proposes to each of us that we transform ourselves, or our lives, by buying something more. This more, it proposes, will make us in some way richer—even though we will be poorer by having spent our money.

Publicity persuades us of such a transformation by showing people who have apparently been transformed and are, as a result, enviable. The state of being envied is what constitutes glamor. And publicity is the process of manufacturing glamor.[14]

Most effective advertising is based on strategies of persuasion, whether a commercial ad uses social currency to persuade someone to purchase a brand-name coffee or a public service advertising campaign uses humor to encourage people to get tested for colon cancer.

People purchase products and services to meet basic needs. Beyond that, they're purchasing transformational fantasies. Every brand sells hope—the ideal this or that, a transformation, whether it's a hope that you'll look better, smell better, or be able to run faster, or whether it's a *hypothetical*, a hopeful speculation, for example, that the money you're contributing to a cause will change the world. And no matter what happens, the ad is saying, this brand is there for you.

Transformation can be about an ideal. In "Love Means Everything," a spot for Gatorade, we hear Beyoncé Knowles narrate a salute to Serena Williams, a role model and one of the greatest athletes of all time. Created by TBWA\Chiat\Day and directed by Jake Nava, Beyoncé speaks of transformation—of Williams's iconic role in sports, monumental growth, and "trailblazing career and how, from the beginning, she beautifully and forcefully embodied the power of loving oneself, and one's true identity, in the face of adversity."[15]

" 'Love Means Everything' is a nearly two-minute tribute to Williams that highlights her contributions beyond the sport. Beyoncé, who [had] released her seventh studio album 'Renaissance' . . . is on hand to narrate the short film and contextualize what Williams represents to her millions of fans: determination, confidence and above all, self-love."[16]

A Well-Crafted Brand Story

No matter how much an individual is inclined to share (or is involved with the brand), a poorly crafted story likely will, first and foremost, go unnoticed amidst a flood of advertising and other attention-seekers and, if noticed, will strike out. "In a market saturated with advertising, finding new ways of speaking to an audience is an imperative. Creative work can be lost in a sea of commercials if we are not looking for new ways to break through the clutter," Phelan told us.[17]

Crafting a Well-Told Story

People want to share a brand story when it touches them, when it speaks to them, when it says something that's hard for them to express.

—Dawit N. M., director and photographer

No matter what kind of brand experience it is, the ad team's burden is to craft a well-told story and, very often, promote the brand-as-hero to their audience. In advertising messages, being authentic and keeping the brand promise is paramount. Beyond that, great advertising stories have some common characteristics.

- There is a change, usually for the better—from negative to positive.
- There is an inciting incident that requires the protagonist to change.
- The protagonist wants something. And the story is good enough that the audience wants to see if the protagonist gets what they want.
- Every element of the story propels the "plot" forward. There might be a conventional plot, or the story might follow an unconventional structure. Either way, every decision the creatives make moves the story along.
- The story entertains, informs, educates, or does something (shock, surprise, misdirect, etc.) to capture people's attention for its entirety.
- The story strikes an emotional or aspirational chord. It sustains an emotional connection throughout.
- It's well-made in terms of film craft, activation, and brand experience— the creatives know what they are doing to make it attractive to their audience. "The audience's attention span has diminished regarding commercials, so every frame needs to be visually captivating from the first scene to the last," Phelan advised.[18]
- Perhaps it hits a cultural moment.
- It aligns with people's values and aspirations.
- It understands people's desires or needs.
- It's fresh or original and jives with the zeitgeist.
- It makes you laugh, or it makes you cry or both, or it makes you cringe (negative emotions work, too).[19]
- The press will write about it.
- It's so powerful it becomes part of popular culture.

Curiosity

Whether it's an Instagram story, original content, or a conventional commercial, people only pay attention to engaging stories. But there's a common ingredient we've noticed.

Have you ever continued watching a movie or reading a book, despite it not being very engaging, just because you were curious about how the story would end? We have. Sure, there's the issue that you've already invested time in a feature-length story and don't want to lose your investment. But we're betting on curiosity.

Advertising doesn't have the luxury of time—it must cultivate your curiosity right off. A good advertising story must make you curious *immediately*. Will she or won't she? What will work? How did that car back up without a driver? What is he doing on his phone when everyone else is celebrating the holiday? What does it mean to "Dream Crazy"?

There are other benefits to cultivating curiosity. In a study at the University of California Davis, researchers found that when the participants were highly curious about a fact, they were 30 percent more likely to recall it.[20] The researchers also found that curiosity activated the release of the neurotransmitter dopamine, which can also enhance the formation of new neural connections, contributing to a stronger memory.[21] Advertising recall is critical.

You can buy a Whopper at McDonald's for one cent. Curious?

For this marketing effort, Burger King's goal was to get people to download their mobile app to use its order-ahead functionality. Agency FCB New York broke that goal into three main corporate objectives: (1) Create top-of-mind awareness of Burger King's app, (2) get people to download the app, and (3) get people to actually use the app. A case study write-up explains:

BK [Burger King] needed to generate excitement for its revamped mobile app with order-ahead functionality. Rather than using a typical coupon, we leveraged a powerful insight: With the new BK App, anywhere can be a place to order a Whopper—even a McDonald's, turning their much larger footprint into ours. Rewarding customers with a $0.01 Whopper (when ordered from McD's), we invited consumers to engage in the trolling fun, hitting #1 on both app stores, generating 1.5 million downloads in just 9 days, and an ROI of 37:1.[22]

BK made people very curious and offered an opportunity to participate in an outrageous troll against a rival. The gain? A $0.01 Whopper (when ordered within 600 feet of a McDonald's) and trolling fun for the audience.

The worthwhile idea: Buy a Whopper for just one cent. The catch: Customers could order it only on the Burger King app "at" McDonald's.

The press, award shows, and BK fans loved it.

Surprise

In his TED Talk, filmmaker Andrew Stanton advises that a sense of wonder is critical to storytelling.[23] The *Cambridge Dictionary* lists one definition of *wonder* as "a feeling of great surprise and admiration caused by seeing or experiencing something that is strange and new."

How about an unexpected six-second Instagram video that asks you to vote on whether "The Cold Dog" is "Stupid" or "Genius"? "The Cold Dog. Is it a stupid snack or a genius dessert? #StupidOrGenius—You decide. Drop a comment below. #KeepItOscar" In partnership with frozen desserts company Popbar, fans can grab a "Cold Dog" for $2 at select Popbar locations in Long Beach, New York City, Atlanta, and New Orleans. The treat is made of flavored frozen gelato, described as capturing an Oscar Mayer dog's smokey, umami notes with a swirl of mustard."[24]

In Australia, chef Nelly Robinson created an eleven-course fine-dining experience for host KFC—the "KFC Degustration." What was Chef Robinson's inspiration? KFC's classic menu items. People's perception of KFC's quality increased by 41 percent in Australia, thanks to the chef and Ogilvy, Sydney. Food critics, journalists, celebrity chefs, and influencers were the first to experience the fine dining experience. At the cost of $75 per person, 20,000 people joined the waitlist for a seat at the table.[25]

At the 2022 MTV Video Music Awards (VMAs), *Saturday Night Live* (SNL) star Chloe Fineman's dress didn't get best-dressed praise, but it did satisfy the celebs in attendance—her dress was filled with snacks, including dried fruit and candy. To promote "Carts," showcases of products curated by pop culture personalities, retailers, and creators, fashion brand threeASFOUR partnered with Instacart to create the "Cart Couture" dress, part of Instacart's "The World Is Your Cart" campaign created with Droga5. The dress is "made with interactive jelly bean-shaped clutches that could hold snack items."[26] To imitate a cart and snack packaging, the dress was made out of holographic vinyl, holographic PU, silver nylon, metallic organza, organdy, duchess satin, and Poly-fil. The campaign also included a film that debuted at the VMAs and a new in-app shopping experience inviting shoppers to play with the idea that the world is your cart.

On October 4, 2021, when Facebook, WhatsApp, and Instagram were down for six hours, Twitter (now X) was flooded with users. The folks at Twitter tweeted, "Hello literally everyone." Although the tech difficulties were a hardship for many people who depend upon WhatsApp and Facebook, brands and celebrities joined in to respond to "Hello literally everyone."[27]

Make a Brand Promise

Laurence Vincent, former chief branding officer at UTA and professor at USC Marshall, wrote, "A brand is a promise."[28] From the outset, any brand story makes a promise to the audience and keeps that promise with a worthwhile journey.

In "Heartwarming the World: School," a spot for Hershey's Milk Chocolate Bar, distributed on YouTube, Twitter, and Facebook, we see a teen looking in a mirror practicing American Sign Language (ASL). His quest? To ask a classmate, "Do you like chocolate bars?" When he actually approaches her, he mistakenly signs, "You chocolate bar?" She enthusiastically responds in ASL, "I love chocolate," and he hands a Hershey Milk Chocolate Bar to her.[29]

Hershey comes through here on their "shared goodness" promise. The company's shared goodness promise has four rungs: shared futures, shared planet, shared business, and shared communities.[30]

System1, an ad effectiveness agency, tests ads on their long-term and short-term efficacy. The star rating system, where an ad can earn between one and five stars (best), captures people's emotional response to an ad. Only 1 percent of ads

WHAT ADVERTISING OFFERS

- Historically, advertising stories most often are about transformation. Advertising, unlike other forms of storytelling, has to offer a transformation or transportation via a brand.
- Activations offer brand experiences.
- Original content offers entertainment or information.
- Social media offers conversations, participation, and the potential for community.

on the system score five stars. "Heartwarming the World: School" earned a five-star rating.[31]

"It's a promise delivered by all of us at Hershey—to see every day as a chance to be successful in a way that makes a difference."[32]

STORY STRUCTURE OR NOT

The burden of most great stories is change. Whether you read Joseph Campbell's *The Hero's Journey* or employ screenwriter Dan Harmon's "Story Circle," the protagonist leaves the ordinary world, reemerging changed from a strange world. That change happens through a desire (or want) plus overcoming the obstacles in the protagonist's way to get what they want.

Here's how we map it out:

Protagonist and/or Brand + Brand Calling (to quench thirst, enhance fitness, etc.) →
Audience Quest (mission to feel safe, desirable, successful, etc.) + Dragon to Slay (obstacle) + Wizard (the facilitator or magician, which is the brand) +
Quest Fulfilled (resolution and call-to-action)

Another way to map it:

Protagonist (represents the target audience) →
There is an Obstacle (conflict) in the way of getting what they want →
The protagonist's Want or need or desire + Brand (facilitator) →
Transformation → Resolution and call-to-action

$$C.O.W. + B \rightarrow T$$

The one thing most effective advertising stories seem to have in common, whether implicit or implied, is the apotheosis stage of the journey—the moment of realization when a hero lets go of their old, unevolved self and embraces their new, better self, which is enabled by the transformation that the brand's product or service provides.

If a brand is a promise, then the apotheosis is the fulfillment of that promise.

THE HERO'S JOURNEY, IN SHORT

The hero's journey is a widely recognized pattern found in stories worldwide. It serves as a valuable framework for creators and strategists in crafting compelling advertising narratives. This framework helps pinpoint and enhance the pivotal moment in an ad story when our protagonist, seeking a transformation in their life, ascends to a higher level of existence due to the brand's influence.

For effective storytelling in advertising, it's crucial to tailor the narrative for different media formats, ensuring it's immersive and engaging. This adaptation should be flexible enough for improvisation and capable of being told in various, yet connected, ways across different media channels. This flexibility allows for responsiveness to audience feedback, current cultural trends, and the unique capabilities of each media platform.

ARCHETYPE HEROES

When BMW and Fallon launched the BMW film series *The Hire* starring Clive Owen in 2003, we saw a move to original content—longer-form advertising as entertainment. This was not simply a sponsorship of other folks' unique content but original content created for the "brand as hero" or, at least in the case of the BMW films, the hero's vehicle of choice, the facilitator. Fallon managed to get esteemed film directors on board, such as John Frankenheimer (*The Hire*: "Ambush"), Alejandro G. Iñárritu (*The Hire*: "Powder Keg"), and Ang Lee (*The Hire*: "The Chosen"). In 2023, the automaker, centered around the i7 M70, debuted its latest film at the Cannes Film Festival, *The Calm*, starring Pom Klementieff and Uma Thurman and directed by Sam Hargrave. "The movie's debut at the Cannes Film Festival will take place exclusively on the 31-inch, 8K 'Theatre Screen' fitted in the back of BMW's i7 sedan, with the automaker bringing 200 i7s to present *The Calm* to guests in the second row of the vehicle."[33]

The Red Bull brand also has become proficient at this form, employing film and daring stunts, such as sponsoring Austrian skydiver Felix Baumgartner's jump from a helium balloon in the stratosphere or, thanks in part to Red Bull Advanced Technologies (RBAT), Scottish BMX athlete Kris Kyle performing tricks 2,000 feet in midair on a specially constructed platform suspended from an extremely large hot air balloon.[34] People can watch Kyle in *Don't Look Down*, the full-length documentary of how the project came together on Red Bull TV.

Heroes can take many forms, such as a girl facing down a bull. They call her *Fearless Girl*. In honor of International Women's Day, the advertising agency McCann New York worked with the investment firm State Street Global Advisors to promote gender diversity in business leadership. Recounting the firm's installation of a bronze statue of a daring young girl in the middle of Wall Street, McCann New York commented, "Why? Because companies with women in leadership perform better."[35] People loved *Fearless Girl* so much that New York City found a permanent home for her facing the New York Stock Exchange.

> To me, purpose-led marketing is here to stay, and I think that is an important thing. Governments are falling short in their main purpose, which is to help people. What an opportunity for brands to fill the gap and positively impact the world. The challenge is to make these purpose-led ideas disruptive. It's not enough to have a bold initiative. You need to deliver it to the world in such an interesting, surprising, and powerful way that it can't be ignored. That's the reason why Fearless Girl not only won every award in Cannes, it won and will continue to win in culture every day.—Rob Reilly, global chief creative officer, WPP[36]

Types of Heroes

As a brand story archetype, the hero archetype rises to meet any challenge and possesses courage and perseverance.

An archetype, from Greek *archetypos*, "original pattern," is a concept popularized by Swiss psychiatrist Carl Jung, which refers to a primordial image or character's role occurring consistently enough throughout literature and art to be considered a universal concept.

With the goal of making a brand more relatable, marketers tie an archetype to a brand in branding or advertising. Essentially, the brand plays an archetypal role the target audience can identify with, which fosters emotional connections with people. Employing an archetype also allows for consistent messaging and experiences across touchpoints. Of course, the archetype must be in sync with the target audience's psychographics, values, and desires.

Brand consulting and design firm Landor & Fitch advises that to create an archetype-driven strategy, consider the following:

- "The archetype description: The personality traits, common behaviors, and brands and characters (fictional or real) that embody this archetype
- The brand idea: How does it tie to the archetype?
- The brand's personality attributes, which should be based on the archetype
- The brand's beliefs and values, which should represent the archetype"[37]

Wouldn't a gym be your hero if it could figure out a way to get you to actually attend the gym? Blink Fitness worked with agency Mischief on Gymnosis, free hypnotherapy sessions that hypnotize you into loving the gym. Blink Fitness held Gymnosis sessions for members and nonmembers in person at some of Blink's locations for one week.

"Logic, reasoning, and willpower are not always enough to convince ourselves to exercise," Carolyn Barnes, a certified clinical hypnotherapist and wellness expert who led the virtual hypno-sessions, told *AdAge*. "Hypnosis is a purely natural state that can offer direct access to the subconscious mind, where our learned behavior pattern-making systems reside. By accessing the subconscious mind, we can start to change the default switch from old patterns that don't serve us, to new ones that do."[38]

The Brand and Literary Archetypes

The Hero: Rises to meet any challenge, possesses courage and perseverance
Marketing niche: Saves the day, improves everything; e.g., American Red Cross, Moderna, Ben & Jerry's, CVS Health, ServiceNow
The Lover: Romantic, passionate, guided by one's heart
Marketing niche: Builds relationships, intimacy; e.g., Hallmark Channel, FTD, Ralph Lauren, Ferrero Rocher
The Magician: Alchemist, harnessed powers, omnipotent
Marketing niche: Helps people transform, grants wishes; e.g., Guide Dog Foundation for the Blind, L'Oréal, Proactiv, Tiffany & Co., the Nature Conservancy
The Outlaw: Rebel, independent thinker, pushes boundaries

Marketing niche: Iconoclast, risk taker; e.g., Harley-Davidson, National Geographic Partners, Red Bull, Away, Virgin Group Holdings, Liquid Death

The Sage: Wise, insightful, knowledgeable

Marketing niche: Helps people, provides practical information and guidance; e.g., Google, NPR, Wealthsimple, Rosetta, Grammarly, Propublica, OpenAI, Khan Academy

The Innocent: Hopeful, pure, sincere

Marketing niche: Trustworthy, strong values; e.g., Lowe's, Aerie, Pure Leaf, Fiji Water, Disney

The Creator: Artist, creativity, ingenuity, steering cultural conversations

Marketing niche: Creative spirit, love of self-expression, e.g., Apple, HBO, Spotify, Tencent, Dove, Adobe, Nike, TikTok, *Fast Company*

The Ruler: Leader, exerts power over others

Marketing niche: Keeps order, omnipotent; e.g., Amazon, Louis Vuitton, Mercedes, *New York Times, Bloomberg*

The Caregiver: Nurturing, supportive, service-oriented

Marketing niche: Serves the public good through service, education, healthcare; e.g., Allstate, Johnson & Johnson, Campbell's Soup, TOMS, NAMI, Vodacom

The Everyday Person: Relatable, unpretentious, your neighbor

Marketing niche: Fits in, regular, a buddy; e.g., Visa, Walmart, Alibaba, Budweiser, Dunkin'

The Citizen: Believes in the humanity of everyone. Works toward the common good

Marketing niche: Advocate, everyman; e.g., Trader Joe's, Reddit, Eileen Fisher, Patagonia, Microsoft, and IBM (three on the Kantar Gen Z sustainability index[39])

The Explorer: Craves new experiences and journeys

Marketing niche: Seeker, adventurer; e.g., Jeep, Airbnb, Viking River Cruises, Impossible Foods, Burning Man

Warrior: Soldier, rises to a challenge, assertive

Marketing niche: Achievement-oriented goals; e.g., HIIT, U.S. Marines, Blizzard Entertainment, Supreme New York

The Jester: Trickster, comic, disarming, insightful through humor, sassy

Marketing niche: Irreverent, light-hearted fun; e.g., Duolingo, Wendy's, Oatly, M&M's, Skittles, Cadbury, Hot Pockets, Scrub Daddy

Vodacom Antihijack Ads/VMLY&R Johannesburg

Most drivers use navigation apps to find the fastest route possible. However, the fastest route is not always the safest. VMLY&R Johannesburg's team used Waze's geo-located ad spots (figure 5.1) "to alert motorists of approaching hijack hotspots (identified using available crime data) and then used Waze's existing technology to offer motorists an alternative route."[40]

5.1 "Anti-Hijack Ads"; Agency: VMLY&R Johannesburg; Chief creative officer: Ryan McManus; Client: Vodacom.

When it comes to the telecoms and technology category, jargon sometimes overwhelms the intention of the brand or product. As Vodacom, we were in the midst of a shift towards being a technology company with purpose at its heart, and we needed a way to make this story real. We were willing to bank on something braver and something that answered the needs of South Africans to show the possibilities that emerge when technology meets the human spirit. That is our story, and we wanted to find the most impactful and demonstrative way to tell it. In the new age of branding, where purpose needs to be proven beyond the billboard, we believed it was critical to tell our brand and tech story through real action. With the Anti Hijack Ads piece of work, we brought the brand vision of using tech for good to life in a practical and impactful way.—Vodacom[41]

The Protagonist

The timeless resilience of accomplished athletes and sports icons is a celebrated phenomenon that transcends generations. "The Golden Son" narrates one South Korean athlete's journey.

"As Premier League soccer kicked off its new season this week, Tiger Beer is targeting Asian soccer fans with a campaign celebrating a South Korean player."[42]

"Golden Son," the spot by Publicis Singapore, "tells the story of Tottenham Hotspur striker Son Heung Min, who recently became the first Asian player to win the Premier League's Golden Boot Award after scoring twenty-three goals in a single Premier League season. It's narrated by the player himself, who touches on the prejudice he faced as an Asian footballer. In the spot, Son Heung Min says, "It took them a while to notice me. Did I come from the wrong place?" The spot goes on to show his rise to fame and fans celebrating his success with, of course, bottles of Tiger Beer.[43]

The "Nominate Me Selfie" for Political Shakti and the *Times Of India* by FCBIndia Group, Gurugram, offers up a much-needed protagonist. Only a fraction of India's parliamentarians are women. This campaign's goal is to catalyze adequate representation in policy making and in power. Tara Krishnaswamy, cofounder of Political Shakti, said, "We brought out the novel idea of using the narcissistic selfie to ask for women's representation!"[44]

Imagine organization expert Marie Kondo magically appearing to tell you that you don't have to throw out anything! In a spot for Google One subscription service, Kondo tells our protagonist, actor Keegan Michael Key, just that. "There's no need for Key to thank photos or files for the joy they sparked before trashing them because Google One will allow him to be the hoarder that he is—just a more organized one."[45] The campaign was created out of L.A.-based Omelet with direction by Terri Timely via Park Pictures. It is running across online video, social, and CRM. Kondo also offers digital organization tips on the Google One site.

BEGINNING, MIDDLE, AND END (OR NOT)

Brand stories are typically ten, fifteen, thirty, or sixty seconds. For this reason, scripts are tightly structured to convey the message in a short time frame. Many stories have a clear beginning, middle, and end.

A TV commercial or online video's conventional story structure has three acts:

1. The first act or setup in a story constitutes around 25 percent of the entire narrative. This initial phase sets the stage for the story, traditionally introducing the quest or the main goal. It's crucial because without a compelling and engaging beginning, audiences might lose interest before reaching the story's conclusion.

2. The second act or journey within a story typically makes up approximately 50 percent of the entire narrative. This section focuses on the conflicts or challenges the hero must face and conquer to accomplish their ultimate goal or quest.

3. The third act, along with the call to action, makes up roughly 25 percent of a story. This final section is where the resolution occurs, marking the achievement of the quest or the main goal. It's also where the call to action, prompting the audience to take a specific step or action, is usually incorporated.

Considerations

Story flow: Understand the storyline's progression and its direct impact on elevating the brand. Does the narrative build anticipation for the protagonist's journey? Does it effectively foster empathy for the protagonist's plight?

Audience relevance: Assess the story's significance for the primary audience. How does it align with their priorities? What concrete benefits does it offer them?

Emotional resonance: Explore how the story resonates emotionally with the audience. What specific emotions does it evoke? How does it connect with their feelings and experiences?

Actionable outcome: Define a clear call to action. What specific action or response do you want the audience to take after engaging with the story? What behavior change or reaction is the story intended to prompt?

The Quest

The quest, representing the protagonist's desires and motivations, serves as the central driving force behind the story. It instills purpose and ideally steers the protagonist's journey and the overall flow of the narrative. This quest is not only pertinent to the brand's essence but also resonates with the audience's needs and desires. It plays a crucial role in establishing empathy and forging an emotional connection between the audience and the hero/protagonist.

A Conflict

In storytelling for advertising, the conflict represents the clash between opposing forces—the barrier or challenge that obstructs the protagonist from achieving their desired resolution. Essentially, it's when the hero wants something, but an opposing element hinders their progress. To resonate with the audience, they need to emotionally invest in the protagonist's struggle. It's crucial to understand the obstacle faced by the protagonist and why they are driven to overcome it. The brand, in this context, serves as the solution or means to surmount this conflict, enabling the protagonist to achieve their goal.

A brand story can fail to resonate when the audience doesn't connect with the protagonist, the conflict lacks suspense, or when the overall narrative lacks emotional depth or fails to strike the right tone. When a story feels disconnected, unrelatable, or overly straightforward without holding the audience's attention, it often falls short. Alternatively, a story may underwhelm if it feels mundane, sounds too much like a sales pitch, or is poorly constructed in terms of its craftsmanship and delivery.

Exploring the conflict's nature involves highlighting the consequences of the protagonist failing to achieve their quest. It's crucial to illustrate the potential outcomes if the protagonist doesn't succeed. This aspect is pivotal because it ensures that the audience cares deeply about the stakes involved and is emotionally invested in what happens to the protagonist.

Transformation

1. *Simple implication*: No prom date
   Wider implication of no self-esteem
2. *Simple implication*: Body odor is offensive
   Wider implication of body odor: Exclusion from society
3. Simple implication: No reliable way to meet others
   Wider implication of no face-to-face social interactions: Loneliness and isolation

Climax

The climax is the dramatic turning point in the story—the pivotal moment when the protagonist is up against the opposing force or obstacle to resolve the conflict. This is where the brand is the catalyst and comes to the rescue or facilitates the win for a resolution.

Whether it's a short film or any traditional plot structure, the climax is the moment when the story arc bends toward a resolution.

Resolution

When positioning the brand either as the hero or as the facilitator enabling the resolution of the quest, clarity is key. The conflict must be definitively resolved, showcasing the brand's role in overcoming it. This resolution moment is crucial as it allows the viewer to grasp the significance of what's been at stake for the hero. As the hero fulfills their quest, the transformation becomes evident, underlining the brand's impact on this journey.

Alignment in values between the brand and the target audience is crucial. Stories should refrain from being opportunistic, disrespectful, or predatory in nature. It's essential to establish a connection based on shared values. Additionally, an emotional resolution within the story is vital, providing a sense of closure or satisfaction that resonates with the audience:

Clarity of the brand's role: Is the brand's role clearly presented in a way that the audience can understand? How effectively does the story showcase how the brand enables the protagonist's transformation or helps in achieving their desires?

Articulation of brand values: Are the brand's core values clearly communicated and integrated into the story? Is the story authentic in representing these values while resonating with the brand, the company, and the target audience?

Relatability and emotional satisfaction: Does the story feel relatable to the audience's experiences and emotions? Does it offer a satisfying emotional resolution that leaves the audience feeling connected or moved?

Beneficial outcome and narrative structure: Does the story's outcome provide a beneficial impact? Does this outcome align with the narrative structure, ensuring a cohesive and logical progression?

Audience engagement: Is the story compelling enough to maintain the audience's interest throughout? Does it provide an engaging and exciting experience that might prompt them to share it with others?

Shareworthy: Is the experience exciting or engaging enough to share with friends, family, or coworkers?

Each of these aspects contributes to evaluating the effectiveness of the story in conveying the brand's message and ensuring resonance with the audience while maintaining their interest and engagement.

Or Not

Conventional advertising storytelling plays chronologically from start to finish. But advertising stories do not have to follow that chronology or any. For Heineken-owned cider brand Orchard Thieves, Irish agency Rothco conceived and created "Start Bold/End Bold," a "reversible" commercial (in Ireland) with "a fully reversible commercial which has a narrative that works in both directions."[46]

Whether viewed forward or backward, directed by Stevie Russell, Russell Curran, the story is the same. "Orchard Thieves is all about finding our own bold way to do things and when the idea of a TV commercial that could be watched forwards and backwards was presented we were instantly intrigued," comments Emma-Jane McKeown, senior brand manager, Orchard Thieves.

"The narrative is built around Orchard Thieves' simple worldview that if you start bold, you'll end bold, and if you end bold, you obviously started bold!"[47]

The brand was looking for a way to push boundaries.

Ray Swan, creative director at Rothco, adds, "Whilst we wanted to shoot a single film that worked forwards and backwards, it was also important that it worked as an engaging story. We didn't want the technical part of the commercial to ever get in the audience's way. I think we've really achieved that."[48]

Aimed at millennials, what starts out as a pedestrian alcohol online ad and TV commercial becomes unconventional halfway through; viewers are urged to rewind and watch the action backwards.[49]

Chinese air conditioner brand Midea wanted to penetrate the U.S. market for the first time. They aimed at New Yorkers with a product that they claim is particularly suited to New York City housing. Ad agency Pereira O'Dell aided in filling that gap for Midea with a creative campaign offering a respite from the heat with ninety minutes of free air conditioning in a movie theater, a place where people could relax comfortably, check their phones, and sit back. The film shown? Midea shot a feature-length film of an air-conditioner visual as it cools a

SP☀TLIGHT

Reddit Inc.—"Superb Owl"/ R/GA

When "r/WallStreetBets," an investor community on Reddit, drove up prices of colorless stocks, a media frenzy ensued in the United States and caught the notice of Washington, DC.

Seizing on this unique opportunity, R/GA, Reddit's agency, capitalized on it and "hacked" the Super Bowl (figure 5.2). Because the Reddit community tends to be anti-advertising, R/GA stayed true to the brand. R/GA had one week to make the commercial, from presentation to production to air.[51]

5.2 "Superb Owl"; Agency: R/GA California; VP, executive creative directors: Bryan Gregg / Chapin Clark; Creative director: Kevin Koller; Associate creative director, studios: Kirstie Bones; Associate creative director, copy: Jocelyn McCanles; Senior copywriter: Scott Steele; Art director: Ben Muckensturm; Client: Reddit; Reddit chief marketing officer: Roxy Young; Reddit senior marketing lead: Dong Chen.

(continued on next page)

(*continued from previous page*)

Their idea? "Let's disrupt the biggest moment in the ad world, just like our Reddit users disrupted the financial world, by airing a low-budget commercial at the Super Bowl, proving that small groups can achieve some pretty massive things."

The ad started with an old-school "'Please stand by' art card, which gave way to a static long-copy slide speaking to the Reddit community and their mindset.

Too long to read in five seconds (on purpose), the ad forced viewers to pause, rewind, or go online to get the message, which was loaded with easter eggs."[52]

The media responded; publications such as *Fast Company* and the *New York Times* covered the Super Bowl "hack," and it drove many to Reddit's site, with a 25 percent spike in traffic.[53]

It won the Cannes Grand Prix Lion for Real-Time Response.

Author Greg Braun interviewed Kevin Koller, group creative director at YouTube, formerly a creative director at R/GA, about "Reddit Superb Owl."[54]

Compared to Super Bowl megabrands, Reddit had a comparatively small advertising budget. How was this disadvantage actually inspiring creatively?

Whenever I approach a problem, I always try to think, "How do you do it opposite from the way that it's always been done before." When we first got this project, we didn't necessarily know it was even going to be a Super Bowl project. Initially, we just wanted to react to all of Reddit's momentum in the news, and, honestly, we started off with things like billboards, but then the proximity to the upcoming Super Bowl got us thinking, "Can we actually pull it off?" which led to the next questions, which were, "How can we pull it off with less than a week to the event?" and "How can we show up in a way that's truly impactful?"

We realized, "We don't have the money, we don't have the time, and we're not going to get a celebrity," but luckily, we had a story that people were really interested in, so we wanted to emulate the spirit of the people on our Reddit platform, which was being disruptive of the system. The idea of the long copy ad kind of came to us, and that was the catalyst. All you really needed was the story for the audience to grab onto, and so we gave that to them.

Why was it important for Reddit's brand story to make people participants in the campaign as opposed to merely witnesses?

That was a big component of it. We purposely wanted to make it something that you wanted to share. We had two things on our side from a technology standpoint. One was that we now all have the ability to pause a commercial, so if something catches our attention, we can do that. Then there's this other aspect, where even if you miss something, you can quickly go online and find the answer as to what it was. By making it something people felt the need to share with others, it created a conversation.

Why would you say it's the responsibility of creativity to challenge the status quo?

I actually think that's how you make impactful work. I feel that we, as humans, get in sort of a zombie state, if you will, and our lives are kind of filled in for us. There are all of these unwritten rules for us about the way things are supposed to be, and I think the way you wake people up from that zombie state is you do something disruptive. It's a healthy exercise to look at the rules and say, "What if you don't do that?" and always start from that posture.

From an executional standpoint, how did your team make it appear that CBS was hacked?

We were only a week before the Super Bowl, and basically, there was a moment where we said, "Should we do something around this moment of Reddit momentum, or should we not?" We were debating it internally, and then there was a moment when both Alexandria Ocasio-Cortez and Ted Cruz came out on the same day in support of this Reddit phenomenon. Then it was like, "Okay, we've got two completely politically opposite people, both on our side. There's never going to be a better opportunity; we've got to go for it." Our clients agreed, so that Friday, we started concepting into the weekend, and then Saturday morning, we came up with the "Superb Owl" campaign. Monday morning, we pitched it to the client, and they were like, "Yes, this is it." We immediately sent our media team to see if there was Super Bowl ad time availability. Because I had worked on the Sprint business previously, I knew there was sometimes leftover Super Bowl media inventory. There are these five-second bumpers, which are not meant for commercials but just meant to get you in and out of the programming. We essentially just bought one of those, which turned out to be a really affordable buy for us.

Our first thought when we were brainstorming was that whatever we aired had to be insanely short. Then we thought, "No wait, what if we flipped it and made the content really long? That would actually be more interesting." Because we broke the rules and did what you're not supposed to do, it was more disruptive as a result.

The campaign closed with the statement, "Powerful things happen when people rally around things they really care about." How did Reddit's "Superb Owl" campaign bring this particular sentiment to life?

Reddit is a community composed of a hundred thousand communities, and a hallmark of Reddit users is that whatever you're passionate about, you're going to find the most passionate, like-minded people in the world here. Whether it's needlepoint or breadmaking, we just wanted to invite people in, to feel that way about other subjects as well. Even if you weren't into stocks, you would now know Reddit was a place for you as well.

(continued on next page)

(*continued from previous page*)

Is there a key insight about the creation of this campaign and brand storytelling that you would like to share?

I would just say that our partnership with the client was key. From the very beginning, having that trust was crucial. The thing is that we didn't know if it was going to work. We were all excited because we were breaking the rules in such a different way, but there was a real feeling of, "This could go horribly wrong, or this could go horribly right." We felt good about the work. But you never know how things will be received, especially when they're so different. It took a lot of courage from our client to have the guts to do that, and I think they deserve all the credit in the world for recognizing a good idea, pouncing on it, and having the courage to go through with it.

In what way is courage an essential ingredient of storytelling?

It is an essential ingredient. We're all looking for new stories and new things, and the only way you get to new things is by being courageous. Jeff Goodby [one of the cofounders of Goodby, Silverstein & Partners] always told us that when you drop a new campaign, it should feel like you're unleashing it on the world. I always liked that. You're not going to just quietly drop it and then watch it fade away. You're going to launch an idea that's so impactful that the world almost isn't ready for it. As humans, we're very simple. We're looking for the new exciting thing to be interested in or to fascinate us, and so I think it's our job as advertisers to figure out how our clients' products fit into that dynamic.

NYC apartment.[50] The insight? New Yorkers will see a film in an air-conditioned theater for a break from the heat.

AUTHENTICITY

In advertising, genuineness equals trustworthiness. Authenticity in advertising means the brand's intentions are not spurious, and their actions are accurately represented. How a brand's advertising communicates authenticity as an integral element has to do with accuracy, real from fake statements and claims, historical accuracy, and how their genuine communication aligns with what people identify as authentic inasmuch as they can research claims on their own with available information on the Internet.

"I think there's a big push towards storytelling now, not only because it helps to cut through the clutter of online advertising, but also because when you tell a story, it feels more authentic. It makes you seem more like a person and less like a third-party disconnected body. It helps you seem more trustworthy and enjoyable, like a friend who is going to give you advice on what to buy," says Jacob D. Teeny, assistant professor of marketing at the Kellogg School.[55]

Teeny also suggests, according to research by Assumpció Huertas, associate professor in communication studies at the Rovira i Virgili University (Tarragona, Spain), that people perceive live videos or disappearing videos on social media as somewhat more authentic.[56]

SP TLIGHT

Kingsford "Preserve the Pit"

Through an immersive fellowship program, one-on-one mentorship with industry leaders, and films, the Kingsford brand partnered with Current Global and Woodward Original to launch "Preserve the Pit," an initiative focused on preserving the cultural history of Black pitmaster barbecue and investing in its future.

A two-minute film delves into the historical and cultural significance of barbeque. "The cooking technique has deep roots in the African American community and has provided opportunities for both innovation and the preservation of traditions. Barbeque joints have long been central to building neighborhoods and communities."[57]

"To kick off the company's initiative to support a new, younger generation of Black pitmasters with grants to barbeque entrepreneurs, Kingsford turned to cultural historian Dr. Howard Conyers, media partners with strong multicultural strategy teams, and its own DEI group to introduce the complex and fascinating story behind a uniquely American cuisine."[58]

**INTERVIEW: LUIZ SANCHES,
PARTNER/CHAIRMAN AND
CCO OF ALMAPBBDO, BBDO
CCO OF THE AMERICAS,
AND CCO OF THE CANNES
LIONS CREATIVE AGENCY
OF THE DECADE**

Luiz Sanches

Luiz Sanches is the chairman and CCO
of AlmapBBDO, where he has worked
for twenty-five years and heads the agency's board. He began as an art director,
became a creative director in 2002, and was soon made general creative director.
He also serves on BBDO's Global Creative Board.

In 2013, he became a partner at the agency. Almap is a four-time Agency of the
Year at Cannes, the best-performing Brazilian agency in the event's history, and
has topped the *Gunn Report*'s ranking four times.

Luiz has received more awards than any other Brazilian creative, including 184
Cannes Lions and sixty-three Pencils at D&AD in London. The *Gunn Report* once
named him the best creative director in the world. In 2018, he served as president
of the Cannes Film Jury.

Over his thirty-year career, Luiz has helped to create indelible campaigns and
reposition Brazil's most iconic and prominent brands. He believes that creativity
fuels his clients' businesses and that, in a world fragmented by the digital revolution, big ideas are crucial for brands to stay relevant.[59]

*You seem like a person who's very comfortable embracing multiple international cultures
simultaneously. How would you say your multicultural outlook has helped you create
breakthrough work?*

I think it's really based on the origins of Brazil, where I'm from, which is a
multicultural country. If you think about Brazil, it's the only country in South
America with the national language of Portuguese, so in order to learn how to
communicate, we became very strong visually. Once we became very strong visually, we started embracing the different ways other cultures around us communicated as well. That and the fact that Brazil is always in a big crisis. That makes
us humble in terms of understanding that we need to do so much with so little.

And with the difficulties that we have, we've learned how to be really creative, not just in terms of having strong insights, but how we then show people these insights in the most impactful ways. We have this huge blend of different cultures in Brazil, and we've learned how to transform that into an advantage by embracing it, not fighting against it.

In your leadership role at BBDO, are you able to bring some of that multiculturalism to other markets as well?

As a network, I can say that BBDO really embraces the importance of diverse cultures. When you walk around the agency here in New York, you can truly see a multicultural agency at work, and you can see the same thing in our other offices around the U.S. So, instead of just promoting ourselves as diverse, I feel that we're actually implementing it. This is all part of the direction that's happening at the agency to really bring different ways of thinking to tackle creativity because creativity is all about having different points of view. It's like you have this colorful palette called diversity, right? So, as a result, we have more colors with which to paint our picture, which is very much a part of the culture here.

You've served on the industry's most prestigious advertising awards juries, often as jury president, including the 2022 Cannes Titanium Lions Jury. Is there a social responsibility involved in sitting on juries of that magnitude?

Yes, there's a social responsibility, and there's also a responsibility to really celebrate the work that brings real solutions and real insights that we can apply in different cultures and to actually understand how a local cultural phenomenon could become something that can then impact global culture. We have a lot of programs inside the agency where we promote diversity in advertising, but in addition to that, I think one of the most important things we can do in order to promote diversity is to represent it in our client's advertising. Supporting diversity within an agency is valuable and might achieve a couple thousand impressions if we were to message that communication to the public. But when we put diverse representation in the work we create for our clients, that's when we're really able to transform things on a large scale, and that relates to one of the responsibilities that you have as an international awards jury member. To really recognize the work that is more than a brand simply trying to promote itself by association but is instead a brand making a true commitment to positive change in society.

Your American Red Cross TV spot, "Bloody Nightmare," called up classic modern horror movies to inspire volunteers to donate blood. Why is it important to harness popular culture to create positive change?

I truly believe that what we generate is content, is entertainment, and is something that has to impact culture. Earlier in my career, looking outside of Brazil, I remember seeing the "Whassup" campaign from Budweiser and the "You're Not You When' You're Hungry" campaign for Snickers. Those campaigns were very popular, and people talked about them well beyond the confines of the advertising community itself. It became a part of pop culture.

This is part of the responsibility that we as creatives have in today's world—to really try to continually reinvent ourselves and to strive to be brave in our work. If we're not creating brave work, then what we create could be considered like a commodity when inherently it's not. Therefore, in order to defy that, you have to challenge, you have to provoke, you have to be bold, and you have to bring the swagger to your ideas. I think the Red Cross "Bloody Nightmare" campaign represents a little bit of this mindset in trying to really connect with popular culture, and the result was beautiful work.

The metaphor that I use is the playlist on Spotify. Since you have only a limited amount of time for engagement during any given day, what are the brands you're going to pick to put on that playlist? Are they the brands that just give you something different and interesting, or are they the ones that offer you an emotional connection? Are they the ones that you relate to, that give you a meaningful conversation, or that give you a unique perspective? Those become the brands that I want to consume every day. Using the Spotify metaphor, in order to become part of people's playlist, we need to offer them something that really captures both their attention and their hearts simultaneously.

Your work often requires audiences to mentally engage with the work and then rewards them for it. One example would be the "True Fashion" campaign for Havaianas sandals, which showed that backstage, off the runway, the fashion model footwear of choice is actually the brand's comfortable signature flip-flops (figure 5.3). Does that respect for the audience's intelligence represent a creative philosophy of yours?

I think the most important thing we're always pursuing in the work is, "What is the human truth?" When you talk about the Havaianas New York Fashion Week idea, we weren't creating any fantasies. That literally happened, so the idea then becomes, "How are we going to best show that to the audience?" It could then be executed differently in terms of tonality, as in it could be funny, it could be emotional, or it could be dramatic, but the thing we had to really start with here was this sweet spot of the truth and then really boost that truth to become the foundation of an amazing idea.

5.3 "True Fashion"; Agency: AlmapBBDO, São Paulo; Client: Alpargatas Havaianas.

In searching for a brand's illuminating truth, what insight would you offer about how to discover it?

Usually, you know you have a valuable insight when it makes you feel uncomfortable. When you're thinking to yourself, "I could get in trouble for this," that's actually your brain telling you that you've discovered a solution that's different from the ones you've been exposed to before. My approach is that I would rather make nine mistakes on the way to having one big winner than to consistently create a body of "just average work" that's ultimately "just okay." I cannot live with "just okay." There's one thing that I always say to my clients, which is, "You may hate it, or you may love it. But you'll certainly never ever forget it." When seeing the work touches you, changes you, or impacts you in some way, then you know you're on the right track to achieving what has to be done.

So many of your successful campaigns focus on environmental sustainability, such as "The Beach Walker Project" for Johnnie Walker, the Greenpeace print ad "Sea Levels," or AmBev's "Drink This Poster." Is it important for our industry to support and promote causes in addition to promoting brands?

Yes, it's important to read the moment and to understand the responsibilities that brands have. We saw what happened during the pandemic, right? We as a society failed when we could have prevented so much of that, but we were not able to because there was a lack of political leadership. In contrast, we saw many brands step up during that time and take on some of the responsibility of guiding the people through the pandemic by saying, "Okay, Let's use masks" and "Let's wash our hands." Here, the brands themselves took on the responsibility to act and led people down the right path.

But there's a time for everything. Sometimes, a brand has to build on different needs as well. Is the purpose of this brand in your life as entertainment? Is the purpose of this brand in your life as inspiration? Ultimately, the brand needs to deliver something that you desire. Otherwise, all the brands will say the same thing in the same way, and that risks becoming just one single indistinguishable voice. So, I think there's a great opportunity to build the social responsibilities of brands, but at the same time, we cannot forget that any successful brand engages you like a human being does. One that knows you and appreciates your desires. It has to be balanced.

Is there any wisdom you can share with the next upcoming generation of advertising professionals?

The other point I'll make about some professionals from the younger generation is that they're trying to copycat when they get into agencies. That's a mistake. Instead, what they can best bring creatively is the kind of work that agencies are not currently doing because, otherwise, they're not needed, right? So, it's a balance. You need to understand the industry, you need to learn the discipline, you need to absorb all the skills and the crafts that you're exposed to, but at the same time, when you get into the agencies, you need to understand that you're not there to repeat what's already been done.

You have to do your own thing creatively because you come from a different generation, bringing ideas that previous generations don't necessarily understand in the same way. My expectation for the younger generation is to "Do what I don't do." And that's the beauty of creativity, right? You're there to make your own mark.

CHAPTER 6

THE NORTH STAR

"Т he best way to describe what happened to our roof is that it peeled back like a sardine can."

That's how Kim Miller, homeowner, described the cyclone that hit Rockhampton, Queensland, Australia, in the short film, *The Story of Resilience*, created by Leo Burnett Australia for the insurance arm of Suncorp, Australia.[1]

For many Australians, extreme weather is becoming commonplace. Gusting winds. Floods. Cyclones. Brush fires. The coldest winters in decades. This existential problem isn't going away. Homeowner insurance protects you when your home is damaged, but what if an insurance company's North Star mission was about resilience rather than protection?

For Suncorp, Leo Burnett Australia conceived a way to create more resilient communities with "One House to Save Many," a prototype house "resilient" to fire, flood, storm, and cyclone, collaboratively designed, built, and tested by experts at the Commonwealth Scientific and Industrial Research Organization, James Cook University, and Room 11 Architects.

The point: See how this house could help save yours.

"After the initial stages of concepting, we had a realization," recalls agency senior copywriter Eric Franken. "Instead of focusing on the protection that comes with insurance, what if we focused more on prevention? Could we make the homes themselves more resilient? As natural disasters cost Australia's insurers upwards of $150 billion a year, the concept of a more resilient Australia was instantly appealing to Suncorp."[2]

"A lot of where purpose [advertising] goes wrong is when it just points a finger at the problem and says, 'that's a terrible problem,'" Leo Burnett

CEO Emma Montgomery told *Little Black Book.* "What's great about this is that the creative solution is the answer to the problem, which is: 'insurance should not be about protection. We need to shift the whole paradigm of the category to resilience.' And that's about everyone in Australia. . . . This is a piece of work that has captured the attention of CEOs, the local government, the federal government, because they see that this is what we need to be doing."[3]

Using existing technologies, novel uses of resilient housing materials, and accessible tools and materials (such as installing mesh screen doors around the balustrade to defend against debris in cyclones and prevent embers from getting through in a bushfire), the expert team designed the home to withstand cyclones, floods, storms, and fire. Leo Burnett launched "One House" with an integrated campaign, a prime-time documentary, and an online hub. Not only did this campaign win major ad awards and earn media attention, but it is now also impacting the future of Australia's building codes.[4] The expert team "devised novel applications of existing technologies to help Australian homeowners keep their homes and communities safe."[5]

"As a jury, we were blown away by the boldness of the idea, the creative bravery of the execution, and the massive societal, environmental and economic impact. One House innovation has started a movement," said Cannes 2022 jury president Cleve Gibbon, CTO, Wunderman Thompson, US.[6]

"What started out as a marketing initiative could help to save lives, livelihoods and lifestyles of Australians," commented Georgia Phillips, COO at specialist brand and communications insights agency Luma Research.[7]

"Several weeks after launch, the Federal Government announced a $600 m[illion] resilience fund for new disaster preparation and mitigation programs. The campaign reached 99 percent of the target audience through paid and earned media and was covered across every major Australian news network, resulting in more than 20 million impressions."[8]

When an insightful North Star idea not only stems from the brand's mission but also underlies all the ad communication, it resonates with the audience. What's so telling about Leo Burnett's "One House to Save Many" idea is that it is a paradigm shift for the brand and brand category—the North Star idea proposes a different understanding of the problem. As Montgomery points out, their creative solution was reframing what insurance should be about—not protection but shifting the category to resilience.

A brand campaign with real human insight always makes it easier for the viewer to relate and therefore want to act, whether sharing, liking, or buying your product.

—Wes Phelan, executive creative director[9]

GENERATING NORTH STAR IDEAS

Polaris, the North Star, is the brightest star in the constellation Ursa Minor, also known as the Little Dipper. It's called the North Star because its position in the night sky is almost directly over the North Pole. "Polaris is attention-getting, because unlike all the other stars in the sky, Polaris is in the same location every night from dusk to dawn, neither rising nor setting," according to astronomer and science communicator Dr. Richard Tresch Fienberg.[10] Due to its constant position in the sky, sailors have used the North Star as a navigational tool and a guide.

Identifying a brand's or a brand campaign's North Star is very useful. It serves to establish a core story concept and keep you on course—a course aligned with your brand's core principles, narrative, essence, strategy, and goals.

Finding a North Star idea that resonates across various media platforms and has the power to captivate audiences begins with a keen understanding of the target audience. It's about creating stories that are impossible for them to ignore. Starting with insights into the target audience is crucial to generating these impactful ideas. As Harsh Kapadia, EVP and chief creative officer of MRM, advises, "People only hear interesting stories."[11] (Read the full interview with Kapadia in chapter 3.)

Here are factors and information to consider when generating a North Star story idea.

THE IDEATION PROCESS

There are idea-generation processes in general use, two of which were popularized by advertising professionals. In 1926, Graham Wallas, an English scholar and cofounder of the London School of Economics, wrote *The Art of Thought*, delineating a four-stage model of the creative process (preparation, incubation, illumination, verification). During the mid-twentieth century, James Webb Young, an advertising executive at J. Walter Thompson, wrote *A Technique for Producing Ideas*, presenting a five-stage ideation process (preparation, incubation, illumination, evaluation, and verification) based on Wallas's framework, popularizing it in advertising. Many people use Webb Young's process today. Webb Young also advocated for combinatorial thinking (combining existing [his word: old] things into new ones) and a Pareto theory approach (the imbalance of inputs and outputs is what is known as the Pareto principle, or the 80/20 rule), saying that an 80/20 mindset helps you to stay focused.

In 1953, Alex F. Osborn, cofounder and vice president of Batten, Barton, Durstine, and Osborn, introduced brainstorming through his books *Your Creative Power* and *Applied Imagination: Principles and Procedures of Creative Thinking*. Osborn was influenced by Wallas's process, as well.

Brainstorming continues to be widely used and is part of current design processes, including design thinking and IDEO's innovation process. Though an individual can employ brainstorming, Osborn considered it a group problem-solving method with the end goal of generating as many ideas as possible, involving spontaneous contributions from all members of the group and subsequent consideration of the ideas to devise a solution to the problem. Osborn had four basic rules: (1) Generate as many ideas as possible; (2) no one criticizes anyone's contributions of ideas, with judgments deferred until the brainstorming process concludes; (3) wild ideas are welcome; and (4) participants can combine ideas and improve on one another's ideas.[12]

Many experts, from psychologists to designers, consider creativity as a novel combination of existing or familiar ideas—what some refer to as combinatorial. However, for it to be deemed creative, the novel idea must be interesting.[13] In her research on artificial intelligence (AI), Margaret A. Boden points out that two definitions of creativity are necessary. However, both require that the novel idea be interesting. "Improbabilist creativity concerns novel and improbable combinations of familiar ideas. Impossibilist or exploratory-transformational creativity concerns novel ideas that, relative to the pre-existing conventions of the domain, the person could not have had before."[14]

About the creative process, Jules Henri Poincaré, a French mathematician, theoretical physicist, and a philosopher of science, pointed out that "ideas rose in crowds; I felt them collide until pairs interlocked . . . making a stable combination."[15] Albert Einstein said, "Combinatorial play seems to be the essential feature in productive thought."[16]

In *The Act of Creation* (1964), Arthur Koestler introduced bisociation—a combinatorial model of creativity in which the brain synthesizes raw material into new ideas. Bisociative thinking occurs when we simultaneously consider a problem or situation in two or more domains or "matrices of thought." Optimally, the two matrices' interaction results in their fusion into a novel synthesis. That novel synthesis can lead to an idea or result in an idea. Paul Thagard, philosopher, cognitive scientist, and author, analyzed one hundred breakthrough discoveries and one hundred historic inventions, showing that, without exception, each could be broken down into a combinatorial product.[17]

MIT's Hal Gregersen has developed a methodology of brainstorming for questions rather than answers, which lets you reframe problems in ways that might spur "breakthrough thinking." You have a problem to solve and invite a group to consider it. The methodology: "In just two minutes describe it at a high level so that you don't constrain the group's thinking. Make it clear that people can contribute only questions and that no preambles or justifications are allowed. Then, set the clock for four minutes, and generate as many questions as you can in that time, aiming to produce at least 15. Afterward, study the questions generated, looking for those that challenge your assumptions and provide new angles on your problem. If you commit to actively pursuing at least one of these, chances are, you'll break open a new pathway to unexpected solutions."[18]

In *The New Art of Ideas: Unlock Your Creative Potential*, author Robin Landa introduced the three Gs framework of ideation. To generate or crystalize an idea, identify the following:

- Goal—What you want to achieve
- Gap—The unmet need or void that the idea addresses
- Gain—The overall benefits of your idea[19]

From her experience in advertising, branding, and academic research, Landa cites the importance of a gap—a missing piece that fills a void—an unmet need, an area not yet explored or underexplored, a question not yet asked, a method not utilized, or a population not addressed or underserved. The gap helps you differentiate your ad idea. Landa notes that people want a benefit, either functional or emotional, from a brand or brand advertising. That led her to see the benefit as the gain in her ideation process.

DON'T FORGET THE INSIGHT

The creative brief sets out the brand strategy and goal for any campaign. That's the starting point. Once the brief is analyzed and scrutinized (it could be skimpy or poorly conceived), no matter which ideation process you use, first seek an insight into the audience.

An *insight* is a realization or revelation about the intended audience's need or belief or about their true thoughts, feelings, or behavior—a human truth or finding no one has yet noticed. That insight or human truth ultimately should warrant a change in how you look at a behavior, situation, product, or service and could be the catalyst for generating an idea. A great insight that leads to an idea usually is about the audience rather than the brand. However, if you pinpoint an insight for each and they work off of each other, that could be a revelation or sweet spot.

Jeff Fromm, president of Futurecast, believes that insights are more about the category than the brand. Insights reveal more about how people want to *feel* than what they think, and insights inspire new ideas—not the same old stuff.[20]

You can think of insights in two main ways: A fixed insight dominates what people say and how they behave over an extended period. A dynamic insight bends with small- or large-scale changes in the audience's needs, behavior, or situation—think of a black swan event of staggering proportions, such as a pandemic or a hurricane of enormous size and scope.

"To me, an insight is something that gives you a new way of looking at a situation. And it has to be something that your brand can have a role in addressing. Not all insights should make their way into the idea. The idea should be born from the insight, and resolve it in some way but that is not the same thing as showing it," explains Bridget Angear, joint chief strategy officer, AMV BBDO.[21]

"Why is a good insight like a refrigerator? Because the moment you look into it, a light comes on," said Jeremy Bullmore, advisory board member to WPP.[22] About Bullmore's statement, Guillaume Martin, managing director and chief strategy officer, Oliver, said, "An insight is a stepping stone that allows you to move to an idea."[23]

Gareth Price, global brand strategist at Facebook, advises there are two broad frameworks that can help guide the process of identifying insights, and both can make use of social data. *Facts plus observations*: "Combining facts with observations" is one of the most effective ways to reach an insight. For creative purposes, insights only matter if they inform ideas or lead to great execution. *Disconnects in the data*: "Looking for disconnects within data" can also be an effective way of identifying insights. This could be a conflicting attitude held by the same group of people.[24]

Beyond the ideation processes cited, let's look at ways to generate North Star ideas that get results.

STRATEGICALLY CREATIVE NORTH STAR THINKING

Any North Star idea should be strategically creative. It should be flexible enough so that each execution is conceptually sound, solves the problem in the brief, anticipates issues (what people might want or need), aims empathetically and appropriately at the top-priority audience, and ultimately benefits the audience. (A benefit can be emotional or practical.) The idea must align with the brand's or entity's values.

The North Star idea must A.L.T.E.R.:

- *Attract*: People must notice it and find it appealing enough to talk about or share.
- *Timely*: Ideas should be opportune, well-timed, appropriate, and judicious.
- *Lodestar*: It entails the central premise, mission, and values. It is the guiding light of the campaign in synchronization with the company's mission, values, and actions.
- *Engage*: It should be involving, stimulating, or ideally participatory. It should prompt or move people to do something.
- *Resonate*: People should find the idea remarkable, relatable, and relevant; and, it should be responsive to their aspirations, hopes, and desires.[25]

Ask: Would the idea make people think or feel something? Change their point of view? Alter their behavior?

Reframing

In the creative process of addressing advertising challenges, at times, creatives immediately start thinking about creative solutions without thoroughly examining the problem's depth or potential interconnected issues. This can limit the scope of their solutions, focusing on one aspect while neglecting a broader or more complex problem.

Reframing involves stepping back from the initial problem statement to analyze if there might be a larger or different issue at play. It's about looking beyond the surface to explore whether the problem could be more extensive, interconnected with other factors, or multifaceted. By reframing, creatives aim to identify a better, more comprehensive understanding of the problem they're trying to solve, which can lead to more innovative and effective solutions.

Think: *Is there an alternative definition or interpretation of the problem?* Leo Burnett's reframing of Suncorp insurance company's message and role led to an extremely creative storytelling and consequential solution.

Reframing involves altering the perspective or viewpoint through which you perceive a problem or goal. It's about considering various angles to gain a more comprehensive understanding.

To begin the reframing process, it's essential to question the initial problem or goal outlined by the client or in the brief. This questioning involves critically assessing whether the problem presented aligns accurately with the actual issue at hand. By posing these questions, you aim to uncover any misunderstandings or limitations in the initial problem definition:

- Validity of the problem: Is the problem defined accurately, aligning with the client's perception or the specifications outlined in the brief? Are there underlying factors that might not have been addressed?
- Identifying misconceptions: Is there a misconception or assumption that might be skewing the perception of the problem? Are there aspects that haven't been considered?
- Revealing layers: Are there additional questions that could be asked to reveal a broader or more intricate problem? Sometimes, the problem statement might not encompass all relevant factors.

Reframing a question can change outcomes. In the TED Talk "Choice, Happiness, and Spaghetti Sauce," journalist and writer Malcolm Gladwell explained how reframing a problem can lead to successful solutions. Prego, in its pursuit of the perfect spaghetti sauce, hired Howard R. Moskowitz, an experimental psychologist who worked in the field of psychophysics. Although Prego was looking for the perfect spaghetti sauce, Moskowitz reframed the assignment based on his data: There is no one perfect spaghetti sauce, only different kinds of spaghetti sauce that suit different kinds of people. Instead of trying to please everyone with one sauce, Prego heeded Moskowitz's advice and created a varied spaghetti sauce product line that generated hundreds of millions of dollars in sales.[26]

One way to initiate a paradigm shift, as Leo Burnett and Suncorp did, is to identify what category of problem you think the brand or entity is examining. For a brand, is the category about sales? Awareness? Connecting with a new audience? A brand personality issue or rebrand?[27]

When the creative brief presents the goal and describes the strategy or situation, be mindful of how all-embracing a look at the problem at hand was given. Is it a superficial examination of the brand? Issue? What was not cited or neglected according to your own (formal or anecdotal) research?

How do you attract more twenty-one- to thirty-four-year-old drinkers to a beer brand? A few years ago, Coors Light introduced their theme, "Made to Chill." Developed with Leo Burnett, the campaign "taps into the cultural insight that younger legal-age drinkers are actively seeking ways to temporarily check out, or step away from lives spent 'always being on and connected,' which can be all-consuming and overwhelming," said Ryan Reis, vice president of the Coors family of brands at MillerCoors.[28]

The campaign launch focused on how Coors Light is the catalyst for chill, with spots showing a young guy having a Coors Light while showering (tapping into the #showerbeers cultural phenomenon) or a young professional woman choosing a Coors Light over a white wine to unwind at home after a day at the office. But more recently, "Made to Chill" became the world's first ad campaign that turned roofs into billboards that help cool down apartments in Miami, a city known for its heat—a purpose-driven reframing of "Made to Chill." DDB Chicago, NORD DDB, adam&eveDDB conceived the reframe.

Roofs in Miami can get up to 170 degrees. Using reflective white paint that reduces the absorption of solar radiation while lowering the internal temperature of the buildings, they painted messages on roofs, cooling down ninety-six apartments.

DDB Chicago, Nord DDB and adam&eveDDB created the world's first out-of-home advertising campaign that no one can see but everyone can feel for

Coors Light. Each roof was painted with a different message to raise awareness around the benefits of these reflective roofs—including reducing the need for AC and lowering cooling costs.

More than 36,000 sq. ft. of roofs were painted—the equivalent of 90 average-sized billboards, helping cool down 96 apartments, and reduce energy use across Miami.[29]

Here, DDB Chicago, Nord DDB, and adam&eveDDB reframed out-of-home and endowed with it a purpose beyond promotional messaging.

Associative Thinking

Associative thinking is a "relatively uncontrolled cognitive activity in which the mind wanders without specific direction among elements, based on their connections (associations) with one another, as occurs during reverie, daydreaming, and free association," according to the American Psychological Association dictionary.[30] It is a stochastic process; random variables are inherent. In design and advertising, creative professionals employ free association during the ideation process, which is thinking without censorship of whatever thoughts come to mind. Some employ mind maps to facilitate this.

Associative thinking occurs when you allow your mind to freely (nonconscious effort) link up ideas, thoughts, observations, sensory input, memory of existing knowledge, and your subconscious. This process allows thoughts to arise that might not happen on a forced focus level. Unlike brainstorming, which was originally intended for group participation, this process happens in one person's mind. It's a kind of mind wandering for creative outcomes.

"One hypothesis I like is that mind-wandering serves the purpose of exploration," explains Zachary Irving, professor at the University of Virginia's Corcoran Department of Philosophy, who researches mind wandering. "Without knowing it, you are generating creative ideas, or broadly exploring a base of ideas."[31]

"We find a pattern that is really similar to what you find in creative thinking tasks," Irving said. "That became a central part of our hypothesis, that mind wandering is this meandering thought that is similar to the thought processes that underlie creative thinking. It fits intuitively, and now we had neural evidence to support that picture."[32]

Once the associative thinking takes place, you permit the conscious selection of goal-relevant thoughts to lead to ideas.

Culture Surfing

Brand ideas can co-opt a cultural moment, such as "Barbenheimer" (the simultaneous release of two popular films in 2023, *Barbie* and *Oppenheimer*), Wordle, British documentarian Louis Theroux's rap, Swiftie (an ardent Taylor Swift fan), Prince Harry's very personal admissions, or the Nepo Baby (individual who benefits from the celebrity associated with their parents or other relatives) discourse. Brand ideas can also be found in a cultural zeitgeist—a collective feeling or spirit of the time—for example, the generative AI craze, scam artists dominating streaming, and musical festival season. How? A creative mind thinks: *How does this relate to my creative brief? To the brand's values and larger story?*

For Burger King's Impossible Whopper, agency David Madrid created the "Confusing Times" campaign: "These are confusing times," ends the ad. "Which is just about the right time to have the Burger King Impossible Whopper. A Whopper made without beef that tastes just like . . . a Whopper."[33]

The advertising idea culture surfs, pulling from the zeitgeist. We see different people dealing with "confusing times." For example, "Emma" discovers that she prefers dating Mark's profile more than dating Mark, or someone orders a book about climate change packed in unsustainable styrofoam peanuts. The dark humor hits the right spot for a vegan audience who wouldn't think to visit Burger King for a vegan burger.

The brand's or entity's core values should guide the North Star idea and all advertising messaging. Co-opting the confusing times we live in wouldn't align with a brand such as Coca-Cola. The "Confusing Times" campaign is infused with dark humor, and Coke is all about sharing and friendship. Hopping on a cultural moment takes interrogation. However, when it does align, it can get into the conversation or *become the conversation.*

To promote flavor remixing, Magnum brand ice cream from Unilever has been remixing classic music videos, such as a new version of Kylie Minogue's "Can't Get You Out of My Head," featuring South Korean dance music artist Peggy Gou. For many years, the creative forces behind Magnum have been bringing the brand together with culturally relevant names, such as Miley Cyrus and Halsey. "Today, branded talent collaborations need to feel authentic, unexpected and most importantly have a strong narrative that underpins the content," explains Katie-Jo Flynn, executive director at Golin London, in a statement.[34]

To promote Magnum in Austria, agency Lola MullenLowe created a music video set to the first movement of Wolfgang Amadeus Mozart's "25th Symphony in G Minor," remixing the classic piece with some twenty-first-century additions. This campaign certainly is an imaginative contemporary reinterpretation, and the video is part of the exhibition *Mozart by Magnum* in Salzburg, Mozart's birthplace. But what does Mozart have to do with ice cream? A letter from Mozart to his father inspired the campaign idea. The public can view the letter (courtesy of the International Mozarteum Foundation), which is part of the *Mozart by Magnum* exhibition.

"In this letter from Paris dating to July 3rd, 1778 to his father Leopold, Mozart tells of his joy over a successful symphony concert performance and that he treated himself to an ice cream afterwards: 'after the symphony I therefore immediately went to the Palais Royale out of joy—had a good ice [cream]—prayed the Rosary that I had promised—and went home.' "[35]

Purpose-Driven Advertising

In a study evaluating over seventy-five brands conducted by Zeno, a communications agency, they found that global consumers are four to six times more likely to trust, buy, champion, and protect those companies with a strong purpose over those with a weaker one.[36]

Brands are engaging purpose-driven advertising ideas—efforts benefiting a social cause—with a variety of initiatives, for example, diversity and inclusion, sustainability, or other causes that align with their core values. For purpose-driven ideas to work, the purpose must align with brand strategy, where a purpose is "authentically baked into the brand."[37]

"The goal of purpose-driven marketing is for an organization to develop a deeper rapport with their consumer base by creating authentic connections based on shared values."[38] Can purpose drive business growth?

"We have seen a massive impact of purpose on long-term sales. For me there are three things to make purpose a driver of growth—the purpose needs to be somehow linked to the industry; it needs to be authentic which means you need to be part of a solution; and the third thing is you need to invest in that purpose. Purpose drives brand power much more than heavy commercial," said

Alessandro Manfredi, chief marketing officer, Dove, at the sixty-eighth edition of the Cannes Lions Festival of Creativity.[39]

"If there is a focus to your purpose then it tells the story of your brand and what you're trying to achieve. If you're genuinely doing good things, then the story of your brand gets narrated itself," added Marisa Thalberg, executive vice president, chief brand and marketing officer, Lowe's.[40]

"Protect Our Protectors," a Coors Banquet program, aligns with Molson Coors' purpose-driven efforts around sustainability and environmental protection. "Protect Our Protectors" supports wildland firefighters in the United States. Created by Mischief and No Fixed Address, the film features actual firefighters with their own equipment, showing them fighting fires to protect the environment and taking risks in the process. "We really wanted to be respectful of all those who devote their lives to this cause in the most authentic and responsible way possible," said Will Dempster, executive vice president of production at Mischief, in a statement.[41]

The numbers of these "heroes in yellow" have been dwindling as wildfire season has grown—today, it's now 105 days longer than just a few decades ago. In California, Oregon and Washington, regions more susceptible to wildfires, the U.S. Forest Service has seen staffing levels drop to 50 percent.

Over the past eight years the Coors Family of Brands has donated more than two million dollars to the Wildland Firefighter Foundation, but the new program and associated campaign, created with Mischief, ramps up the support.[42]

Craig Bagno, managing director, global strategic excellence, McCann Worldgroup, advises that purpose-driven ideas should aim to shine a light on an injustice in the world, but they also need stopping power, whether it's fermenting outrage in the audience to mobilize collective action or comes from finding an issue that has been "flying under the radar." "Often the magic is in the mechanism—how we go about identifying the injustice as opposed to what the injustice is. Spotlighting gives the topic gravitas and lends heft to the brand's role and beliefs."

Bagno goes on to note that the best purpose-driven ideas offer actual solutions. "Some efforts create conditions that will support a solution in the future. Others galvanize a constituency to make a difference. Others still set an example for other brands or industries to follow. Solutions give brands the credibility and permission to play in this space."[43]

Disruptive Thinking

Challenging the status quo involves questioning conventional or established norms and approaches. It's about breaking away from traditional thinking patterns to explore new ideas or strategies. Disruptive thinking isn't merely about doing something different for the sake of novelty; instead, it's a strategic and creative approach aimed at generating fresh ideas.

As David Suarez, associate partner and coexecutive creative director of Goodby Silverstein & Partners NY, told us, "I think people share things that surprise them. Society is inundated with messages from brands all the time, and there's a preconceived notion of how ads or brands will act. But when you subvert those expectations, people appreciate it."[44]

What if an ad were a social experiment?

Skyn brand condoms and Tokyo agency UltraSuperNew did just that with a brand campaign, "Soft Love." To reawaken the exciting feelings of intimacy when people first meet, they created a social experiment by hypnotizing a couple, Haruka and Chiaki Hatakeyama, who have been married for ten years. Their aim? They wanted to remind couples why they married and stayed together. "Simply, because they liked each other," said Annie Hou, head of business development APAC at Skyn. The film's director and a hypnotist auditioned the couple.

"At first, we had reservations if this idea would work, because they would have to completely erase each other's existence and memories they've built up over the years," added Yousuke Ozawa, creative director at UltraSuperNew. "But when the hypnosis worked, needless to say we were in awe. When they started to open up to each other, that is when we felt something magical was happening before our eyes."[45] The short web film runs online, on social media channels, and on digital out-of-home in the Shibuya neighborhood of Tokyo.

"I wonder who will save the Oreos," tweeted a concerned fan.

In 2020, when NASA reported that Asteroid 2018VP1 was headed toward Earth's atmosphere, an Oreo fan posted that tweet, which would inspire a disruptive campaign. Inspired by the fan's tweet and by "doomsday" seed vaults, Oreo launched a cross-agency activation campaign to save the cookie for future generations by building the "asteroid proof" Global OREO Vault in the permafrost region—Svalbard, Norway (78°08'58.1"N, 16°01'59.7"E), and documenting the entire journey.[46]

On to a serious topic—how can a victim of domestic abuse signal for help when confined at home or to the abuser's vehicle?

A girl who had been reported missing flashed a hand signal from a car on the Kentucky interstate. She appeared to be waving. "But one person in a nearby car recognized the signal from TikTok and knew it was no ordinary wave. The girl, sixteen, was using a new distress signal, tucking her thumb into her palm before closing her fingers over it, according to the Laurel County Sheriff's Office."[47]

After receiving a 911 call, sheriff's deputies pulled the car over and rescued her. For the Canadian Women's Foundation, Juniper Park\TBWA, a Toronto-based creative agency, "developed a hand gesture as a silent call for help, to be used without leaving a digital trace" for people to indicate that they are at risk of abuse and need help, which had spread largely through TikTok.

"With no media budget available, we purposely built a campaign for social media: our options for amplifying the message were limited. But we were confident that with the volume of time and the attention people were paying to social media, the message would travel and garner attention with every share. People were aware of the increase in violence against women and sharing Signal for Help would make it easy for them to help."[48]

How do you reach and call a young audience to action about antiknife crime?

To do that, Engine Creative's David Dearlove and Richard Nott conceived "Long Live the Prince," for the Kiyan Prince Foundation. "Created out of Engine, the campaign imagined what would have happened had Prince lived and turned him into a playable soccer pro character in EA Sports' FIFA21. His stardom was also highlighted in ads for JD Sports and Match Attax trading cards."[49]

"Selling to teens is a very hard thing to do, so you almost have to sneak that purpose in. You've got to find a way to get to teens in a way that doesn't turn them off. It almost has to feel undetectable," explains Rob Reilly, Titanium Lions jury president and global chief creative officer at WPP. The campaign "is one of the most disruptive ideas I've ever seen," Reilly said during the Cannes Lions Awards press conference. Moreover, it "moved us so much."[50]

Two years earlier, Dearlove and Nott had read a book written by Kiyan Prince's father, Dr. Mark Prince OBE. "The goal was to deliver an anti-knife crime campaign that was audience-first and multi-creative practice; approaching the subject from a positive angle, as opposed to focusing on the negative consequences, and inspire young people by showing them what the top footballer Kiyan would have become through reimagining his legacy virtually in EA SPORTS FIFA," agency Engine notes on LinkedIn.[51]

Chipotle and e.l.f.'s collaboration nearly broke the internet. Both brands had experienced great success on TikTok. Movers+Shakers agency website case study notes, "We wondered what could happen if two like-minded disruptors came together. . . . The campaign garnered 4 billion press impressions (*NY Post*, *Forbes*), unsolicited celebrity endorsements (Stephen Colbert, James Charles, Drew Barrymore), and a tidal wave of fan love."[52]

Their creative solution: "We broke the internet by launching a limited-edition e.l.f. collection: an avocado makeup sponge, spicy salsa lip gloss, and a palette inspired by Chipotle's serving trays. e.l.f. and Chiptole lovers united and within 44 minutes products sold out online."[53]

Combinatorial Thinking and Intersections of Factors

Combinatorial thinking leverages your wealth of knowledge; the more you know about the brand, industry, consumer, popular culture, and the more general knowledge you possess, the easier it becomes to link diverse information in your mind. With ample experience and knowledge, seeking creative solutions allows you to connect seemingly unrelated pieces. These fresh connections often lead to innovative ideas. Some agency creatives specialize in identifying problems rather than just solving them. At AREA 23, their working model is called What If. The idea for "Sick Beats" by Woojer wasn't born out of a client ask.[54]

For children living with cystic fibrosis (CF), airway-clearance therapy is part of their daily treatment and is challenging. The Area 23 creative team had been thinking about how they could improve the experience and spoke with children living with CF and their families to find out what might do that. They connected the dots among different things: an existing Woojer vest, musical beats, and airway clearance.

"Sick beats by Woojer is the world's first music-powered airway clearance vest prototype for CF, using the clinically proven modality of soundwave therapy in an awesome treatment experience. The prototype, a redesign of Woojer's consumer vest, syncs with a smartphone to pull therapeutic 40Hz frequencies from music and send them to the chest. The SICK BEATS experience uses a curated Spotify library of thousands of 40Hz songs. Kids can find new 40Hz music and create custom therapeutic playlists for the vest, all in the Spotify app."[55]

To identify thousands of songs with 40Hz, Area 23 used an AI-enabled sniffer to search 30 million songs for therapeutic frequencies in the Spotify library. "Since its launch, 2,000+ CF families within the Claire's Place Foundation network have access to the vest—on a rolling basis, free of charge."[56]

To ensure people would respond on a sensate level, Mastercard leveraged combinatorial thinking to appeal to several of our five senses. Beyond the visual appeal of their brand identity, Mastercard employed sound by launching its first album, "Priceless." "Even the Mastercard products have a typical sonic signature. When one completes a transaction, he or she hears a specific sound. This gives the user a sense of ratification and completion," said Raja Rajamannar, chief marketing and communications officer, Mastercard.[57]

To appeal to our sense of smell, Mastercard launched two scents, created in partnership with Firmenich, a Swiss fragrance and flavor company. To give people's taste buds a go, for their "Priceless" initiative, they partnered with Ladurée and the launch of its temporary restaurants in cities worldwide, offering original macarons.

Mastercard has a Touch Card, an inclusively designed card with a series of notches so that it can be easily identified by people who are partially sighted or living with blindness.[58]

SP☀TLIGHT

Samsung: iTest with Brett Colliver/ DDB Group New Zealand

Some audiences are tougher to persuade than others. Apple iPhone owners are among them. How do you convince Apple iPhone users to try a rival? DDB Tribal Aotearoa Auckland, New Zealand, had a combinatorial idea for Samsung: iTest—hijack a rival's device to allow people to "test drive a Samsung from the comfort of their own iPhone." They combined the concept of people taking a car for a test drive with trying out a communications device (figure 6.1). Here, the combinatorial and confluence factors include technology, demographics, trends, different sectors (automotive and communication), and brand rivalry.

(continued on next page)

(*continued from previous page*)

"In a bid to give iPhone users a taste of what they're missing out on, DDB Tribal Aotearoa created iTest, a web application that mimics the operating system of an Android device, allowing consumers to experience navigation, app interaction, settings, texting/calling, and even the camera features. Designed to replicate Samsung's intuitive 'OneUI' user experience for Android, Tribal went

6.1 "Samsung: iTest—hijack"; Agencies: DDB Group Aotearoa / New Zealand / Tribal Worldwide NZ; Creative directors: Brett Colliver / Mike Felix, DDB Group New Zealand; DDB creative experience lead: Daniel Castillo, DDB Group New Zealand; Executive creative director: Hayd Kerr, Tribal Worldwide NZ; Client: Samsung.

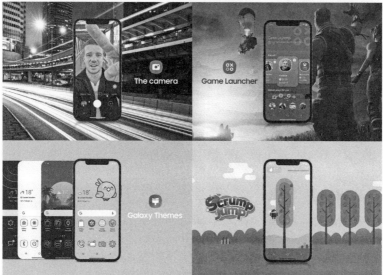

6.1 (continued)

through the challenge of developing such an application that would convert even the most ardent of Apple fans."[59]

It worked. Over 12 million iPhone users have test-driven a Samsung, and millions of others have seen the iTest thanks to thousands of user-generated demos being posted by tech bloggers and influencers.[60]

We asked Brett Colliver, chief creative officer, dentsu Aotearoa, formerly at DDB NZ, about the campaign.

(continued on next page)

(*continued from previous page*)

The key to the castle

After being added by Apple in 2018, this button made it possible to add iTest to the user's home screen, allowing for full functionality.

6.1 (*continued*)

How did you realize the insight?

We were given a brief to launch the Note 20 and, as part of that, convince iPhone users of its benefits. In the briefing, one of the big topics of conversation was that iPhone users are daunted by the prospect of switching to a Samsung device. They think they're going to have to learn a new language in order to use it and, therefore, never even consider it.

The myth that Android is "complicated" and hard to use has been around for over a decade and, having been iPhone users ourselves, was something that we'd experienced first-hand. However, we knew that if you actually manage to get a Samsung into the hands of an iPhone user, they see very quickly that their fears are misguided.

But that insight wasn't right for the Note 20 brief, as we needed to promote features contained within that specific device. But alongside the work that answered the Note 20 brief, we also presented what would eventually become iTest.

The client was enamored with it from the start. To their credit, they said, "We love it, but it's so much bigger than just one handset. This is something we should build for the entire brand."

How did you generate the idea?

We knew that if we could get iPhone users to try the Samsung UI, they would quickly discover how intuitive it actually is.

But test driving a phone in-store, where there are often salespeople hovering, isn't ideal. We wanted to give people the opportunity to experience it at their own pace and wherever they felt comfortable.

So we simply asked, "Could they do it from the comfort of their iPhone?"

Simple in theory... much trickier in reality.

iTest wasn't simply about showing people what the Samsung UI looks like; it was about them getting to *feel* what it's like.

Therefore, it needed to appear to actually transport users to the Samsung operating system. That meant that alongside all of the apps and features that needed to be built, every tiny detail, such as gestures and animations, had to be faithfully replicated as well.

If we could have built an app, achieving that might have been reasonably simple. But, of course, Apple would never have allowed us to put an app like that in the App Store.

Turns out, however, Apple had left a key to their castle under the doormat.

A critical factor in pulling this off was a technology known as "Progressive Web App" technology, or PWA for short. This is something that didn't exist on iPhones until 2018, when Apple added it into their native Safari browser.

The PWA feature enables people to save websites to their home screen in what looks and functions like an app. And this was critical, as it allowed us to fully take over the screen and to build not only the big things, like the camera and a fully functioning game, but equally as importantly, ensure that every single animation, every swipe, and every gesture felt exactly like the real thing.

Because you have to remember, while this looks like a fully functioning operating system, it's actually a website *mimicking* a UI.

So, while the leap from insight to idea was relatively simple, pulling it off was far more challenging.[61]

UNLOCK CREATIVITY WITH DATA

Do you think you could use data to generate an idea?

For adidas, Havas Middle East's team had an insight into the audience. Around the world, 32 percent of women feel uncomfortable swimming in public. Moreover, in the Middle East, it's 89 percent. Havas and adidas produced a swimmable liquid billboard situated at one of Dubai's popular public beaches, encouraging women to swim in public and become brand ambassadors for adidas' new inclusive swimwear collection (regardless of an individual's ethnicity, shape, or ability to navigate the water). What resulted was a worldwide conversation across sixty countries about making swimming more inclusive as a sport.

"So when we were talking about how to create a piece of communication to close the gender gap in swimming, these data points told us that we needed to bring a discussion to the Middle East and highlight what's important for women here," Fabio Silveira, general manager at Havas Creative Middle East, told Contagious.[62]

"The global data came with the brief, and after we received the brief we worked with wonderful research partners to understand women in the UAE and compare the data points. So our insights came from our research partner as well as from adidas," Silveira added.[63]

The liquid billboard is part of an integrated campaign. Cameras inside the billboard swimming pool filmed the swimmers, and the footage was edited in real time. Then it was transmitted directly onto a digital screen above the Dubai Mall Ice Rink, next to the adidas flagship store. To enhance the experience for the swimmers, Havas personalized each swimmer's photo and printed posters for them. They also gave them images for sharing on social media.[64]

SP☀TLIGHT

Jardim Sonor's "Blended with Nature"/ Dentsu Creative Portugal

To design the poster campaign for Jardim Sonor, the international electronic music festival in Portugal held in the Keil do Amaral Garden in Lisbon, the creatives employed Midjourney, an AI-based image program that generates images based on text prompts.

The creative team input the names of top festival performers—Todd Terje, Jeff Mills, Jan Blomqvist—along with words like *birds, butterflies, leaves,* and *trees* to Midjourney. They refined the output.[65] About the attention-grabbing posters (figure 6.2), Ivo Purvis, executive creative director on the project, told us the following:

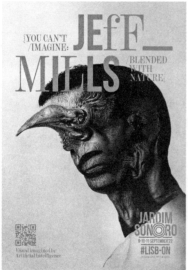

6.2 "Jardim Sonoro: Blended with Nature"; Agency: DENTSU CREATIVE Portugal; Chief creative officer: Lourenço Thomaz; Executive creative director: Ivo Purvis; Creative director: Gil Correia; Art directors: Gil Correia, Ivo Purvis; A.I. prompt master: Fred Van Zeller; Copywriter: João Moura; Designer: Emanuel Serôdio, Tiago Rodrigues; Motion graphics: Fabio Magalhães; Client: Jose Diogo Vinagre, Director Jardim Sonoro.

(continued on next page)

(*continued from previous page*)

In a year that marks the return of the festival in a physical format, Lisbon flourished with a new name—Jardim Sonoro—and with a new concept, "Blended with Nature." Even more camouflaged and merged in nature, the festival gains oxygen and a new breath, moving its roots to a bigger park, the lung of Lisbon, and an idyllic natural stage for the emergence of new flora.

For fans, this makes it hard to predict everything that is coming, as it is difficult to idealize an even more natural symbiosis of this year's lineup with a new environment in a new garden.

Thus, in the inability to rationally conceive what is to come, we challenged technology to imagine what the unimaginable Jardim Sonoro 2022 will be.

Looking at the results of this experience, we think that this project portrays and illustrates that our creative frontiers need to expand, and AI will force us to do it like any other new tool did in the past. In the end, we believe that it's all about the talent and capacity to master any kind of tool. That's how you create your own language.[66]

SP☀TLIGHT

Nike Fiftieth Anniversary, "Never Done Evolving: The Greatness of Serena Williams"

To celebrate their fifty-year anniversary, Nike celebrated Serena Williams, whose legacy will inspire generations to come. Harnessing advanced AI, Nike and AKQA (studios in Melbourne, Portland, and São Paulo) created an eight-and-a-half-minute film, *Never Done Evolving*, a match between 1999 Serena Williams when she won her first Grand Slam title, and Serena Williams when she won the 2017 Australian Open. Machine learning modeled each era's playing style: decision making, shot selection, reaction time, recovery, and agility, based on archive footage. Models were brought to life by rerendering them into an entirely new scene and having them appear to be playing and responding to each other.

We spoke with Diego Machado, chief creative officer at AKQA São Paulo. Machado said,

When AKQA's Brand Story Team was concepting, we imagined all of the athletes in the Nike universe—thinking about Serena Williams, Michael Jordan, Cristiano Ronaldo, Andre Agassi, and Joan Benoit. We thought about what makes them the best, asking, what are the criteria? We focused on performance and the markers of athletic excellence. Is it speed? Strength? How high can someone jump?

Once we landed on displaying Serena Williams's extraordinary athletic evolution, we brought in the tech team to create a film where we see the two Serena Williams playing each other across 130,000 games and five thousand matches.[67]

It is a new and accessible format for tennis experts to experience and interpret data.

1.7 million viewers watched the grand final via YouTube, an increase of 1,082 percent in organic views compared to other Nike content. "Never Done Evolving" broke all Nike's organic views records on YouTube.[68] Luciana Cani, executive creative director AKQA Portland told us, "Our challenge was to take the future of sports analytics to a more human-readable data visualization."

INTERVIEW: SUSAN YOUNG, EVP/GLOBAL EXECUTIVE CREATIVE DIRECTOR, MCCANN-NEW YORK

Susan Young

Susan Young has created award-winning campaigns for iconic brands like AT&T, Microsoft, Mastercard, and Tide, as well as nonprofits like March for Our Lives, Girls Who Code, and Color of Change. She is passionate about work that is brave, beautiful, and makes a difference—but she will settle for at least one out of the three. Her work has been recognized by Cannes Lions, the One Show, D&AD, Webby's, and Clios. She has been featured in *Adweek*'s Creative 100, *AdAge*'s Creatives You Should Know, and was an A-List Awards Creative Director of the Year finalist. Susan has also had the honor of being a jury member for D&AD, Cannes Lions, ADC Awards, and Dubai Lynx. She lives in Brooklyn with her supportive husband, brilliant child, and crazy COVID puppy.

Throughout your career, you've worked on several of the world's biggest brands. Why is it particularly important for big brands, with big voices to tell relatable stories?

Sometimes, it's something that marketers forget, and it's always great when marketers know how important that is. We're not talking from machine to machine. We're trying to connect to other people. So, obviously, the best way to do that is to show that you understand people and that you relate to them on that level. I've also done a lot of business-to-business advertising, and we always approach it as *business-to-person* because, at the end of the day, you're not talking to annual reports or some other business entity. At the other end of whatever message you put out, there's an actual human being. It's your mom, it's your brother, it's your kid; whoever it is, it's still a person who is important and who ultimately has to feel something about the brand.

For Microsoft's "#makewhatsnext," you told the story of underrecognized women inventors through the eyes of female grade-school science students. Why were those honest perspectives so crucial to the message being shared?

The whole brief was about girls and STEM, and we specifically honed in on inventors and patents, but it was also for International Women's Day. We were trying to speak specifically to celebrate women and encourage women and girls.

This campaign actually started out as a true experiment on our part. We thought, "Hey, this is a thing. You never really hear about any women inventors," and as we started to do some research, we saw there's actually a fair amount of them. But do people know this? Do kids know this? And so, we actually sold through the first part of the concept to the client by literally just having people in the agency ask their kids if they could name any female inventors and then filming it.

And so, there were a couple of things that we learned. First, I learned that filming a *proof-of-concept* spec video (a test video to share with clients) is a great way to sell through an idea. I'd never really quite done that before, and now I feel like we do that all the time. Secondly, almost everyone's kid came back and literally could not name a single female inventor. We were like, "Wow, that's insane." Especially coming from the children of people who thought of themselves as being more feminist. I know I personally try really hard to have my own daughter look at all kinds of positive stuff, so that was really surprising, and just the power of us seeing the results of that particular experiment was, "Oh, this is how we need to frame it because it's so shocking."

And what I loved about the girls we did end up filming for the campaign was just seeing that they were realizing it as well and how kind of messed up it was. Seeing the light bulb go off for them was super powerful. They were smart enough to know that it wasn't their shortcoming, but they were thinking, "Yeah, why, aren't we learning this? Why isn't this being taught to us?"

It was never in any way about shaming the girls for a lack of knowledge. It was quite the opposite. It was about how there's a bigger problem with a system that's let them down a little bit, and that's what we wanted to get at.

We wanted to have an action come out of the campaign beyond just awareness, so we followed up with the patent program for women. I give the Microsoft clients a ton of credit for really pushing hard within the organization because it was more than just a marketing initiative. Through the project, they helped people actually do the legal paperwork and learn how to patent ideas to start getting more patents by women. They worked with the whole company to make this program a reality, and they did it.

For "Tactile," you told the story of some of the first participants in Microsoft's patent program for women, where six MIT students created a device to convert printed text into braille in real time, potentially transforming the lives of people in the blind community. Can you talk about how modern brand storytelling is no longer limited to traditional mediums, such as a TV commercial or magazine ad?

I've always thought that's the most exciting part of our business. While I do love a good TV spot, and I love to create great storytelling on film, I also think the exciting part of the industry right now is that there are so many different mediums. It really is a matter of, "What's the craziest thing we can do with this idea?" It's the purest form of creativity because it's just having an idea and then determining where it would live best. I feel like literally anything's on the table. It's almost truly back to really being all about ideas.

During the development of the campaign, there were so many points where we could have just given up on the "Tactile" project or just said "No," but then we'd go back at it another way. I remember for me, I was fairly new at the time, and I think I had just been promoted to executive creative director. For me, it was such a huge learning curve just trying to keep people motivated, myself included, when it was so incredibly frustrating because you loved an idea so much, and it kept changing and was, at times, on the brink of extinction. And then just trying to come back again and again, and not just trying to motivate myself but trying to keep the team from being completely demoralized and giving up. But we had a super team who was very tenacious and very resilient. I keep going back to the importance of resiliency. Every now and then, you'd have to go back and say, "Okay, so let's just rethink this, and now come back with the next thing."

Regarding Microsoft's "Tactile" campaign, this is where it really helps to have strong client relationships because you are asking more of them. For some clients, it's too much, and they really do just want to do what's easy, but when you have a great client that's going to get as excited as you are and devote themselves to figuring it out with you, then that's when the possibilities are amazing. For the really big ideas or the radically different ideas, you really do need to have the client on your team who is a true partner.

Speaking of being resilient, why is it an important quality of any successful professional storyteller in media or marketing?

I think you have to be. Anything worthwhile requires resilience, and you have to work at it. I feel that sometimes people think just having the idea is enough, and it's not. The "idea" itself is necessary and important, but being able to protect the idea, shape the idea, and continually evolve the idea is the only way to make it in this business right now.

When we inevitably fail on occasion, I also think it's important to let yourself grieve a little or get upset, but then you've got to move on quickly and find some joy in the process. I think that's actually the thing I have really finally learned is to celebrate the wins along the way. They matter, it's important, and you've got to enjoy each of the successes you have, so when we inevitably experience some failures along the way, we understand that's just part of it too. So allow yourself to enjoy all the little wins.

March for Our Lives was a massive protest by students against gun violence in schools. The "Price on Our Lives" campaign calculated the millions in campaign contributions accepted by politicians from the gun lobby, divided by the millions of young people in Florida, which came to a total of $1.05. The cost of a young life was then symbolized by an iconic price-tag bracelet that supported the movement (figure 6.3). How did distilling a complex dynamic empower an important cause like this one?

The producer we worked with was an alumna of the high school in the Parkland community, so that's where it all started. We all were distraught, and of course, your first reaction is, "What can I do to help?" Our producer was still in touch with a lot of the students and teachers from the school, so once they formed the "March for Our Lives," she reached out directly and just said, "Hey, is there anything that we can do?"

6.3 "Price on Our Lives"; Agency: McCann New York; Client: March for Our Lives, Washington, DC.

What really seemed to spark for them was the idea of having some kind of symbol that would be a powerful statement for the people that would be in attendance there. When we printed all the "Price on Our Lives" tags and we went to the march, we weren't sure if they would actually use them because we left the choice up to them. To their credit, the Parkland students were very focused on their core message, which was something we always respected. But once we saw that they started to use the tags on stage, and were passing them out, and that people were wearing them, it felt like this symbol had actually struck a chord with people. It was actually making an impression as intended, and its impact was meaningful.

Why is it important for people like yourself with professional stature or influence to take on projects like this?

I love creativity. I love problem solving. I love a lot about advertising. I don't love feeling sometimes like I'm pushing consumerism. So that means I have a responsibility as a citizen of the world to actually try to make the world better. I have a lot of respect for people who choose professions that do that in a very clear, meaningful way, so I look for every opportunity to try to bring some of that into what I do professionally because you have to figure out the ways to make what you do matters and feel like you're making a difference.

What is your opinion of the importance of brands aligning with purpose?

I love it, and I think it's great. It especially matters for younger genera-tions. With Gen Z, they're conflicted because they want to do things that are purposeful, and they want to support brands that are doing good, but they also want instant gratification, fast fashion, and cheap prices, so it's hard to align your values with your purchases, but the more you can do so the better. Some people, and even some clients as well, feel that brands have no business trying to be purposeful unless it's very specific to their brand and how they operate, but I think it's always important. It's imperative that businesses help drive some of this change because what corporations do matters, given that they have a ton of power. As long as there is some truth to the purpose and it's not just for show, or it's not just fluff, that's the crucial thing. It really bothers me when brands try to just do awareness initiatives that aren't then backed up by actions. Authenticity is important, and it makes a big difference in the brands people want to engage with. It all goes back to the concept of brand relationships being like human relationships. Who do you want to associate with? Who do you want to hang out with? Who do you want to support? I feel it really does matter.

The United States is home to over 1,800 Confederate statues that are a constant reminder of a painful past. In light of social justice, many of those statues were finally removed, and The Color of Change "Pedestal Project" found a way to repurpose the empty pedestals where they once stood. Instagram users were given the ability to use AI to virtually replace symbols of hate with symbols of hope, such as civil rights activist John Lewis. Why was it so important to give audiences an active, as opposed to passive, role in telling this story of racial healing?

Especially during that time, and given the recent George Floyd tragedy, having people feel empowered, or at least feeling that they are part of the process, is important. I strongly believe that it's not enough just to not be racist. You have to be antiracist. You have to actively engage in some of these constructive conversations and actions.

At its core, the "Pedestal Project" was still just about the idea of transforming these symbols of hate and oppression into something positive. It felt like a powerful thing to put out in the world, and I thought it was really beautiful for people to have the means to be able to share in that experience.

Is brand storytelling still relevant in today's technologically focused world?

Yes, it is, but it's about using data and technology in ways that enhance creativity instead of trying to give them more importance than creativity because, at the heart of our business, it still really is about creative ideas. People can't lose track of that, and you have to keep that concept front and center because technology is simply one of many tools at your disposal.

Is there any other piece of wisdom or insight about brand storytelling that you would like to share?

Once again, you have to enjoy the process. You have to really take pleasure in the whole journey, and of course, it's the best when your campaign actually gets made and it gets attention within the industry, but if you're only looking for that, you're going to be miserable. Every step of the way has to bring you some kind of joy, so you have to figure out how to just love the act of creating. I actively remind myself to be grateful that I get to make stuff up, and think, and tell stories for a living, and it's a gift as long as you remember that.

CHAPTER 7

BRAND AS ACTIVIST

Diversity, Equity, and Inclusion

AN EQUITABLE APPROACH

"What is love?"

That's the enduring question people ask Amazon's Alexa in a documentary-style film, *What Is Love?* as part of the #LoveHasNoLabels multifaceted, collaborative campaign, directed by Rodney Lucas, an award-winning Brooklyn-based documentary filmmaker from the South Side of Chicago. In the film, created in partnership with the Ad Council (2022), we hear actual people's voices and the acts of love "they show to or are shown by others from different identity labels," with the intent to inspire greater acceptance.[1]

Lucas saw this campaign as an important initiative, "I saw these films as groundbreaking moments within advertising, but also a uniquely important initiative for a Black director to lead.

From its conception, to the voices it highlighted, to the crew behind the scenes, diversity, equity and inclusion were at the core of this campaign."[2] In another publication, Lucas added, "Amazon's Alexa has been asked millions of questions about love, and the new campaign aims to educate listeners and encourage them to take meaningful actions to combat bias and spread inclusivity."[3]

The Ad Council's "Love Has No Labels" campaign launched in 2015 to promote "acceptance and inclusion of all people across race, religion, gender, sexual orientation, age and ability," notes the Ad Council website.[4] Agency R/GA created the original campaign.

A Walkers brand campaign asks a very different kind of question which resonates with its audience through humor, featuring a diverse cast of talent—"Are crisps best enjoyed in or out of sandwiches?"

Crisps are better known as potato chips outside the UK. In their campaign, "#CrispIN or #CrispOUT," Walkers brand and their UK agency of record, VCCP London, reignited a national hot-topic debate in England. (Sandwiches top the nation's favorite lunch options; many people eat crisp sandwiches, that is, crisps between two slices of bread with or without other sandwich components.) The fun debate struck a resounding chord with consumers, and so did the spot's broadly diverse cast.

"Walkers' 'Crisps in or crisps out?' campaign's inclusive narratives had universal appeal and rocketed its social conversation," wrote Sebastian Parker, insights researcher at Creative Equals, in *Campaign US*. Why would an inclusive campaign not only create brand affinity but resonate mightily to boot? Parker goes on in that article to explain that brands can build trust that way.[5] People not only responded to Walkers' brand message but also to the diverse messengers.

The goal of a recent Microsoft study was "to understand if inclusive advertising drives trust, builds loyalty, and leads to purchase intent for Gen Z. The answer is mostly yes. Seventy percent are more trusting of brands that represent diversity in ads."[6]

A recent research report conducted by Adobe of more than two thousand people found, "38 percent of consumers, in general, are more likely to trust brands that do well with showing diversity in their ads. This percentage is even higher among specific consumer groups including Hispanic (85 percent), Black (79 percent), Asian/Pacific Islander (79 percent), LGBTQIA+ (85 percent), millennial (77 percent), and teen (76 percent) consumers."[7] According to the 2021 U.S. Census data, multiracial, Hispanic, and Asian communities have driven the most population growth (percentage-wise) over the last ten years.[8] Clearly, if companies are only thinking about profit rather than the triple bottom line, these are crucial audiences, based on purchase power, for any marketer to gain trust.

Conversely, a brand can erode trust when they employ tropes, perpetuate stereotypes, overindex white cisgender straight men, leave out particular groups of people (e.g., people living with disabilities), or misrepresent.[9]

Perhaps seeing diverse representation in advertising builds trust because people see it as fair. In *Finding Fairness: From Pleistocene Foragers to Contemporary Capitalists*, Justin Jennings argues that we have an evolved visceral expectation for fairness.[10] This desire for fairness, according to Jennings, was a catalyst for societal change.

When brands tell stories that represent diverse voices, they acknowledge many—an equitable approach broadens, diversifies, and connects. According to a survey conducted by Female Quotient in partnership with Google and Ipsos of 2,987 U.S. consumers of various backgrounds, when asked if they believe that in order to be inclusive and diverse, it is important for brands to be conscious of gender identity, age, body type, race/ethnicity, culture, sexual orientation, skin tone, language, religious/spiritual affiliation, physical ability, socioeconomic status, and overall appearance in their advertising campaigns, it was found that "people are more likely to consider, or even purchase, a product after seeing an ad they think is diverse or inclusive." That same report goes on to state that "in fact, 64 percent of those surveyed said they took some sort of action after seeing an ad that they considered to be diverse or inclusive."[11]

Beyond consumer appreciation for diversity and inclusion, telling brand stories with an equitable approach acknowledges the corporate social responsibility that comes with telling public stories. Doing otherwise is not relevant in a diverse world and, worse, is complacent and complicit with cultural hegemony.

Inclusive brand storytelling, the telling or representation of someone's experience or perspective, must move forward to be "storiestelling." Whether it's in the fictional realm, for example, Disney+'s *Ms. Marvel*, a recent series that introduces superhero Kamala Khan, a Pakistani American teen growing up in Jersey City, New Jersey, or it's the actual origin story of a company or brand, representation provides the opportunity to assimilate diverse lives to our own, to start to see the world through other lenses. It is crucial that corporate and brand narratives and messages avoid dehumanization and stereotypes, as such narratives not only hinder the opportunity for assimilation but also inflict harm.

A focus on diversity, equity, and inclusion (DEI) brings stories to the fore that have not been told, brings people to the fore who have not told their stories or have been in the shadows, and calls forth the power of representation in every role, yielding diverse stories—multiple perspectives, multiple voices, diverse representative experiences, diverse images, intersections, and all with the purpose of elevating equity through business, through representation/visibility, role models, and ultimately building trust.

"More representation at the table, more diverse voices will elevate the thinking in the industry; creativity doesn't just come from safe choices or employing the usual people," Sophie Gold, executive producer of Eleanor, told us.[12] Representation of marginalized groups in advertising and elsewhere in the media matters because a deficiency contributes to a lack of understanding of a diverse population. Establishing expectations with each team on the ground floor is optimal.

INCLUSIVE "STORIESTELLING"

Inclusive storiestelling leads to truthfulness, to accurately portraying people's lives, and to the much-desired authenticity that everyone talks about. When a diverse group has seats at the table, from start to finish, it fosters the creation of legitimate portrayals of underrepresented communities. Authenticity requires multiple perspectives encompassing others' points of view and representing the full spectrum of your audience's experiences. The storyteller must be congruent with their own story. Reflecting people's stories is key to authenticity. Best practice dictates that people tell their own stories. What you might think is authentic to a community to which you don't belong might actually be a trope. How do diverse voices and inclusion at every level of creative work elevate the thinking in the industry? As Wes Phelan, executive creative director, told us, "Having many voices and stories to inspire the process and output is vitally important. New ways of thinking often lead to new solutions to existing problems."[13]

When people threatened to boycott Ulta Beauty, the largest beauty retailer in the United States, after the company included Dylan Mulvaney, a trans TikTok celebrity, on Ulta's "*The Beauty Of . . .*" podcast, Ulta held their ground for inclusivity. They responded by saying, "We believe beauty is for everyone. And while we recognize some conversations we host will challenge perspectives and opinions, we believe constructive dialogue is one important way to move beauty forward."[14]

Their stand is consistent with their ad campaign titled "Beauty&," which featured a diverse cast to "spark dialogue, shift perceptions, and showcase how expansive beauty truly is." Ulta also is donating to the Jed Foundation, a nonprofit that supports teen and young adult mental health.[15]

Most companies realize that backlash often accompanies taking a stand on social issues or featuring celebrity spokespersons. For example, in 2023 on Instagram, Bud Light featured trans influencer Dylan Mulvaney, who has more than 10 million followers on TikTok and nearly 2 million on Instagram. Due to the political contention, Anheuser-Busch suffered a significant market share decline.[16]

Responsibility Checklist

Creative professionals, clients, and all who contribute to advertising have a responsibility to respect and uplift all members of society, including those of different ages, races, ethnicities, socioeconomic status, religions, beliefs, gender identities and expressions, sexualities, people living with disabilities, and people who are unhoused. In that spirit, here are questions to ask when you create advertising because systematic inequality represented in pop-culture artifacts can inadvertently shape thinking and ideas. Additionally, encouraging existing hegemonic systems can be especially dangerous in advertising, which sets out to persuade its mass audience.

   On interrogating ideas, stories, images, and copy:

- Have you interrogated every aspect of the idea, story, images, and copy for meaning? Do any perpetuate stereotypes or tropes?
- Does the story, imagery, and copy represent fairly, truly, or negatively?
- Is a stereotype or trope being employed relative to race, ethnicity, gender sexuality, religion, ability, or age?
- Have you properly researched stereotypes of the group you are depicting and made a conscious effort to eschew them?
- Have you tried swapping the image/audience for that of another race, ethnicity, gender, neurodiversity, age, sexual orientation, person living with disabilities (physical or intellectual), socioeconomic group, or religious group? If so, do any stereotypes emerge? Is the image/audience still appropriate?
- Have you considered how people of different communities might identify with what you are creating?
- Is the solution respectful? Does it denigrate, dehumanize, or diminish any group, even with humor? Is tokenizing involved?
- Is it a caricature or a historically offensive portrayal of a group or race? Is it a distortion?
- Is an immutable human characteristic used as a punchline?
- Have you sought multiple perspectives? Feedback from a diverse group?
- Have you considered intersecting identities? (For example, BIPOC [Black, Indigenous, people of color] who are trans or who are living with a disability)

On power:

- Who holds the power in your representation? Does the ad purposely exclude or oppress?
- Have you thought about how someone from a different group would experience this?
- Does the solution build on a stereotype or trope of who holds power and who is subordinate?
- Does the solution contribute to any hegemonic systems of oppression?
- Would any group be marginalized by this representation or message?
- Have you thought about the intersectionality of identities represented in terms of power?
- Does a characterization uplift or undermine?
- Does the solution read from multiple perspectives?
- Does the solution offer alternative readings?
- Have you tested various scenarios?

On appropriation:

- Are you employing another's narrative or culture? Is it yours to appropriate?
- Is cultural value lost due to the idea, representation, or copy?
- Are you respecting another culture's traditions and customs, particularly those that are held sacred?
- Is there any suggestion of another culture being less developed than another?
- If employing a narrative or culture other than your own, have you done appropriate research?
- Is it reasonable to assume that members from the portrayed culture would represent themselves or their customs in a similar manner?
- Are any aspects of the culture being represented out of context?
- Is credit properly given?

On storyline and settings:

- Are you considering socioeconomic status, race, and disability status lines?

- What is the objective of selecting a metropolitan, suburban, or rural location? Does the story and setting accurately capture the diversity of your audience's socioeconomic situations?
- Is any derogatory/discriminatory language employed (e.g., "inner city")?
- Are gender stereotypes employed? For example, women gathering in a cafe or men gathering on a basketball court, cuisine stereotypes, unsheltered stereotypes, or mental health tropes
- Is consideration given to an intersectional lens? Intersectionality credits an individual's whole identity. As Kimberle Crenshaw points out in her seminal paper, "Because the intersectional experience is greater than the sum of racism and sexism, any analysis that does not take intersectionality into account cannot sufficiently address the particular manner in which Black women are subordinated."[17]
- When casting, can real families be used rather than built?
- Does casting reflect diverse representation?

Bottom line: Do not contribute to hegemonic systems currently in place through your solutions.

> After all the intelligent discussions about equality, empowerment, and inclusion, it all comes down to this: We're in a creative business. And creativity has never been about sameness.
>
> —Will Chau, Global VP of Creative & Design,
> Whole Foods Market[18]

FIVE DEI POINTS

How can brand storytelling thrive through the challenges of intense global competition and socioeconomic crises? By harnessing the power of inclusion and the positive emotional consumer response that generates an authentic link between the brand stories and its audience's values and actual composition, storytelling can evolve into *storiestelling*. We see five fundamental points to consider that will ensure you are telling advertising stories that resonate, elevate, and are worthy of sharing: who the public sees representing the brand; building inclusion into the creative process; elevating equity; reflecting the zeitgeist; and amplifying DEI.

Front Facing: What the Public Sees

Who the public sees representing the brand in brand stories on every platform can foster a sense of belonging, an awareness that there is a community larger than oneself. Identifying with another individual's story could connect people. According to Uri Hasson, professor of psychology and neuroscience at Princeton University, as a listener hears a story being told, their brain waves start to synchronize with the storyteller.[19] "I'm trying to make your brain similar to mine in areas that really capture the meaning, the situation, the schema—the context of the world," Hasson told NPR.[20]

Viewing a narrative has the potential to produce changes in something as central as the viewer's self-concept. Researchers Marc Sestir and Melanie C. Green believe that two factors, identification (identifying with the character) and transportation (the state of feeling immersed in the narrative), are the primary moderators of the relationship between a person and the narrative. "Traits exhibited by media characters may spill over into the self-concept of the viewer."[21]

In one chapter of her book, *Inventing Human Rights: A History*, Lynn Hunt, a distinguished research professor at UCLA, writes about torture and cruel punishments. She points out that torture ended not "because judges gave up on it or because Enlightenment writers opposed it" but because "the traditional framework of pain and personhood fell apart, to be replaced, bit by bit, by a new framework, in which individuals . . . recognized in other people the same passions, sentiments and sympathies as in themselves."[22] Recognized shared desires and feelings might certainly aid understanding others, but there must be fair and accurate representation in media messaging.

Adobe's inclusive Instagram account features diverse artists, talent, and content from people of different races, genders, sexual orientations, ethnicities, ages, and people living with disabilities. Adobe seems to understand what feeling seen might mean to many people.

When author Robin Landa interviewed NiRey Reynolds, global director of creative excellence, Momentum Worldwide, for her book *Strategic Creativity*, she asked how advertisers can become more sensitive to how identities are represented or marginalized. Reynolds replied:

Representation is a word as powerful as its meaning. I want everyone who is reading this right now to think back to their youth and all the media that had an impact on them. How many actors, characters, or models looked like you or had families that looked like yours? How many times were you included? Know that not everyone had the luxury of these experiences. In the United States, this melting pot of cultures, ideals, and nationalities, not everyone has representation on public platforms. We have the ability in this industry to show not only diversity but people in positions of power, and we need to realize the impact these decisions have.[23]

As the entire advertising industry begins to seriously embrace inclusion, they must consider the entire spectrum of communities and groups. Most often, the visibility of disability in advertising is low except when it's focused on products that treat disabilities. Rarely do ads show people living with disability in everyday life, such as working, parenting, doing chores, or enjoying activities. On the presence of people living with disabilities in advertising creative, a Nielsen report states, "In a custom analysis of Nielsen Ad Intel data, we looked at nearly 450,000 primetime ads on broadcast and cable TV in February 2021. Of those ads, just 1 percent included representation of disability-related themes, visuals, or topics."[24]

"Many brands are embracing the need to engage and include people with disabilities. But when they include people with disabilities in creative content, we need to be seen for who we are—beyond our disabilities—without ignoring the fact that we have one," said Christina Mallon, head of inclusive design and accessibility, Wunderman Thompson.[25]

Stella Young, an Australian journalist, comedian, and activist, writing in *Ramp Up* (2012), an Australian publication focused on disability, penned the term *"inspiration porn"* and also addressed the issue in a TEDx talk. The term caught on. Young deliberately used the term *"porn"* to provoke because such images, such as a child running on carbon fiber prosthetic legs " . . . objectify one group of people for the benefit of another. . . . We're objectifying disabled people for the benefit of non-disabled people. The purpose of these images is to inspire you, to motivate you, so we can look at them and think, 'Well, however bad my life is, it could be worse. I could be that person.' "[26]

To change the narrative of how advertisers use images of people living with disabilities, U.K. broadcaster Channel 4's "Super.Human" campaign to promote its coverage of the 2021 Paralympics depicted the multifaceted struggles and joys of Paralympians' road to athletic greatness. "The idea showed the athletes with all their flaws and everyday frustrations, correcting the idyllic yet distorted depiction of Paralympians—what some might describe as 'inspiration porn'— of the brand's previous Grand Prix–winning ads 'We're the Superhumans' and 'Meet the Superhumans.' "[27]

We asked Eoin McLaughlin, deputy executive creative director, Channel 4 (and bestselling children's author), about the story behind the "Super Humans" campaigns for Channel 4. McLaughlin's response follows.

"THE STORY OF SUPERHUMANS" BY EOIN McLAUGHLIN

Advertising can never change the world.

Except, sometimes it can.

When Channel 4 started broadcasting the Paralympics in 2012, it was seen as a bit of an Olympic sideshow. The media generally presented the athletes as inferior amateurs who "tried their best." Unsurprisingly, the viewing figures were terrible. And this largely mirrored perceptions of people with disabilities in general.

So, when we won the rights to broadcast the Paralympics, we had a clear business problem to solve: How could we turn the Paralympics into a mainstream event? And if we could succeed, we knew there was a bigger prize on offer. We had the opportunity to affect real social change. We saw that if we could change people's perceptions of Paralympians, we could change people's perception of disability as a whole.

As with all great ideas, we started by doing something extremely simple. We just flipped current perceptions on their heads. Instead of presenting the athletes as inferior, we told the truth. These people are a hell of a lot more impressive than Olympians.... And so we repositioned the athletes as "superhumans."

Once we'd made that strategic step, the executional direction became clear. Everything we did would show the Paralympians as stronger, more dedicated, and downright badass than any other athlete out there. We'd give them a swagger that nobody else had. This would not be a campaign about disability; this would be a campaign about elite athletes kicking butt and taking names.

That was over ten years ago. And here's where it gets really interesting. Three Summer Paralympic Games later, "Superhumans" has become [one of] the most

(continued on next page)

(*continued from previous page*)

successful advertising works of all time. Three Cannes Lions Film Grand Prix and three D&AD Black Pencils. It's taught on the UK school syllabus and is used by the United Nations. Two separate prime ministers have called out its genius. And most importantly, it's helped to radically change perceptions of disability all over the world.

It's rare for advertising to change popular culture; it's even more rare for it to continue to do so for over a decade. But just like the idea itself, the secret to "Superhumans'" continued success is as simple as the idea itself. Just because the 2012 work was successful, we weren't afraid to break it and do something different.

In 2016, we broke the definition of *"superhuman."* Instead of just featuring athletes, we used it to talk about all disabled people. Our film featured the largest disabled cast ever assembled. We also hired more presenters [living with disability] and film crew than ever before, and presenters who are not living with a disability are now the minority on our coverage. These things have had a huge impact on the representation of disability on both sides of the camera.

In 2021, we quite literally broke the word *"superhuman"* (figure 7.1).

Before we started work on the newest campaign, we spoke to disabled journalists, artists, writers, athletes, academics, and comedians. Everyone told us that "Superhumans" had been so successful that it had unintentionally spawned a new stereotype: "the invincible disabled sports terminator." Our work had accidentally "othered" the athletes by setting them up as superheroes.

7.1 "Super. Human"; In-house agency: 4Creative / London; Production company: Somesuch/London; Client: Channel 4.

So, this time, we told a different truth. Instead of focusing on what made the athletes "super," we showed what made them "human." Including all the screaming toddlers and popped blisters of reality.

Aside from all the strategic smarts and executional pizazz, the thing that's made the work successful is the tone of voice. More and more brands are doing work with a purpose, but very few are brave enough to have a sense of humor as they do so. That's Channel 4's point of difference. Nothing closes the gap between two people quicker than a joke. Humor humanizes. As we all try to make more of a difference and reach out to marginalized groups, let's not always make the same earnest advertising with the same plinky-plonky, pity-me piano music in the background. That's not inclusion, that's othering. **Just because we've found a purpose, let's not lose our sense of humor.**

Working on a campaign like this has been a huge privilege. And it's taught me a few things that will stick. Before you start working on anything with a "purpose," or which engages in a cultural conversation, you need to listen widely. To solve a problem, you need to change perceptions. *Just because you're talking about something serious doesn't mean you need to take yourself seriously. And when you've done something well, don't be afraid to break it next time.*

Unilever's Rexona brand's "#MoveYourWay" campaign aims to level the proverbial playing field and break down barriers to movement. For all Unilever brands, #Unstereotyping advertising is a core policy. For Rexona, this means representing movement in diverse, equitable, and inclusive ways. "From our products to our communications, we will ensure diversity and inclusion are embedded at the core of everything we do as we continue to inspire communities of all abilities across the world to move," said Emily Heath, Rexona senior brand manager.[28] On International Day of Persons with Disabilities, Rexona partnered with One City Disability, an award-winning program of football activities run by City in the Community, "to ensure that every person who joins the program is able to participate and develop football skills regardless of their disability or impairment"; supported professional athletes and grassroots activities; and shared lessons and successes of diversity champions.[29]

SP☀️TLIGHT

P&G "Widen the Screen"

We each have our own perspective, our own worldview shaped by our experiences, communities, families, and education. This personal perspective is the obvious lens through which we see the world and ourselves in it. Too often, the media—whether it's entertainment programming, news coverage, or advertising—portray some groups of people through a narrow lens. Stereotypes and tropes still abound. Creative professionals in advertising who hail from majority communities often create many of the portrayals of BIPOC, women, and other groups that we see day in and day out.

With "Widen the Screen," Proctor & Gamble (P&G) aims to widen the lens to empower Black creators to tell their stories and portray their communities with nuance, breadth, and depth. Damon Jones, P&G chief communications officer, told *Muse by Clio*:

> The idea originated from the knowledge that 6 percent of writers, directors and producers of U.S. films are Black. The visual of that narrow screen [which appears in the interview clips] inspired the idea and program name. Because Black filmmakers are not given enough opportunity to share real stories of Black life, the images that we are shown in advertising, media and film are stereotypes that reflect that limited narrow and racist view of the Black experience.[30]

"Widen the Screen" is a comprehensive initiative focusing on content creation, nurturing talent, and forming partnerships. Its primary aim is to combat racial bias and racism by expanding the limited portrayals of Black experiences in visual media. This initiative actively champions equal representation and the inclusion of Black storytellers within advertising, film, and television, thereby unlocking opportunities across the entire creative and production spectrum for more Black creators.[31]

About the initiative, P&G's website notes,

> Sustained action and investment are necessary to address the systemic bias and inequality in advertising and media. Widen the Screen is an expansive content creation, talent development, and partnership platform that celebrates creativity and enables Black creators to share the full richness of the Black experience. Only when we Widen the Screen to Widen Our View can we all broaden the spectrum of the images we see, the voices we hear, the stories we tell, and the people we understand. Fully.
>
> This is how P&G is showing up for Black creators–both behind the camera *and* on the screen.[32]

Building Inclusion into the Creative Process

As important as it is for representation in the front-facing media, it also is critical to ensure inclusion and diversity at the outset, during the entire creative and production processes:

Ideation process: creative teams, storyline, character development, research
Preproduction: casting/talent, setting/location, roles
Production: directors, crew, photography, video, illustration, product
    imagery, language and voiceover, makeup and hair, costume/clothing
Postproduction: editing, retouching, music, accessibility, and testing
Virtual or hybrid event design: events and experiences must be accessible to all
Distribution: modify reach and existing messaging

One associate creative director of color at the table does not represent all voices. Inclusion is key to getting narratives right and fair. Crafting multifaceted stories that challenge stereotypes and nurture a feeling of belonging requires the involvement of diverse voices at all stages. Collaborating with diverse creatives allows for a broader connection to a wider community.

"When films are just directed by white males, they can't possibly resonate because they are not reflective of what the general populace thinks and feels. Safe choices don't work—they are not noticed," Sophie Gold of Eleanor told us in conversation.[33]

"You're a woman, what do you think?" is a question author Robin Landa has heard many times when she was the only woman seated at the ideation table. One woman isn't enough.

In 2021, no women of color directed Super Bowl spots. In 2022, out of seventy-eight Super Bowl commercial directors, there were ten spots with diverse directors.[34] For example, Best Director Academy Award winner Chloé Zhao (represented by Superprime for spots) directed the Budweiser's Clydesdale spot for Vayner Media. In 2023, four women and one Black director helmed spots.[35]

Wieden+Kennedy's New York head of integrated production, Nick Setounski, said that year-round, W+K makes concerted efforts to diversify behind the lens. "It is absolutely a priority for our production department and our producers to shift the tide of who we award jobs to. We look for underrepresented directors—people of color and female directors—as a matter of course."[36]

Google's "Real Tone"

Many manufacturers of mobile phones with cameras neglected "to design software to capture everyone's complexion. Camera technology has been notoriously non-inclusive when it comes to showing the full richness of darker skin tones."[37]

"'Real children could not see themselves in the picture,' said Hugo Veiga, global chief creative officer at AKQA, who led the jury for the Cannes Lions mobile category, about how mobile cameras had not been designed initially for inclusivity. Now, it 'allows people to see themselves as they truly are,'" Veiga added.[38]

Google explains:

Historically, camera technology has excluded people of color, especially those with darker skin tones. A lack of diverse testing means that today's cameras can carry that same bias, delivering unflattering photos for people of color.

What is Real Tone? Google's mission to make our camera and image products work more equitably for people of color. We vastly improved our camera tuning models and algorithms to more accurately highlight the nuances of diverse skin tones with Real Tone software.[39]

The Google "Real Tone" campaign was created in partnership with the *New York Times*' T Brand Studio, Wieden+Kennedy New York, and Gut, Miami.

Elevating Equity: Diverse Workforce, Inclusive Teams

Defining a company's core values clearly at the outset allows the values to drive and steer communication. People align with companies whose values they share. Well-defined core values provide a foundation for all creative solutions and, when articulated in a creative brief, ensure creative compliance. Articulating core values allows the company and the advertising to represent the company to the public consistently and on their own terms. Of course, people form their own perceptions of brands and advertising. However, maintaining and committing to core values aids in projecting an authentic portrait and a competitive advantage. It's not about pleasing the core audience as much as being committed to ethical behaviors guided by key values.

"Built by Dyslexic Thinking" reframes dyslexia and also reframes several of the brand's core values communicated through a campaign.

SP   TLIGHT

"Dyslexic Thinking"/FCB Inferno

"Brands have the power to change the world for the better. Virgin is a brand that has always challenged conventions because it was shaped by a dyslexic mind. Where others saw problems, Sir Richard Branson saw solutions. Dyslexia allows people to think more creatively, see problems differently and lead with empathy. Dyslexic Thinking is an idea that reframed dyslexia, championed neurodiversity and captured the spirit that built the Virgin brand," Owen Lee, chief creative officer, FCB Inferno, told us.[40]

The creative team wanted to encourage people to view dyslexia as a skill. To do this, their insight was to reframe dyslexia, for companies to promote it as a benefit, which might "embolden people with dyslexia to come forward."[41] Their idea? Virgin Group partnered with Made by Dyslexia, LinkedIn, and Dictionary. com to turn the phrase *"dyslexic thinking"* into a positive skill people with dyslexia possess (figure 7.2).

"To raise awareness, LinkedIn changed its platform to feature Dyslexic Thinking as an official skill available for the 810 million users to add to their profiles. Dictionary.com then vetted it through their rigorous accreditation process and added it to their dictionary. By recognizing dyslexic thinking in such high-profile ways, we were finally able to begin shifting people's perceptions."[42]

The campaign set out to shift people's view of neurodiversity in the workplace. There was a 1562 percent increase in positive online sentiment towards the word *"dyslexia,"* with a move towards being recognized as a positive skill. "By recognizing Dyslexic Thinking as a skill, we have given the 1 in 5 people

(continued on next page)

(continued from previous page)

7.2 "Built by Dyslexic Thinking"; Agency: FCB Inferno / London; Client: Virgin Group, Made By Dyslexia, LinkedIn.

in the world who are affected by dyslexia the confidence to embrace their unique way of interacting with co-workers and employers," notes FCB Inferno's website.[43]

  Clients: Virgin, LinkedIn, Dictionary.com

Zeitgeist, Contemporary Issues and Culture: How the Stories Reflect the Times and Issues

In an effort to end race-based hair discrimination, with the National Urban League, Color of Change, and the Center of Western Law and Poverty, in 2019, Dove established the Crown Coalition. Dove sales rose 8 percent in 2021, its fastest growth in eight years, which Unilever credits to its purpose marketing; the companywide growth rate was 4.5 percent.[44]

  "Dove 2021 Crown Research Study for Girls," found that 53 percent of Black mothers said their daughters experienced hair discrimination. Some of those experiences began as early as the age of five. The study also found that approximately 86 percent of Black teens who endured hair discrimination

did so by the age of 12, while 100 percent of Black elementary school girls in
majority-white schools who said they experienced hair bias said they did so
by the age of 10.[45]

Created by WPP agencies Ogilvy and Swift, with input from JOY Collective,
the "As Early as Five" campaign depicts three scenarios of "race-based hair discrimination experienced by a girl starting in elementary school at age 5, in high
school and into adulthood—all inspired by real life events." It is "part of the brand's
ongoing commitment to take action, raise awareness and lead on the issue of race-
based hair discrimination and advocate for the passing of The CROWN Act—
legislation to make race-based hair discrimination illegal in all 50 US states."[46]

Out of the Shadows/Amplification: How the Stories Amplify DEI

In the United States, LGBTQIA+ Pride Month is celebrated each year to honor
the 1969 Stonewall Uprising in Manhattan, New York, which was a tipping point
for the gay liberation movement. Pride Month is a time when many advertisers show their allyship with the LGBTQIA+ community. For example, Skittles
partnered with GLAAD, a North American nongovernmental media monitoring
organization, working toward accelerating acceptance for the LGBTQIA+ community. Skittles asked six artists from the LGBTQIA+ community to design Skittles packages to represent how they see the rainbow (https://skittles.com/pride).
For every pack purchased, one dollar goes directly to GLAAD. Skittles started
to generate buzz in May, ahead of Pride Month, which is not the usual approach.

Support during Pride Month is good. Support of the LGBTQI+ community
year-round is better. On the flip side, rainbow washing is a common practice;
brands and companies that do not do tangible work to support LGBTQIA+ communities at any other time during the year only "signal" support during Pride
Month. Some advocacy is better than silence—however, true support comes
through dedicated action.

"Representation requires voice. If companies are committed to supporting the
LGBTQ+ community, they need to stop making assumptions and do the work to
really listen. Ask how people want to be portrayed and supported. Think beyond
advertising: Think about the health insurance they provide, where they make
their products available, the way their forms are set up, the kinds of media where
they choose to place their products, the events they sponsor, the mentorship

programs in place, and certainly, the politicians they support," Cait Lamberton, distinguished professor of marketing at the Wharton School, told *Penn Today*.[47]

During Pride Month, Boy Smells featured *Hacks* star Megan Stalter and *Boys in the Band* star Charlie Carver for a Pride campaign called "Nurture Your Nature." In the campaign, Boy Smells' new Marble Fruit candle "pays homage to the beauty of the LGBTQIA community, representing their uniqueness and resilience," and benefits the Gay, Lesbian, and Straight Education Network, a nonprofit that aims to end LGBTQ+ discrimination in K–12 schools.[48]

But it's not enough to just *market* inclusiveness or diversity. As Deloitte's "Authentically Inclusive Marketing" study shows, 57 percent of consumers

SP☀TLIGHT

Indeed/"Rising Voices" Campaign

Indeed is a job site, a platform to help people find employment. Indeed's "Rising Voices" campaign's tagline is, "We believe that talent is universal, but opportunity is not."

Indeed, Ventureland, 271 Films, and PRETTYBIRD filmmakers and program mentors Calmatic, Paul Hunter, and Melina Matsoukas selected the ten winning screenplays and supported the filmmakers throughout the program and productions.[50]

"Indeed's *Rising Voices* not only levels the playing field for BIPOC creators in Hollywood by creating opportunities for individuals to be seen, heard and represented, but also empowers the next generation of storytellers, providing access to funding, on-site skill, career development and mentorship," actor and producer Lena Waithe said in a statement. "Our continued mission at Hillman Grad Productions is to ensure that program mentees are truly set up for success as they continue to grow within their individual careers."[51]

Indeed has significantly increased its investment in *Rising Voices* season 2 and added a new program called The Lab, developed by Indeed and Hillman Grad, which is a twelve-month nonexclusive residency that will sponsor three *Rising Voices* season 1 filmmakers. "Modeled after Indeed's incubator program, which funds new product ideas internally, Hillman Grad will work with the filmmakers to develop ideas and create content for Indeed."[52]

are more loyal to brands that *commit* to addressing social inequities in their actions.[49]

Instead of spending $1 million on a conventional TV commercial, Indeed invested that $1 million in ten BIPOC filmmakers for each to make a short film about the meaning of work—*Rising Voices*. The idea: Jobs have the power to change us all.

To uncover, invest in, and mentor the next generation of BIPOC filmmakers across the United States, Indeed collaborated with Emmy Award–winning writer, creator, and actor Lena Waithe and her company Hillman Grad Productions.

Simon Usifo; Photo by Sammy Hart.

INTERVIEW: SIMON USIFO, PRESIDENT AND MANAGING DIRECTOR, 72ANDSUNNY AMSTERDAM

Creativity you can't ignore as an effective solution to business problems is what Simon Usifo is passionate about. Prior to joining 72andSunny, Simon spent five years in Berlin as a board member, managing director, and, most recently, chief client officer of Ogilvy Germany.

At Ogilvy Shanghai, Simon was the director of digital strategy. He spent over five years advising global brands such as Sprite, LVMH, Chanel, Philips, Unilever, Nestlé, and Huawei. Before moving to China, Simon lived in London, working in account management at Wunderman and Ogilvy with brands such as IBM, Ford, and Microsoft. Today, Simon is looking after Europe for 72andSunny out of their Amsterdam office as president and managing director. In addition, Simon sits on the advisory board of Upfeel as an advisor and investor. The Paris-based startup helps companies to take care of the mental health and well-being of their employees.

He is also an advisory board member of Beyond Gender Agenda, the most significant network for diversity, equity, and inclusion in the German economy. As a former middle- and long-distance runner and ex-member of Germany's junior national athletics team, Simon is still a passionate runner and loves to explore new running routes in Amsterdam, where he lives with his wife and his seven-year-old daughter.

Is there an inherent advantage to having a diverse outlook?

I personally don't like the term "diversity, equity, and inclusion" very much. It sounds engineered to me. In fact, for the largest part of my career, I tried to elegantly avoid this topic area. Maybe because it hurt too much? I've dealt with unconscious bias, microaggressions, and racial profiling on a daily basis all my life, but no one ever really seemed to care or to be able to relate to it. The lack of diversity, equity, and inclusion in the context of my advertising career during my early years as an advertising professional has been omnipresent but remained unnoticed.

Until George Floyd came into the picture. I realized that maybe something fundamental had changed across the world through the events in the U.S. and that even people who weren't personally affected suddenly became aware of their privilege and got the sense that something was off. Something had to change. This new situation made me reflect a lot about my own identity, my upbringing, and challenges along the way. I thought more consciously about how my very personal story and situation impacted my ability to navigate the corporate world over the years, from being an intern during my time at university to being a C-level executive, overseeing three German offices of Ogilvy, one of the most successful advertising networks in the world.

Interestingly, I realized that throughout my life, what could have been seen as adversity actually turned into an unfair advantage for me in business. The more the market space got impacted by an increasingly complex, uncertain, and fast-paced world, the more it seemed people with a diverse background like me would naturally be adept to deal with the challenges ahead and would be suitable to help more diverse teams find solutions for clients, partners, and internally.

But what do I mean when I say, "people like me"?

As a half -Black, half-white son of Nigerian and French immigrants born in Germany, a country that is famous for many things except for being warm and welcoming, the tension of standing out and wanting to fit in seemed to be a common challenge for many young people with parents that immigrated or were mixed race.

At the same time, the advantage of speaking multiple languages comfortably (for example) was one of the hints that there might also be a beauty of being different. Having different perspectives became more and more like a weapon. Mainly because I developed a special form of empathy and a more diverse outlook. I was also realizing that no matter where I go, there is no country in the world where people look like me, and I will always be kind of a misfit. Which means you have to earn yourself a certain chemistry with people and the comfort of intuitively knowing how to behave the hard way.

What kind of behaviors can leaders adopt to make change?

The more we rely on GenY and Gen Z, the pure bonus-and-incentive scheme won't cut it unless the OKRs [objective and key results] are rooted in the cultural values that go beyond financial performance. What gains in importance is an environment that identifies and removes toxic behavior fast and rewards true leadership that focuses on empowering others to grow and setting up everyone around you for success. It doesn't sound like the traditional definition of leadership but seems to find more and more its way into a modern interpretation of it. Leadership as a behavior, not a rank.

How much room an empathy and compassion-driven leadership style receives across an organization and whether it can fully enable the organization to unlock its full potential is directly linked to how much the most powerful group of people at the very top care about it. The board, the C-levels, the founders, the leadership team. Only they can turn it into a central building block for the culture of a company every day.

What role should DEI play in corporate strategy and culture?

If we look at the discussion around leadership we are having right now, it becomes obvious why diversity, equity, and inclusion is more than ever a central topic. It embodies the question of what the culture of a corporation looks like and whether it can be the perfect breeding ground for transformation and personal growth. The philosophy behind DEI needs to be hard-coded into the DNA of a company, like human rights are in the constitution of a democratic nation. It's an equally fundamental component of the recipe for future-proofing the company and its commercial success and relevance. It should sit at the heart of the corporate strategy, next to sustainability, mental health, and personal growth of the employees.

How do equity and inclusion affect impact?

It's the anomaly, the outlier, the misfit, the friction, the adversity that opens our eyes, makes us leave our comfort zone, and helps us to anticipate more accurately what is needed to grow and adapt in line with the change around us. In the old world, where change was linear and the world appeared less fragmented and complex in our perception, we got away with a lot of complacency. Today, I truly believe that both as an individual and as an organization, we will only thrive if we fully embrace diversity, equity, and inclusion as the absolute new normal in everything we do.

I think that diversity is the part that, in particular, has to turn into a hygiene factor and won't be a strong enough differentiator in the performance game in the long run. It is the equity and inclusion aspect that will be especially reflective of a modern, empathy- and compassion-driven ideal of leadership that will drive the success and impact of companies in the future. It puts the human back at the center of everything, and I strongly believe that, once all aspects of our lives are fully digitized, this is what a postdigital world will be about.

You've lived and worked in different countries. How does this experience impact your leadership philosophy?

The real key to navigating the different perspectives was empathy. An empathy that you learn automatically when you grow up with or in between different cultures, skin colors, or socioeconomic realities. Also, empathy has to do a lot with the ability to listen, which requires a certain level of humbleness, which people gain in different ways. Hardship seems definitely to be one of them. You combine empathy with a bit of compassion, and you receive a leadership culture which was often undervalued in the past but seems to build the most resilient corporate cultures in today's world. A world that is increasingly being referred to as the *vuca* world (volatile, uncertain, complex, and adverse).

When it comes to future-proofing, what type of change is necessary?

While structural change is always required in order to truly advance a transformation, unless there is cultural change, a company is not going anywhere.

Fundamentally, what makes any advertising campaign worthy of sharing?

Successful campaigns are usually based on an extremely strong but simple, single-minded idea that doesn't necessarily need to look and feel like a campaign. In the context of the overall power shift from brands to consumers, it's the added value for either the individual or the collective of our society that is more important. It solves a problem, makes us laugh, or cry, or fall in love, inspires us, etc. These types of ideas can only take off with the help of outstanding storytelling, of course, but could be shared for many different reasons. What unites them all is that they usually touch us in a way that makes them stand out in a sea of sameness. They work their way through the algorithms and a very noisy and fragmented media environment for a very good reason. My observation is that this unique ability to make people share a campaign voluntarily often comes with four specific qualities: **1. Very insightful:** They are based around such a sharp insight that reveals a truth in a very simple and relatable way **2. Great timing:** The theme and tone, as well as the content, the mechanic, or the solution itself, are culturally dialed in and either ride on the zeitgeist in a very smart way or are even ahead of the curve and help push the overall conversation. **3. Outstanding craft** is what often elevates an already strong idea through an execution that is just incredibly beautiful, or technologically smart, or both. **4. Authenticity:** Last but not least, I have to say that all the previous points will be useless and not lead to a sharable campaign unless we feel the authenticity. It needs to be real and believable instead of opportunistic and fake. Unless brands are able to prove through tangible and sustainable actions that they are walking the talk, none of their campaigns will be successful in today's environment.

What are the dynamics of agency culture that continually inspire breakthrough unconventional creative solutions?

Agency cultures thrive on the diverse backgrounds, personalities, and mindsets of people who work in them but also from the input of the diverse clients and industries they work for and with. The key advantage in the context of creating unconventional creative solutions is that there is a constant learning curve and nearly unlimited potential for collective inspiration with every new industry, category, product, or service an agency has to get its head around.

As technology has radically changed content consumption and creation, what are the constants of great brand storytelling that you feel have remained unchanged?

While technology has triggered a significant powershift between brands and consumers, forcing us to approach the way we operate and develop our work differently, the key success factors in the field of brand storytelling have not really changed. Strong insights, cultural relevance, outstanding craft, and authenticity are still key for powerful ideas.

The industry is still talking about purpose and purposeful partnerships. How can collaboration lead to purposeful initiatives between brands and individuals, other organizations, and communities?

To me, it starts with ourselves. Whether we are an individual or an organization, we need to find the discipline and maturity to truly get to the very core of who we are and what we believe in. Because these core values and beliefs will form the DNA of everything that follows, once we are clear about these fundamentals, we can seek partners, companies, and personalities that share the same vision and mission but also the same understanding of how to get there. That's where purpose comes alive in a meaningful way that adds value to the society but also to everyone involved on a very individual level. Because it's authentic and real to begin with. Points of view can change and should change as we constantly learn. Our very core beliefs and values shouldn't. In times of volatility and uncertainty, it becomes even more important to be able to rely on this constant. This is why our ability to join and build great purposeful-partnerships always starts with solid work on our very own organization and brand. Only if the brand identity, the brand positioning, brand strategy, with all their effects on the corporate culture, are clear and clean internally, the organization will be ready to drive purposeful work externally. In fact, ideally, whatever work or collaboration is being developed in the future, it will hopefully just be purposeful by design because it's very much in harmony with who this company and brand truly is.

TORRENTS OF TRUTH / NEBO / UKRAINE AND 72ANDSUNNY / AMSTERDAM

Torrents of Truth is a cyberaction that bypasses Russian censorship to spread the truth about the Ukraine war.

Context

On March 7, 2022, as a response to economic sanctions, the Russian government authorized the piracy of content from countries deemed as "unfriendly," encouraging Russian citizens to pirate popular Western entertainment.

Idea

To circumvent censorship within Russia, Nebo and 72and Sunny initiated "Torrents of Truth," (figure 7.3) orchestrating a cyber-offensive that transformed widely-used peer-to-peer (P2P) platforms into a vast information conduit. This strategy enabled journalists to camouflage their unfiltered accounts of the Ukraine war as pirated torrents of movies, TV series, music, software, and books.

Twenty-One Torrents Uploaded

The journalistic reports were uploaded across P2P platforms popular in Russia and reached Russian citizens who were attempting to pirate content, such as *The Batman*, *Doctor Strange*, or Adobe Photoshop 2022. In total, twenty-one torrent files have been uploaded and seeded on RuTracker, Demonoid, the Pirate

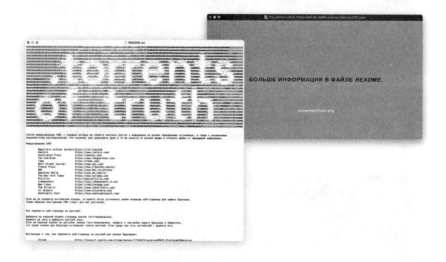

7·3 "Torrents of Truth"; Agencies: 72andSunny Amsterdam and Nebo Kyiv. "Torrents of Truth was conceived and developed as part of a collaboration between 72andSunny Amsterdam and Kyiv-based Ukrainian creative agency Nebo, which saw the Kremlin's decision to encourage citizens to pirate Western entertainment content as a huge opportunity to strike a blow for freedom of speech in Russia. "The aim is to get the people who download Torrents of Truth videos to 'seed' them across platforms. By sparing a bit of bandwidth to download and share the hidden files, anyone, anywhere can help to tackle censorship in Russia and spread the truth about the horrific invasion of Ukraine."

Bay, 1337x, and other torrent trackers popular in Russia. Each torrent embeds a report from a journalist on the Russian invasion of Ukraine camouflaged as a pirated film, series, software, music, or book.

Four Journalists Enabled

While punishments range from fines of $45,000 to prison terms of up to fifteen years for anyone going against the Kremlin disinformation narrative, our cyber action has enabled four journalists to speak up about the truth of the war in Ukraine—opening up an undercover channel to keep spreading unbiased, trustworthy news in a country where TV and newspapers aren't allowing it anymore.

More than Eighteen Thousand Torrents Downloaded

To make the torrents popular, we needed high numbers of seeders (uploaders), so we thought: Let's make it public. That's why anyone, anywhere, could help spread the truth in Russia by seeding the torrents from their own computer. And while it is impossible to know precisely how many times in total the torrents have been downloaded in Russia, we can tell how many times they've been downloaded from our own servers. On the day of the launch, it had around four hundred downloads. As of 2023, this total is so far over 18,500 downloads and counting.

DEI STORYTELLING CONSIDERATIONS

Can a brand be a social activist? A brand's origin story and mission can *organically* align with a social issue or cause; a brand can have substance and not simply hawk their wares.

- Know your audience (of course).
- Positive portrayals effect positive change.
- Inclusive narratives represent and instill trust.
- Inclusive storiestelling, when done respectfully and creatively, can hold emotional power.

(continued on next page)

(continued from previous page)

- Invite and listen to diverse perspectives to avoid cultural insensitivity.
- Be authentic (no "washing").
- Support communities throughout the year, not just during Pride Month, Black History Month, Women's History Month, and so on.
- Consult with DEI officers and build diverse, inclusive teams.
- Diversity and inclusion should be part of the brand's purpose.
- Consider intersectionality.
- Everyone gets a seat at the table during ideation and production.
- Does your DEI effort in advertising storiestelling align with your values, mission, and actions? Do you have the right to speak in this space based on this?
- Subvert stereotypes; no tropes.
- Anticipate and prepare for backlash (e.g., Nike's "Dream Crazy" and Ulta Beauty's podcast with trans TikTok star Dylan Mulvaney).

Valerie Cheng-Madon

INTERVIEW: VALERIE CHENG-MADON, CHIEF CREATIVE OFFICER SOUTH EAST ASIA, MCCANN WORLDGROUP

Valerie Cheng-Madon's love for painting since five spawned a career of more than twenty years across brand-building and integrated creative solutions for major brands such as Zespri, Caltex, Hewlett-Packard, Procter & Gamble, Singapore Airlines, HSBC, Burger King, VISA, Singapore Tourism Board, Changi Airport, Central Provident Fund, Shell, GSK, Cycle & Carriage, Friesland Campina, and many others.

Over the years, Valerie has made her mark at Cannes Lions, D&AD, One Show, London International, Effies, Golden Drum, Spikes Asia, Adfest, and the Webby's. Prior to joining Meta, her most recent achievement in managing VMLY&R Asia was helping her team in India win the rare WHITE PENCIL and 2 WOOD PENCILS at D&AD 2022. Following that, a Grand Prix at Cannes 2022, silvers and bronzes, including a silver for a much-coveted Innovation Lion and a bronze for Glass Lion.

Valerie is also regularly invited to be a judge at all the major shows (Cannes Lions, One Show, New York Festival, Spikes Asia), including as jury president for the D&AD.

If you were to give a speed workshop on storytelling for advertising, what key points would you stress?

(1) Every story must have highs and lows. The more extreme, the better. Get people onto an emotional roller-coaster. (2) The best inspiration comes from real-life situations or experiences that people can relate to. (3) Don't try too hard to be funny if you are not a genuinely funny person. Humor is best scripted by comedians. Humor with universal appeal internationally is also difficult to achieve because some humor doesn't travel beyond its own cultural context. (4) Don't get too indulgent. Many films are unnecessarily long without being entertaining. We can get too in love with our own work and forget that most viewers have very little time.

So much of your work succeeds in successfully engaging multiple cultures simultaneously. What is your approach to realizing that, and what is your advice for other creative leaders hoping to achieve that as well?

The first thing that I always tell myself and my creatives is this: Never assume that if you live most of your life in one country that you understand the people, the culture, the behavior, and the mindset of people in every other country. Just consider how extremely diverse Asia alone is. If you don't live a culture, you don't understand what the people there go through day in and day out. Consider creating work for Japan, where the culture is extremely nuanced. They have a unique language, unique slang, unique ways of life, and belief systems that are very distinct to that culture and can't be generalized. So, with international differences, we have to be deliberate in our approach. There's so much risk these days in making such assumptions. At times, I still get clients who say, "Oh, let's just replicate a campaign from this country to that country." Firstly, it's dangerous. Secondly, you're not really making the maximum impact compared to when work is really natively created for the specific country in order to be culturally and socially relevant. Whenever I get a brief, I always ask what my key markets are, and then I'll reach out to my global offices, which I'm a stickler about. A lot of people love to take the shortcut and say, "Oh, let's just read up on some papers (secondary data) about the market." But no papers can really tell you the full story as opposed to actively working with individuals who are true-blue inhabitants of a country. I believe in gathering those ideas, and I got to practice that every day, working very closely with our global team on brands like Mastercard and L'Oréal. As a senior person, whether you're a regional or global leader, I think your role is to curate and fine-tune the work, but let the ideation come from the source.

As an industry leader, what changes have you witnessed or experienced that indicate that consumers expect positive social and environmental commitment from the brands that they have relationships with?

Brands who have managed to do this successfully enjoy real organic sharing on social media and mass media PR [public relations], such as what was generated by REI's Black Friday "#OptOutside" campaign and Nike's Colin Kaepernick "Dream Crazy" campaign. Beyond the campaigns themselves, brands that have causes built into their DNA, like The Body Shop and Oatley, stand out as unique due to a clear vision that the world can get behind. I wouldn't say that all brands have to make their CSR [corporate social responsibility] efforts evident to be successful, such as Apple, but for those who choose to get behind a cause, they have to do it with commitment and credibility.

What should advertisers be aware of when incorporating CSR into a brand's communication?

It needs to come from the DNA of the brand itself. It's not something that can be adopted overnight, especially if the brand's practices do not live up to it, because it can backfire if it's not sincere. People and the media, as well, are very quick to pick up on superficial campaigns and messages and call them out as a result. A brand has to be ready with genuine answers for real-world questions and commit to living up to a cause 24/7, both externally and internally, within their organization.

Prior to McCann Worldgroup, you were the chief creative officer of VMLY&R Asia, where you and your team developed "the Adeli Movement" campaign in India for the client Unipads to address a longstanding prejudice (figure 7.4). The campaign explains that women who are menstruating are often called "Adeli," which translates to "unclean" in Guharati; and they are frequently banned from restaurants as a result. Please tell us about your idea and how launching the Adeli Café on International Women's Day was a way to enable advocates and empower women.

That campaign is a perfect example of a hyperlocal approach. It addresses a problem that is specific to parts of India, although taboos surrounding a woman's period are seen in other Asian countries as well. Not being able to go in the kitchen to cook for one's family was an issue that we wanted to address in partnership with

7.4 "The Adeli Movement"; Client: Unipads; Agency: VMLY&R Asia.

our client at Unipad, who is a longtime activist for women's rights. Our client even runs a school that teaches young women how to embrace their periods positively and how not to feel "less than." Our client had been promoting education essentially door-to-door from the ground up, so our role as the agency was to somehow leverage communication to amplify the message in a much bigger way. Especially given that organizations like these often don't have the kind of money to buy big mass media.

The agency team in India came up with the idea of directly disputing the idea that eating food cooked by women having their periods will harm you. Their simple idea was, "Let's prove it untrue." Let's create a restaurant where the meals are purely cooked by women who are having their periods, absurd as it may sound, and serve them to whoever wants to come and stand and be an ally. And it was great to see all the advocates who all came out to show their support, including male supporters, journalists, state officials, and celebrities. They got so much PR from the event that it really helped spread the word, and while initially, they activated the Adeli Café for one Indian state, they're now taking that same model and running it in many additional states as well. It was really encouraging seeing the cause generate that much earned media, and that's what creativity is all about. Whenever people question whether there's a role for creativity, that's what great creativity brings—it's earned growth.

Another breakthrough campaign you developed with your team at JWT Singapore is the "Guardian Angel" wearable for the Association of Women for Action and Research (AWARE). The necklace is equipped with a discreet button, so when a woman is in a potentially harmful situation, she can press it to generate a fake call to her own cell phone, thereby creating an excuse to break the chain of events (figure 7.5). If the situation persists, the user can press and hold the button to send a SOS to a designated number, such as a parent, guardian, or trusted friend, along with a Google map location. How did an insight into consumer behavior inspire your team to create this important solution?

The main insight that inspired this idea came from speaking with the AWARE women's group in Singapore. Again, it's about understanding the real problem behind abuse and the kinds of threats that women face. Statistically, most abuse actually comes from people you know, whether it's, sadly, a spouse, a relative, or even a close friend, and many times, women are stuck in a position where it's very

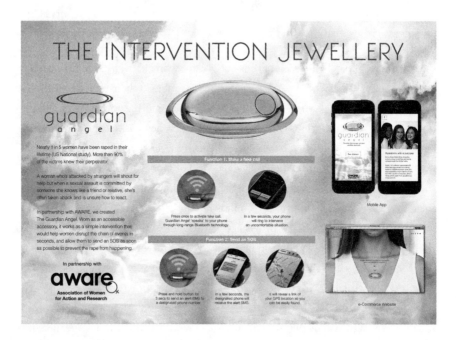

7.5 "Guardian Angel"; Client: AWARE (Association of Women for Action and Research); Agency: JWT Singapore.

difficult to make the decision to call for help because of those relationships. In a hostile situation, confronted with someone you know, there are a lot of barriers to screaming for help.

So, how do you do it in a way that's subtle enough that you feel safe to do so? That was the inspiration behind creating a piece of jewelry that could be activated without raising suspicions. The wearable was designed to allow someone to disrupt a certain cycle to get them out of a situation before it can escalate. How it works is that the first click generates a fake call to your cell phone, giving you an excuse to say, "Hey, hang on a minute. Can I pick up a call?" And, if threatening behavior persists, you can also click and hold to actually call for proper help.

The wearable was not easy to produce, and I bring this up because it was such a huge learning curve for the team. As a creative agency, we're not structured to create hardware prototypes, but I think what we felt really proud of was the fact that we put ourselves in the very uncomfortable situation of learning to accomplish something we'd never done before. That's why, even today, when a creative tells me something can't be done, I tell them, "It's all in your head." We've got networks of like-minded thinkers out there all around the world, and you'd be surprised how many people are hungry for opportunities to do work together when it's meaningful and when it's a chance to do something that hasn't been done before. Anything is possible.

When you first started your career in advertising, it was particularly challenging for women to reach upper management in the industry. What insight can you offer about your success that might offer encouragement to women entering the industry today?

My message to women in our industry would be—please don't ever think that your ability to succeed is based on your gender because that mentality already places you on the back foot, and that's very dangerous. I can't say that every woman would have the same experiences I've had in having my male colleagues embrace me wholeheartedly and see me as equal, and I know there are instances where people suffer in a boardroom or in a meeting and feel that their voices aren't heard, and promotions aren't given. But just remember to speak up and speak with the belief that you are equal, and never think that you are less than because the moment you start thinking that way, you will naturally retract. If you believe we're all equal, then people start seeing you as equal.

Is there one piece of additional wisdom you can share with the upcoming generation of advertising professionals?

I would say that a good creative is someone who is constantly open-minded. Open-minded to collaborating, open-minded to being told that they may be wrong, and not being precious about what you initially thought was the best idea. I think it's important to have that sense of humility. Of course, as creatives, we treat the idea as our baby, and hence, there is a tendency to want to protect it. But the truth is the best ideas are constantly being shaped and molded, and they never remain 100 percent the way they first started. It's really like sculpting. An idea is a piece of clay that you keep molding and shaping and touching, and sometimes, it requires a few additional people to come in and help you. Hence, with an open mind, invite more perspectives and listen to more people because if you only see it through your own eyes, then it's always going to be a little bit biased and also limited in its ability to become something so much bigger. The thing I would leave creatives with is this: Never believe that the idea you first came up with is as good as it gets because it can always be better.

CHAPTER 8

WHAT'S THE NEXT STORY? HOW TO TELL A STORY WITHOUT A PLAYBOOK

THE ART OF STORYTELLING IS CONSTANT, HOW THEY'RE TOLD IS EVER-CHANGING

Let's talk about cat food.

In the 1960s, there was a phenomenon in the advertising industry known as the creative revolution.[1] It was led by the ad agency Doyle Dane Bernbach, who created the famous "Think Small" campaign for a then unusual and unknown imported car called the Volkswagen Beetle.[2] In the current era of marketing, we're looking at another revolution in brand storytelling that is marked by a willingness to embrace or activate platforms in new mediums for new forms of consumer engagement and a movement to integrate purpose into brand building. As evidence of these two shifts, one only has to look at some of the recent solutions created in some of the oldest brand categories.

One novel example occurred for canned cat food, which, as a product category, has been in existence since the 1930s and, over the decades, has been advertised in magazines, television commercials, and other mediums in decidedly traditional ways.[3] But in 2019, when Sheba sought to reiterate its commitment to sustainably sourced fish as one of its product's ingredients, the brand endeavored to try and do more by redefining how a billboard functions for the simple reason that fish are ultimately only sustainable if their environment is as well.[4]

The issue is an urgent one given that scientists indicate that 90 percent of coral reefs around the world are at risk of dying this century, possibly even as early as the year 2043.[5] Reef destruction on this scale would have negative ramifications for the global food supply, coastal protection from storms and flooding, and even the economic future of tourism-based societies.[6] In light of these compelling facts, Sheba and its ad agency AMV BBDO/London created a break-through underwater billboard supported by the United Nations and the World Wildlife Fund, located off the island of Bontosua in Indonesia's Coral Trian-gle.[7] It features forty-six-foot-high, thirty-foot-wide letters spelling out the word *Hope*, and it is continually growing.[8] The living "Sheba Hope Reef" is made of rapidly growing reef stars and is actually viewable from space on Google Earth. This billboard generated 2.5 billion earned media impressions worldwide, and in just two years, the coral reef went from 99 percent dead to 70 percent alive. It was all a part of the more than $10 million in reef restoration the brand and its parent company, Mars Inc., has invested over the last decade, along with $1 bil-lion invested through its Sustainable in a Generation Plan. Since the implemen-tation of the Sheba Hope Reef, Australia, Mexico, The Maldives, Seychelles, and the U.S. Virgin Islands have all adopted the Sheba reef-building system as well.[9] Professor David Smith, Mars Inc.'s chief marine scientist, said, "We hope our efforts inspire others to join us so we can all play our part in helping prevent the extinction of our coral reefs." Eventually, the healthy coral growth will envelop Sheba's innovative living billboard and obscure it completely, which is, of course, the whole point.[10] As Sheba succinctly says in its brand communications, "More coral today. More fish tomorrow."[11]

It's a powerful story and one that would have, perhaps, seemed incomprehen-sible, at least from a media planning perspective, to past stewards of the brand. It utilized the timeless art of storytelling while capitalizing on ingenious new platforms to present them. Consider the media channels that are most aligned with your consumer's behaviors, interests, and, above all, values, and the canvas for your next important brand story may end up being the one you invent.

THE NEXT GREAT ADVERTISING STORY MAY LOOK NOTHING LIKE ADVERTISING

Sometimes, the most compelling brand stories don't look and feel like brand sto-ries at all. In 2019, a significant portion of international TV audiences were glued to the epic season finale of *Game of Thrones*—to the tune of 19.3 million viewers worldwide, a record for the biggest episode in HBO history.[12] A common refrain from the TV series is "Winter is coming." Coincidentally, during the same year, an especially severe winter caused the Red Cross to miss out on thousands of blood donations.[13] In fact, the season's polar vortex brought the coldest air in a generation and forced the Red Cross to cancel no fewer than 370 blood drives nationwide, leaving some 11,500 blood donations uncollected—a potentially dire situation for the organization, considering blood donations are perishable and can only be replaced by other donor volunteers.[14] A breakthrough solution was needed and, therefore, HBO, the Red Cross, and their ad agency partners Droga5 and Giant Spoon implemented a most unlikely partnership to accomplish that goal.[15] The campaign didn't look or sound anything like what's commonly considered advertising and instead immersed donors in a story that they already followed and loved.

The campaign created a partnership between the Red Cross and the *Game of Thrones* series and was aptly titled "Bleed for the Throne." Here, a show known for copious amounts of bloodshed now mobilized its devoted fans to donate it.[16] An immersive *Game of Thrones* experience was created at South by Southwest (SXSW), an annual festival in Austin, Texas, complete with costumed actors, an epic medieval hall, and, of course, the Iron Throne itself.[17] At the SXSW experience, all visitors had to do for a chance to earn one of multiple trips to the *Game of Thrones* world premiere was "bleed for the throne" in the form of a much-needed blood donation.[18]

Was this decidedly atypical ad campaign successful? The HBO and the Red Cross #BleedForTheThrone partnership included blood drives in forty-three states across the country,[19] and the campaign resulted in 21 percent more first-time donors and over 350,000 U.S. blood donations, which amounted to thirteen times what was initially lost over the winter shortage.[20]

This highly effective ad campaign that looked nothing like traditional advertising is just one of many examples of how rejecting conventions can also be a rejection of limitations. The next brand story you tell may be unrecognizable as an ad, and that can be a very good thing in terms of engaging your audience in new and powerful ways.

Jaime Robinson, the cofounder and chief creative officer of JOAN, *Adweek*'s 2022 Small Agency of the Year, said this about the inherent ability of each one of us to create *the next* innovative brand story:

> Any preconceived limitations about the kind of work you can put into this world are nothing but vapor. Don't be restricted by the humdrum status quo's lack of imagination. You only have three responsibilities: (1) to your client and their business objectives (know them, understand them, live them) (2) to your

audience and the things they want to experience (be honest, why should they care?) (3) to your own creative heart (don't spend your life making things you don't LOVE). Other than that, anything goes. You can create your own media, you can carve your own path, you can build your own dreams, you can secure your own funding, you can make your own connections, you can build a network. Believe and you'll see—the rules are fake. This goes for pretty much everything.[21]

THE NEXT STORY YOU TELL COULD MAKE ALL THE DIFFERENCE

In the communication business, the story we're telling is often in the service of a brand, and that's a generally useful thing. In a free market economy, advertising is an engine that drives business, and when done with an ethical foundation, society can benefit. But sometimes, the purpose of an ad campaign is literally the promotion of our highest ideals, such as equality and social justice. That was the case when the American Civil Liberties Union partnered with the agency DeVito/Verdi in New York to address the growing issue of racial profiling. For example, in Florida, 80 percent of those stopped and searched while driving were Black and Hispanic, even though they constituted only 5 percent of all drivers.[22] The ad (figure 8.1) ran in the *New York Times* and the *New York Times Magazine*, and its headline appeared in bold type on a distressed canvas above two imminently noteworthy figures. The headline read, "The man on the left is 75 times more likely to be stopped by the police while driving than the man on the right." On the left was a photograph of Martin Luther King Jr., and on the right was a photo of Charles Manson.[23] Author Greg Braun created the ad as a young art director, along with his writer partner, under the leadership of esteemed creative director Sal DeVito; its power as a piece of communication was amplified due to the fact that it wasn't just some statistic thrust at readers, but it was instead framed as a powerful story about prejudice and injustice.[24]

Ellis Verdi, president at DeVito/Verdi, said:

> This ad has had a life of its own. Not only does it remain on the walls at the ACLU many years after its publication, it's also used as an example by many to describe a "strong concept." Those ads that are "strong concepts"

8.1 "Manson"; Agency: DeVito/Verdi New York; Client: The American Civil Liberties Union.

are typically ageless. They are, in fact, classic. They communicate something so basic and truthful that even years later they resonate. The art direction or look might be dated, but the idea or concept is timeless. In this particular case, unless racism finally disappears once and for all, there remains a place for this ad—we have received many calls in the past few years for a copy.[25]

The ad went on to garner widespread industry success, including winning a Gold One Show Pencil[26] and being named *Advertising Age*'s Best Magazine Ad of the Year, but industry recognition was never the point then, and it isn't the point now.[27] That particular ad for the ACLU ran approximately twenty years ago. Unfortunately, the consequences of social injustice are every bit as important today, and one only has to consider the tragic murder of George Floyd to know how much work is still to be done.[28] In the era in which the ad was created, Facebook, Instagram, and TikTok didn't yet exist.[29] Augmented reality, virtual reality, consumer response marketing, and experiential were all profoundly limited in comparison to today. Which brings us to this question for you: Given all the foundations of engaged storytelling we've discussed in this book, how would you continue this message today? How would you enhance marketing communication, empower audiences as participants in the cause, make them cocreators in the campaign, make them co-owners in its success, amplify their voices across platforms, and ultimately promote a movement for society? How would you make the message a story worth sharing among the audience's reference groups and, therefore, one that is ultimately shareworthy? Positive change will be impacted by the new stories this generation chooses to tell.

BECOME SHAREWORTHY

In this book, we've analyzed brand storytelling in depth in terms of emotional appeals, rational appeals, narrative construct, and the integration of purpose. It's important to note that the purpose of this text isn't to create a checklist but rather a mindset.

Stories themselves aren't inherently valuable until they engage, enlighten, and motivate audiences in ways that result in action. Action can take the form of consumer behavior or even changes in consumers' attitudes regarding a cause or an initiative. It's fundamentally about placing the audience at the center of each story told.

It's an understatement to say that the practice of storytelling has only become more complicated in our time, given not only the massive proliferation of media platforms and artificial intelligence (AI) but also the responsibility of brands to authentically embrace purpose. And yes, audiences' expectations have expanded in kind. The number-one brand value in 2022, as identified by consumers, is integrity at 58 percent. Two-thirds of consumers report that they no longer purchase from brands whose values don't align with their own, and 74 percent state that transparent communication is now more important than it was before the pandemic. These are all national trends initiated by millennials and furthered by Gen Z.[30] In other words, what a brand says and what a brand does are equally as important to its success. A company's values plus a company's actions, uniquely expressed, must be the foundation of a brand's story. Once achieved, that story is then co-owned by the audience, who give it vibrancy, relevancy, and prominence through the simple act of sharing. It has then become shareworthy.

Guan Hin Tay; Photo by Shooting Gallery, Singapore.

INTERVIEW: GUAN HIN TAY, CREATIVE CHAIRMAN, BBDO SINGAPORE, AND PRESIDENT, ASIA PROFESSIONAL SPEAKERS ASSOCIATION

Guan Hin Tay is the creative chairman of BBDO Singapore and the former founder of TGH Collective. He is a seasoned creative leader with experience at top agency networks like JWT, Grey, Saatchi & Saatchi, and Leo Burnett. Guan has a proven track record of delivering impactful creativity that leverages digital and innovative engagement to drive brand preference for clients such as Visa, AIA, Shell, Johnson & Johnson, Abbott, P&G, HSBC, and Unilever. He is a sought-after speaker on vertical storytelling and has spoken at Adfest, Content Marketing Summit in Korea, and E-Commerce Expo in Singapore. He is also the president of the Asia Professional Speakers Association and has served as the first Asian Cannes Lion jury president.

If you were to give a speed workshop on storytelling for advertising, what key points would you stress?

1. Stories are nothing without any tension. Tension can come in the form of an enemy or problem that arises during the hero's journey.
2. Stories need to evoke emotions and trigger relevant themes that are relatable to anyone.
3. Stories that are real and authentic resonate on a personal level. Predictability is the death of any good stories, so always be unboring.

Some scholars say the tenets and structures of storytelling are universal. As a creative leader with an international outlook, what's your perspective?

Stories need to be universally accepted but culturally sensitive. You can start from typical familiar structures but give them a twist. Tap into the familiar so that audiences can relate to it, but always have a layer of surprise that keeps the viewer on their toes. Set up one structure, but break free from the expected and then add an element of surprise.

In summation, the best stories are *relatable* to our everyday lives, *relevant* to what the world is going through, and *real* for us to believe in the characters and the story arcs. The [three] Rs are essential for any story to be successful. *Real. Relevant. Relatable.*

As an industry leader, what changes have you observed that indicate consumers expect positive social and environmental commitment from the brands they engage with?

Doing good is good for business. As Sir Richard Branson said, "Never has there been a more exciting time for all of us to explore this next great frontier where the boundaries between work and higher purpose are merging into one, where doing good really is good for business."[31]

When your customers know they are making a difference in someone else's life or helping the environment, it not only puts a smile on their faces but also keeps them coming back for more. If not, customers will abandon brands that don't support today's values and philosophies and pay more for those that do. It's therefore important to discover your customer's motivation beyond price and quality by understanding what social or environmental issues interest them that fit your brand's long-term vision.

Can storytelling provide a competitive advantage for brands in the marketplace, and if so, how?

There are so many facts inundating our lives that we are sometimes confused with too much information. You may have a product or service that's superior to your competitor's, and telling a story helps consumers better remember your brand; stories are more engaging, and help to make your products more distinguishable. The most profitable companies have purposeful stories behind them that evoke a sense of larger purpose and meaning in what they do. People prefer to buy from companies that they believe in, and telling the right stories can turn average fans into passionate evangelists.

Let's discuss Visa's award-winning vertical video campaign #WhereYouShopMatters, " '9X16' Stores" (figure 8.2), which achieved over 10 million impressions and a view-through

8.2 " '9 × 16' Stores"; Agency: BBDO Singapore; Client: Visa.

rate of 65.62 percent, surpassing industry averages. Given the impact of COVID-19, why was it especially important for Singaporean small independent businesses to have the ability to move online?

In Singapore, COVID accelerated the already substantial digital movement, yet many of the mom-and-pop shops have been operating their businesses in the exact same way for generations and don't want to change the way they do things. For example, there is a chocolate cake shop near my place that's still using penciled notes in a huge book to manage their orders, so I think it is important that these mom-and-pop shops understand that there are helpful options for them. These independent businesses actually have a huge heritage, and we want to preserve the traditions of so many small shops that have contributed to the Singapore economy and society.

Each video ingeniously starts by depicting the charmingly cramped quarters of quintessential small independent Singaporean businesses, such as a florist, tailor, or convenience store, that then magically expand beyond the confines of the screen and, as a result, expand the businesses themselves. How was this Visa campaign conceived?

How we created the work was very simple. We started by asking ourselves, "How do you show small business in a way that's not been shown before?" and the thought of cramming small businesses inside of a small phone was the birth of this idea. It was all about using the specifications of the media as the medium to create a store-within-a-store.

Why was it essential to custom create the Visa "'9X16' Stores" campaign for smart-phones as opposed to simply repurposing existing television assets, for example?

Most of us hold our phones vertically, so in order to reach a mobile-savvy audience, we needed to create work that tapped into the existing behavior of our consumers. So, this campaign ran on Instagram stories as fifteen-second vid-eos; it highlighted the creativity of the medium and created something engaging and talked about at the same time. For this particular campaign, it was shot on a film set that was literally built to the dimensions of nine by sixteen, the exact vertical aspect ratio of a smartphone, which was quite challenging but, at the same time, enabled us to offer consumers something very different from what had been seen before.

Do you have a parting thought about the creation of shareworthy brand storytelling you can offer?

I've said this several times, and these words keep coming through, which are: *Facts tell, stories sell.* Storytelling in creativity is still key. Whether you're telling stories through digital platforms, or on a stage, or to your kids, I think how you tell stories has evolved, but the ingredients of engaging storytelling have never changed. So, maintaining the craft of storytelling, no matter what the platform, is more critical today than ever before.

INTERVIEW: PANCHO GONZÁLEZ, COFOUNDER AND CHIEF CREATIVE OFFICER, INBRAX—SANTIAGO, CHILE

Pancho González holds an MBA from Berlin School and is a VP board member of the IAB Chile and a Marketing Circle Member of Icare.

His work has been recognized over 250 times at awards shows, such as Cannes, ADC, LIA, One Show, NYF, Effie, Webby, The Drum, AME, Epica, Cristal, Cresta, AdStar, and IAB Mixx.

Pancho was named to the Top 25 CCOs and Top 100 Influencers by Cre-ativepool four years in a row; a Top One Creative Director, a Top 10 ECD, and a Top 10 Creative Agency at Bestadsontv in 2017 and 2021; Agency of The Year at WINA 2020–2022; Digital Agency of The Year at TopFICE 2020–2022; Top 10 Crema Ranking 2014 and 2020 by Adlatina.

He's also been a juror of global advertising competitions, including Cannes (twice), Clio, D&AD, One Show, NYF, ADC, LIAA, Dubai Lynx, Effie, and Webbys, and was the jury chair for the AME, The Drum, and WINA awards.

As an industry leader, what changes have you witnessed or experienced that indicate that consumers expect positive social and environmental commitment from the brands that they have relationships with?

It's very simple. I've seen people in the supermarket taking two of the same products and ending up placing the product with the least environmental impact, as expressed on the label, in their cart, even though it's more expensive than the nonselected product. I have seen equity grow for retail brands that have shifted their strategic focus to conscious marketing. People prefer those brands that have a positive impact.

Do you find that consumers in Chile have unique expectations in terms of corporate social responsibility regarding the brands that they purchase?

Absolutely, our country is going through a social "restart." Our new president took office in 2022, and his followers are demanding a fairer and more transparent world; therefore, I think it is the best time for brands to act with a CSR focus and connect with this new audience. One that is specifically more concerned about positive impacts.

Modern consumers will now quickly call out brands that prioritize profits at the expense of social responsibility. What are common mistakes advertisers make when incorporating social causes or existential issues (such as sustainability) into a brand's communication?

The most common problem that brands exhibit is not demonstrating a legitimate or authentic link between their core business and the social issue which they are leveraging as part of their marketing strategy. A second mistake often made is that once the conscious marketing strategy has been articulated, they do not have strong leadership in the area that allows them to sustain a strategy with a positive impact over time. Especially considering that the most damaging thing company leadership can do is alienate a social issue's collaborators.

Your agency recently partnered with the World Wildlife Federation to create the campaign "Footprints of Extinction" (figure 8.3) that used AR (augmented reality) to reintroduce active, moving, extinct animals into children's homes for the purposes of education. How was this successful program conceived?

8.3 "Footprints of Extinction"; Agency: Inbrax Chile; Client: WWF Chile.

The first thing is to contextualize the moment in time when this idea was created because the COVID quarantine in Chile was especially heavy and one of the heaviest in the world. We were all still in lockdown at home, so at that time, people were doing their best to survive themselves. The problem was that, unfortunately, suddenly nobody was focusing on the survival of animals. The World Wildlife Federation (WWF) came to us with the goal of creating awareness of the situation because the continuing plight of animals had basically disappeared from the country's mass media coverage in light of the pandemic.

Our goal was to help elementary teachers create awareness of the situation amongst students (and their parents) by using augmented reality to bring extinct animals, such as the nebulosa panther, great auk, and dodo bird, back to life using this technology.

In partnership with the WWF, we carefully researched the behavior of these extinct animals, the habitats they once lived in, and even their physical movements, which all became a learning opportunity for the students. And amidst that learning, we were able to make the point that if human behaviors don't change, in the future, many more animals will also only sadly exist in a virtual world, not in the physical one.

In a single month, the WWF campaign generated over twenty-eight thousand unique website visitors, over fifteen thousand AR animal interactions, with a conversion rate of 3.3 percent, and a total campaign audience of over ten million, so clearly, it resonated with audiences. What was the key insight that allowed this creative solution to break through?

Here, augmented reality gave us the chance to introduce the topic of conversation by bringing these animals into your own environment at home, whether inside your apartment, your living room, or even in your backyard. This campaign started organically, meaning that we did not attach paid media to it but instead deployed an earned media strategy. CNN supported us and featured the campaign on their program, as more media coverage followed, along with widespread social media sharing from sympathetic citizens who supported our message. There were a lot of Instagram comments appearing from kids saying things such as, "I can't believe it! There's a giant penguin (great auk) in my backyard!" Since the most important conversations happen in the home, we brought the extinct animals inside the home to be part of that most important conversation.

We're now developing a second edition with the WWF because they want to scale up the idea to track all of the animals that are currently disappearing. Because we're continuing to lose more and more species every year, and it's critical that we take action today.

What is your opinion about the positive or negative effect that advancements in AI technology will have on creative storytelling in advertising?

To me, the answer to that question is that AI is like a knife. You can use the knife to hurt someone, or you can use the knife to slice the bread and put the butter on it. To me, it's the same thing. If you know how to use AI, then you have to use it with the intention of creating beneficial solutions, which is our goal as creative people, and that comes from operating with an ethical code of conduct as an industry. We talk a lot about ROI (return on investment) in our business, but the ultimate return on investment must be the well-being of people over dollars.

NOTES

INTRODUCTION

1. "A New Jingle for a New Era," Gold Edelman, accessed October 27, 2023, https://www.aaaa .org/index.php?checkfileaccess=/wp-content/uploads/GOLD_EDELMAN_A-NEW -JINGLE-FOR-A-NEW-ERA.pdf.
2. Gold Edelman, "A New Jingle for a New Era."

1. WHY SHOULD A BRAND TELL A STORY?

1. Flash fiction by Robin Landa.
2. "Binge Drinking," Centers for Disease Control and Prevention, updated November 14, 2022, https://www.cdc.gov/alcohol/fact-sheets/binge-drinking.htm.
3. Tim Nudd, "Why This Brewer Let Other Brands Take Over Its Bottle Caps," *Muse by Clio*, February 20, 2020, https://musebycl.io/advertising/why-brewer-let-other-brands -take-over-its-bottle-caps.
4. Nudd, "Why This Brewer."
5. Daniel Smith, Philip Schlaepfer, Katie Major, Mark Dyble, Abigail Page, James Thompson, Nikhil Caudhary et al., "Cooperation and the Evolution of Hunter-Gatherer Storytelling," *Nature Communications* 8, no. 1853 (November 2, 2017): https://www.nature.com /articles/s41467-017-02036-8#citeas.
6. Jennifer Aaker, "Harnessing the Power of Stories," Stanford: VMware Women's Leadership Innovation Lab (website), accessed September 29, 2023, https://womensleadership .stanford.edu/stories.
7. Kateylyn Polantz, "Special Master Dearie Unhappy with Mar-a-Lago Document Progress: 'Where's the Beef? I Need Some Beef,'" CNN, October 19, 2022, https://www.cnn.com /2022/10/18/politics/special-master-dearie-mar-a-lago-beef/index.html.
8. Greg Hahn, interview by author Greg Braun, July 21, 2022.

2. IT'S NOT ABOUT THE BRAND—IT'S ABOUT THE AUDIENCE

1. Amazon, "Rapunzel Doesn't Need a Prince," YouTube video, 0:30, https://www.youtube .com/watch?v=A-CISJyXICk. See also ReVal Davis, "Amazon Prime's Rapunzel Commercial

Is Exactly the Fairy Tale Every Girl Needs," *Forbes*, October 27, 2021, https://www.forbes.com/sites/ravaldavis/2021/10/27/amazon-primes-rapunzel-commercial-is-exactly-the-fairytale-every-girl-needs/?sh=164517b358da.

2.   Amazon, "Rapunzel Doesn't Need a Prince."

3.   Amazon, "Rapunzel Doesn't Need a Prince."

4.   Jo Shoesmith, interview with author Greg Braun, September 1, 2022.

5.   Nidhi Arora, Wei Wei Liu, Kelsey Robinson, Eli Stein, Daniel Ensslen, Lars Fielder, and Gustavo Schüler, *Next in Personalization 2021 Report* (New York: McKinsey & Company, 2021), https://www.mckinsey.com/capabilities/growth-marketing-and-sales/our-insights/the-value-of-getting-personalization-right-or-wrong-is-multiplying.

6.   Stylés Akira, interview by the author, October 1, 2022.

7.   "Gold Renaissance—Canadian Club Damn Right," Effie Awards Index, accessed October 2, 2023, https://www.effie.org/case_database/case/NA_2009_3517.

8.   "Canadian Club Whisky—Damn Right," WARC Strategy, last modified 2009, https://www.warc.com/content/paywall/article/canadian-club-whisky---damn-right/en-gb/en-GB/89539?.

9.   Effie Awards Index, "Gold Renaissance—Canadian Club Damn Right."

10.   Derek Sherman, email message to author, January 18, 2023.

11.   "The One Show" [Grandma—2010 One Show—Advertising], The One Club for Creativity, accessed January 22, 2023, https://www.oneclub.org/awards/theoneshow/-award/11535/grandma/grandma.

12.   "Canadian Club: Your Dad Had Groupies," *AdAge*, November 16, 2007, https://adage.com/creativity/work/your-dad-had-groupies/2933.

13.   WARC Strategy, "Canadian Club Whisky—Damn Right."

14.   Effie Awards Index, "Gold Renaissance—Canadian Club Damn Right."

15.   Sherman, email message.

16.   Nathalia L. Gjersoe, Emily L. Hall, and Bruce Hood, "Children Attribute Mental Lives to Toys When They Are Emotionally Attached to Them," *Cognitive Development* 34 (2015): 28–38, https://www.sciencedirect.com/science/article/pii/S0885201414000689.

17.   "2020 Silver Household Supplies & Services: Lysol Laundry," Effie Awards Index, accessed October 3, 2023, https://www.effie.org/case_database/case/US_2020_E-5227-834.

18.   Naveed Saleh, "Which Toys Do Children Anthropomorphize?" *Psychology Today*, December 22, 2015, https://www.psychologytoday.com/us/blog/the-red-light-district/201512/which-toys-do-children-anthropomorphize#:~:text=In%20an%20important%E2%80%94yet%20somewhat,to%20anthropomorphize%20similar%20favorite%20toys.

19.   "Campaign of the Week: Lysol, Teddy Repair," *Contagious*, April 15, 2019, https://www.contagious.com/news-and-views/lysol.

20.   *Contagious*, "Campaign of the Week: Lysol, Teddy Repair."

21.   Kate Bullivant, "The Metaverse and Its Possible Effects on Mental Health," February 22, 2022, in *WSJ Podcasts*, podcast, 6:17, https://www.wsj.com/podcasts/google-news-update/the-metaverse-and-its-possible-effects-on-mental-health/2bb244e9-545c-4c48-96bd-5ab00b097384.

22.   Thomas E. Gorman, Douglas A. Gentile, and Shawn C. Green, "Problem Gaming: A Short Primer," *American Journal of Play* 10, no. 3 (2018): https://link.gale.com/apps/doc/A556693754/SCIC?u=usocal_main&sid=bookmark-SCIC&xid=61a6a5f6.

23. Inspired by Iceland, "Introducing the Icelandverse," YouTube video, 2:23, https://www .youtube.com/watch?v=enMwwQy_noI&t=2s. See also Suzanne Rowan Kelleher, "Video: Icelandic Tourism's Epic Trolling of Mark Zuckerberg Is Genuinely Meta," *Forbes*, November 12, 2021, https://www.forbes.com/sites/suzannerowankelleher/2021/11/12/video-icelandic -tourisms-epic-trolling-of-mark-zuckerberg-is-genuine-meta/?sh=1f964a542849.

24. "Welcome to the Icelandverse," The One Club for Creativity, accessed September 16, 2022, https://www.oneclub.org/theoneshow/showcase/2022/-item/44715.

25. Tim Nudd, "Visit Iceland: Welcome to the Icelandverse," June 28, 2022, in *Tagline* (season 2, episode 9), podcast, 31:55, https://musebycl.io/tagline/visit-iceland-icelandverse.

26. Karen-Nelson Field and Erica Riebe, "How Advertising Attracts Attention," WARC, last modified September 2018, https://www-warc-com./content/article/how-advertising -attracts-attention/123122.

27. Amy Rodgers, ed., *The Health of Creativity*, WARC, last modified 2021, https://www.warc .com/newsandopinion/news/health-of-creativity-a-minority-report/en-gb/43258.

28. "What You Need to Know about the Australian Effies Database Analysis," WARC, last modified September 20, 2019, https://www-warc-com./newsandopinion/news/what-you -need-to-know-about-the-australian-effies-database-analysis/42666.

29. Effie Awards Index, "2020 Silver Household Supplies and Services: Lysol Laundry"; The One Club for Creativity, "Welcome to the Icelandverse."

30. Will Feuer, "Iceland Mocks Mark Zuckerberg's Metaverse Ambitions in New Tourism Ad," *New York Post*, November 13, 2021, https://nypost.com/2021/11/13/iceland-marketing -campaign-mocks-mark-zuckerbergs-metaverse-in-tourism-ad/.

31. Procter & Gamble, *2021 Citizenship Report* (Cincinnati, OH: Procter & Gamble, 2021), https://us.pg.com/citizenship-report-2021/.

32. Energy Saving Trust, *Save Energy in Your Home* (Edinburgh, Scotland: Energy Saving Trust, 2017), https://www.energysavingtrust.org.uk/sites/default/files/reports/EST_11120 _Save%20Energy%20in%20your%20Home_15.6.pdf.

33. "Reduce Hot Water Use for Energy Savings," Energy.gov, accessed October 3, 2023, https:// www.energy.gov/energysaver/reduce-hot-water-use-energy-savings.

34. "Turn to Cold with Tide," Tide, accessed October 4, 2023, https://tide.com/en-us/our -commitment/turn-to-cold.

35. Charles Taylor, "Why the Tide and NFL #TurnToCold Collaboration Is a Winner," *Forbes*, August 31, 2021, https://www.forbes.com/sites/charlesrtaylor/2021/08/31/why-the-tide -and-nfl-turntocold-collaboration-is-a-winner/?sh=30d3aefca6ec.

36. "Ad Trust Is Low but News Media Are Worse," *Mediapost*, August 3, 2022, https://www -warc-com./content/feed/ad-trust-is-low-but-news-media-are-worse/7067.

37. Rob Clapp, "77 percent of Consumers Think It's Now Harder to Trust Brands," WARC, last modified December 2019, https://www-warc-com./content/article/warc-datapoints /77-of-consumers-think-its-now-harder-to-trust-brands/130766.

38. Eric Sylvers, and Margherita Stancati, "Italy's Economic Pain Shows Burden of National Coronavirus Lockdowns," *Wall Street Journal*, April 7, 2020, https://www.wsj.com/articles /italys-economic-pain-shows-burden-of-national-coronavirus-lockdowns-11586271238.

39. Heather Haddon, "Covid-19-Closed Restaurants Are Reopening. Running Them Is Still a Battle," *Wall Street Journal*, March 8, 2021, https://www.wsj.com/articles/covid-19-closed -restaurants-are-reopening-running-them-is-still-a-battle-11615207758.

40. "One Show—Creative Effectiveness—Shutter Ads," The One Club for Creativity, accessed January 21, 2023, https://www.oneclub.org/awards/theoneshow/-award/43350/shutter-ads.

41. Cristiana Boccassini, email message to author, February 16, 2023.

42. The One Club for Creativity, "One Show—Creative Effectiveness—Shutter Ads."

43. Boccassini, email message.

44. The One Club for Creativity, "One Show—Creative Effectiveness—Shutter Ads."

45. The One Club for Creativity, "One Show—Creative Effectiveness—Shutter Ads."

46. The One Club for Creativity, "One Show—Creative Effectiveness—Shutter Ads."

47. Michael M. Grynbaum, "After Another Year of Trump Attacks, 'Ominous Signs' for the American Press," *New York Times*, December 30, 2019, https://www.nytimes.com/2019/12/30/business/media/trump-media-2019.html.

48. Eileen Sullivan, "Trump Says Newspapers Are 'In Collusion' on Championing a Free Press," *New York Times*, August 16, 2018, https://www.nytimes.com/2018/08/16/us/politics/trump-news-media-collusion.html; Grynbaum, "After Another Year of Trump Attacks."

49. Jaclyn Peiser, "The *New York Times* Joins Effort to Combat Trump's Anti-Press Rhetoric," *New York Times*, August 14, 2018, https://www.nytimes.com/2018/08/14/business/media/trump-news-media-editorials.html.

50. Grynbaum, "After Another Year of Trump Attacks."

51. Amy Watson, "Most Popular News Platforms in the U.S. 2022, by Age Group," *Statista*, September 25, 2023, https://www.statista.com/statistics/717651/most-popular-news-platforms/.

52. *News in the U.S.*, Dossier no. did-16566-1. N.p.: Statista, 2022, https://www-statista-com./study/16566/news-in-the-us-statista-dossier/.

53. "The *New York Times*: The Truth Is Hard. Cannes Creative Lions, Bronze, Creative Effectiveness Lions, 2018," WARC, last modified 2018, Ann-Christine Diaz, " 'The Truth is Hard,' says The New York Times' first-ever Oscars ad," *Ad Age*, February 23, 2017. Accessed December 1, 2023, https://adage.com/article/advertising/truth-hard-york-times-oscars-ad/308069.

54. WARC, "The *New York Times*: The Truth Is Hard"; Stephen Whiteside, "Cannes Report: The *New York Times* Blends Purpose, Principles, and Process," WARC, last modified June 2018, https://www.warc.com/content/paywall/article/cannes-report-the-new-york-times-blends-purpose-principles-and-process/en-gb/en-GB/122410?.

55. New York Times, "Awards Show TV Commercial | the Truth Is Hard | the *New York Times*," YouTube video, 1:22, https://www.youtube.com/watch?v=y64d2HUvnR0.

56. WARC, "The *New York Times*: The Truth Is Hard."

57. Whiteside, "Cannes Report."

58. WARC, "The *New York Times*: The Truth Is Hard."

59. WARC, "The *New York Times*: The Truth Is Hard."

60. WARC, "The *New York Times*: The Truth Is Hard."

61. Whiteside, "Cannes Report."

62. WARC, "The *New York Times*: The Truth Is Hard."

63. Laurel Wentz, "Cannes Swept by PR, Integrated, Internet Winners," *AdAge*, June 29, 2009, https://adage.com/article/special-report-cannes-2009/cannes-ad-festival-swept-pr-integrated-internet-winners/137630.

64. Antonio Ferme, " 'Drawn Closer' Brings a Middle School Play to Life with Facial Capture Technology," *Variety*, April 2, 2021, https://variety.com/2021/film/news/drawn-closer-animated-short-film-nexus-studios-1234942926/.

65. Mike Bokman, email message to Greg Braun, February 1, 2023.

66. Ferme, " 'Drawn Closer' Brings a Middle School Play."

67. "2022 One Show- Interactive, Online& Mobile Hidden Spots," The One Show, last modified 2022, https://www.oneclub.org/awards/theoneshow/-award/44082/hidden-spots.

68. "Heinz Finds *Call of Duty* Snacking Spots to Help Gamers," *Contagious*, February 22, 2022, https://www.contagious.com/news-and-views/campaign-of-the-week-heinz-targets-gamers-with-call-of-duty-snacking-spots.

69. *Contagious*, "Heinz Finds *Call of Duty* Snacking Spots."

70. "2022 One Show-Interactive, Online & Mobile Hidden Spots," The One Club for Creativity, accessed October 30, 2022, https://www.oneclub.org/awards/theoneshow/-award/44082/hidden-spots.

71. Kaylee Hultgren, "Heinz Reveals 'Hidden Spots' for Snack Breaks in *Call of Duty Warzone Pacific* Caldera Map," Chief Marketer, January 7, 2022, https://chiefmarketer.com/heinz-reveals-hidden-spots-for-snack-breaks-in-call-of-duty-warzone-pacific-new-caldera-map/.

72. Greg Braun, "Advertising Week New York" (conference session at Fan Power: The Many Shades of Super Fan Loyalty and Its Impact, New York, NY, September 30, 2014), https://archive.advertisingweek.com/events/ny/2014/calendar/-newyork-2014-09-30-fan-power-the-many-shades-of-super-fan-loyalty-and-its-impact.

73. Felix Richter. "Super Bowl Pales in Comparison to the Biggest Game in Soccer," Statista, February 10, 2023, https://www.statista.com/chart/16875/super-bowl-viewership-vs-world-cup-final.

74. Joanna Durkan, "10 of Bill Shankly's Best Liverpool FC Quotes," This is Anfield, Accessed December 1, 2023, https://www.thisisanfield.com/2022/09/10-of-bill-shanklys-best-liverpool-fc-quotes/.

75. Michael Starr, " '*Walking Dead*' Premiere Breaks Cable Ratings Record," *New York Post*, October 18, 2014, https://nypost.com/2014/10/18/walking-dead-premiere-breaks-cable-ratings-record/.

76. "One Show Branded Entertainment—the Walking Dead Chop Shop," The One Club for Creativity, accessed January 27, 2023, https://www.oneclub.org/awards/theoneshow/-award/21569/the-walking-dead-chop-shop.

77. Braun, "Advertising Week New York."

78. One Club for Creativity, "One Show Branded Entertainment—the Walking Dead Chop Shop."

79. Gregory Schmidt, "At New York Comic Con, Growing Pains Come with the Crowds," *New York Times*, August 9, 2014, https://www.nytimes.com/2014/10/10/business/new-york-comic-con-expands-reach-and-draws-criticism.html.

80. Jo Shoesmith, interview with author Greg Braun, September 1, 2022.

3. WELL, IT IS ABOUT THE BRAND, TOO

1. "About Us: Timeline," Ben & Jerry, accessed October 6, 2023, https://www.benjerry.com/about-us#1timeline.

2. Merrill Fabry, "Ben & Jerry's Is Turning 40. Here's How They Captured a Trend That Changed American Ice Cream," *TIME*, May 4, 2018, https://time.com/5252406/ben-jerry-ice-cream-40/.

3.   "Ride the Wind in This Dreamlike Burberry Film from Megaforce," *Little Black* Book, October 19, 2021, https://www.lbbonline.com/news/ride-the-wind-in-this-dreamlike -burberry-film-from-megaforce.

4.   *Little Black Book*, "Ride the Wind."

5.   "The Annual: Burberry: Festive Commercial," *Creative Review*, accessed October 6, 2023, https://www.creativereview.co.uk/burberry-festive-commercial/.

6.   *Creative Review*, "The Annual: Burberry: Festive Commercial."

7.   United Colors of Benneton, "Clothes for Humans—Manifesto," produced by James Southward, 180 Amsterdam, YouTube video, 1:23, accessed September 14, 2022, https:// www.youtube.com/watch?v=jDUJ_FSyWZk&t=3s.

8.   "Manifesto," Lululemon, accessed September 14, 2022, https://info.lululemon.com/about /our-story/manifesto.

9.   "Lululemon Manifesto," Pentagram, accessed September 14, 2022, https://www.pentagram .com/work/lululemon-manifesto/story.

10.   Tanya Gazdik, "Colombia Launches Brand Manifesto: 'Most Welcoming Place on Earth,' " MediaPost, May 2, 2021, https://www.mediapost.com/publications/article/362884/colombia -launches-brand-manifesto-most-welcoming.html.

11.   Gazdik, "Colombia Launches Brand Manifesto."

12.   Katie Deighton, "Why Cadillac's CMO Has Literally Rewritten Its Brand Manifesto," *The Drum*, February 11, 2020, https://www.thedrum.com/news/2020/02/11/why-cadillac-s -cmo-has-literally-rewritten-its-brand-manifesto.

13.   Katie Deighton, "Why Cadillac's CMO."

14.   Melissa Brady in email conversation with Robin Landa, November 9, 2022.

15.   "The Mozilla Manifesto Addendum," Mozilla, accessed September 24, 2022, https://www .mozilla.org/en-US/about/manifesto/.

16.   Lars Bergkvist and Charles R. Taylor, "Reviving and Improving Brand Awareness as a Construct in Advertising Research," *Journal of Advertising* 51, no. 3 (April 20, 2022): 294– 307, DOI: 10.1080/00913367.2022.2039886.

17.   Mireille Silcoff, "Dove's Latest Stand in the Virtue Wars," *New York Times*, July 20, 2022, https://www.nytimes.com/2022/07/20/magazine/dove-advertising-beauty.html?referring Source=articleShare.

18.   Silcoff, "Dove's Latest Stand."

19.   "Ogilvy: Dove's Reverse Selfie," WPP, accessed October 12, 2023, https://www.wpp.com /featured/work/2022/06/ogilvy-doves-reverse-selfie.

20.   WPP, "Ogilvy."

21.   Elizabeth Paton, "The Queen of Slow Fashion on the Art of a Slow Exit," *New York Times*, August 13, 2022, https://www.nytimes.com/2022/08/13/fashion/eileen-fisher-retirement .html?referringSource=articleShare.

22.   Paton, "The Queen of Slow Fashion."

23.   Carrie Battan, "Eileen Fisher Meditates on What's Next," *The New Yorker*, October 9, 2022, https://www.newyorker.com/culture/the-new-yorker-interview/eileen-fisher-meditates-on -whats-next.

24.   EileenFisherNY, "Circular By Design," YouTube video, 1:21, https://www.youtube.com /watch?v=FdOaniEjnSA.

25. Shauna Moran, "A Virtually Imperfect Life," GWI, accessed August 29, 2022, https://
www.gwi.com/connecting-the-dots/curated-online-self?utm_source=linkedin&utm
_medium=organic+social&utm_campaign=211213+CTD22+T4:+The+curated+online+self
+web+page|&utm_content=.

26. Sitecore, *2022 Report: Brand Authenticity: What U.S. Consumers Expect from Their Favorite Brands* (Copenhagen: Sitecore, 2022), https://www.sitecore.com/brand-authenticity
/north-america.

27. Paige O'Neill, "Three Ways to Win Over Customers, Retain Them, and Ensure Their
Loyalty," *AdAge*, July 21, 2022, https://adage.com/article/marketing-news-strategy/3-ways
-win-over-customers-retain-them-and-ensure-their-loyalty/2423796.

28. Sitecore, *2022 Report*.

29. "The LEGO Group Unveils 'Fly Away Isles,' a New Playful Installation by Artist
Hebru Brantley that Celebrates the Imaginations of Children," LEGO, August 10, 2022,
https://www.lego.com/en-gb/aboutus/news/2022/august/build-the-change-new-york
-city-installation#:~:text=New%20York%2C%20USA%20%2D%20AUGUST%2010,
community's%20most%20creative%20minds%3A%20children.

30. "Corona Spearheads Eco-Tourism with Corona Island, the World's First Blue Verified,
Single-Use Plastic-Free Island," *BusinessWire*.com, August 9, 2022, https://www.business
wire.com/news/home/20220809005308/en/Corona-Spearheads-Eco-Tourism-with
-Corona-Island-the-World%E2%80%99s-First-Blue-Verified-Single-Use-Plastic-Free-Island.

31. "What Is BeReal and What Does it Mean for Brands," Movers + Shakers, August 22, 2022,
https://moversshakers.co/the-playlist/what-is-bereal.

32. Sara Spruch-Feiner, "K18, E.l.f. and Inn Beauty Project Are Paving the Way for Brands
on BeReal," *Glossy*, August 9, 2022, https://www.glossy.co/beauty/k18-e-l-f-and-inn-beauty
-project-are-paving-the-way-for-brands-on-bereal/.

33. "Converse Collaborations: See the Latest Collections from Miley Cyrus, Vince Staples,
and Tyler, the Creator," *Billboard*, May 3, 2018, https://www.billboard.com/photos/converse
-collaborations-miley-cyrus-vince-staples-tyler-the-creator-collections/1-miley-cyrus/.

34. E. J. Schultz and Jade Yan, "20 Brands Graining Gen Z Attention Right Now," *AdAge*, July
28, 2022, https://adage.com/article/marketing-news-strategy/20-brands-gaining-gen-z
-attention-2022-second-quarter/2423651.

35. "Converse Gallery: Family Is . . . ," Converse Gallery.com, accessed October 11, 2023, https://
converse.gallery/found-family/.

36. Jacyln Diaz, "The Story of a Uvalde Victim's Green Shoes Capture the White House's
Attention," NPR, June 7, 2022, https://www.npr.org/2022/06/07/1103577387/matthew
-mcconaughey-green-converse-shoes-sneakers-uvalde-maite-rodriguez.

37. Schultz and Yan, "20 Brands Gaining Gen Z Attention Right Now."

38. "Timberland About Us: Our Vision," Timberland, https://www.timberland.com/en-us
/about-us.

39. "Timberland CONSTRUCT 10061 Enters the Metaverse," Business Wire, June 9, 2022,
https://www.businesswire.com/news/home/20220609005851/en/Timberland%C2
%AE-CONSTRUCT-10061-Enters-the-Metaverse.

40. "Moldy Whopper by Ingo, David Miami & Publicis Bucharest for Burger King | The One
Show 2020," YouTube video, :45, https://www.youtube.com/watch?v=f9B9HGQsxok.

Also see Ben Kesslen, "Burger King Announces Move to Be Preservative-Free with Moldy Whopper Ad," NBC News, February 19, 2020, https://www.nbcnews.com/news/us-news /burger-king-announces-move-be-preservative-free-moldy-whopper-ad-n1138566.

41. Tim Nudd, "Fernando Machado on the Making of 'Moldy Whopper,' Burger King's Craziest Ads Yet," *Muse by Clio*, February 19, 2020, https://musebycl.io/advertising/fernando -machado-making-moldy-whopper-burger-kings-craziest-ads-yet.

42. Bella DePaulo, "9 Ways the Most Boring People Will Bore You," *Psychology Today*, September 28, 2014, https://www.psychologytoday.com/us/blog/living-single/201409/9 -ways-the-most-boring-people-will-bore-you.

43. "The E.V.A. Initiative," Volvo, accessed August 30, 2022, https://developer.volvocars.com /resources/eva/.

44. Jeff Beer, "The Purpose-Driven Marketer: How Patagonia Uses Storytelling to Turn Consumers into Activists," *Fast Company*, November 19, 2014, https://www.fastcompany.com /3038557/the-purpose-driven-marketer-how-patagonia-uses-storytelling-to-turn-consume.

45. Yvon Chouinard, "Earth is Now Our Only Shareholder," Patagonia, accessed October 12, 2023, https://www.patagonia.com/ownership/.

46. John Elkington, "25 Years Ago I Coined the Phrase 'Triple Bottom Line.' Here's Why It's Time to Rethink It," *Harvard Business Review*, June 25, 2018. https://hbr.org/2018/06/25 -years-ago-i-coined-the-phrase-triple-bottom-line-heres-why-im-giving-up-on-it

47. "Core Values," Patagonia, accessed October 12, 2023, https://www.patagonia.com/core -values/.

48. David Gelles, "Billionaire No More: Patagonia Founder Gives Away the Company," *New York Times*, September 14, 2022, https://www.nytimes.com/2022/09/14/climate/patagonia -climate-philanthropy-chouinard.html.

49. "Aerie Flips the Social Media Algorithm Positive for Spring 2022," Bloomberg, March 15, 2022, https://www.bloomberg.com/press-releases/2022-03-15/aerie-flips-the-social-media -algorithm-positive-for-spring-2022.

50. "How PayPal and Independent Creatives Worked to Capture this Year's Holiday Spirit," Paypal, November 12, 2020, https://newsroom.paypal-corp.com/2020-11-12-How-PayPal -and-Independent-Creatives-Worked-to-Capture-this-Years-Holiday-Spirit.

51. "The *'No' Grants*: Pure Leaf Tea," Edelman, accessed October 12, 2023, https://www.edelman .com/work/pure-leaf-nogrants.

52. "Allyson Felix and PepsiCo's Pure Leaf Partner Up to Empower Women in the Workforce," *Little Black Book*, accessed August 31, 2022, https://www.lbbonline.com/news/allyson-felix -and-pepsicos-pure-leaf-partner-up-to-empower-women-in-the-workforce.

53. Dawit N. M., LinkedIn message with Robin Landa, August 23, 2022.

54. Elliot Leavy, "When Should Brands Interact With Culture?" *Creative Salon*, April 27, 2022, https://creative.salon/articles/features/qotw-cultural-moments.

55. Kaitlyn Wylde, "The Odd Appeal Of Sylvanian Drama TikTok," *Bustle*, February 8, 2022, https://www.bustle.com/life/sylvanian-drama-tiktok-explained.

56. Maggie Griswold, "Style: This TikTok Soap Opera Turned Into Burberry Sponcon That I'm Actually Obsessed With," *Cosmopolitan*, April 15, 2022, https://www.cosmopolitan .com/style-beauty/fashion/a39729813/burberry-lola-bag-tiktok/.

57. UN Broadband Commission for Sustainable Development, *Cyber Violence Against Women And Girls: A Worldwide Wakeup Call* (New York: UN Broadband Commission for Sustainable

Development, 2015), https://www.broadbandcommission.org/publication/cyber-violence
-against-women/.

58. Richard Huntington, *What the Fuck Is Going On?* (London: Saatchi & Saatchi in Partnership
with Meet the 85% and Yougov, February 2022), https://saatchi.co.uk/news/what-the-f.

59. Meg Carter, "EE's 'Not Her Problem' Wins TV Creativity Award: Saatchi & Saatchi-Cre-
ated Film Is the Latest Thinkboxes Winner," *Campaign Live* UK, September 27, 2022, https://
www.campaignlive.co.uk/article/ees-not-problem-wins-tv-creativity-award/1799767.

60. With permission from Saatchi UK.

61. Movember, "Movember Launches World's First Non-Fungible Testicles (NFT) That Could
Save Your Life," April 17, 2022. https://us.movember.com/story/world-s-first-non-fungible
-testicles-nft-tokens.

62. Harsh Kapadia, "Non-Fungible Testicles—Movember,", Vimeo, 2:02, https://vimeo.com
/708929345.

63. Harsh Kapadia, "Non-Fungible Testicles—Movember."

4. CAN YOU FEEL IT? BRAND AFFINITY

1. David Mesfin, email interview by the author, July 31, 2022.

2. J. A. Conger, "The Necessary Art of Persuasion," *Harvard Business Review* 76, no. 3 (1998):
84–95, https://hbr.org/1998/05/the-necessary-art-of-persuasion.

3. Mesfin, email interview.

4. Lucas M. Bietti, Ottilie Tilston, and Adrian Bangerter, "Storytelling as Adaptive Collective Sensemaking," *Topics in Cognitive Science* 11, no. 4 (October 2019): 710–732, https://
doi.org/10.1111/tops.12358.

5. "Donate Life California and Canadian Transplant Association: Second Chances," WARC,
last modified 2021, https://www.warc.com/content/paywall/article/Cannes/Donate_Life
_California_and_Canadian_Transplant_Association_Second_chances/en-GB/137669?.

6. "The Work that Matters, 'Second Chances' Organ Donation for Donate Life California by Casanova/McCann LA," YouTube video, 2:15, https://www.youtube.com/watch?v
=rpS-97v1EtU. See also WARC, "Donate Life California and Canadian Transplant Association: Second Chances."

7. "The Work that Matters, 'Second Chances' Organ Donation for Donate Life California
by Casanova/McCann LA."

8. WARC, "Donate Life California and Canadian Transplant Association: Second Chances."

9. WARC, "Donate Life California and Canadian Transplant Association: Second Chances."

10. WARC, "Donate Life California and Canadian Transplant Association: Second Chances."

11. Rick Nauert, "Are Emotions Universal?" PsychCentral, January 27, 2018, https://psych-
central.com/news/2018/01/27/are-emotions-universal#1.

12. Shazia Ginai, "Great Stories Build Brands," WARC, July 27, 2021, https://www.warc.com
/newsandopinion/opinion/great-stories-build-brands/en-gb/4341.

13. Ted Anthony, "Why the Thai Cave Rescue Captivated the World," *Business Insider*, July 18,
2018, https://www.businessinsider.com/thai-cave-rescue-captivated-the-world-why-media
-circus-2018-7; Kate Lyons, " 'The Great Escape': Newspapers Around the World Share Joy of
Thai Cave Rescue," *The Guardian*, July 10, 2018, https://www.theguardian.com/news/2018
/jul/11/the-great-escape-newspapers-around-the-world-share-joy-of-thai-cave-rescue.

14.   Jonah Berger, *Contagious: Why Things Catch On* (New York: Simon & Schuster, 2016).

15.   Chinching Chang, "Increasing Mental Health Literacy via Narrative Advertising," *Journal of Health Communication* 13, no. 1 (2008): 37–55, https://uosc.primo.exlibrisgroup.com /permalink/01USC_INST/273cgt/cdi_informaworld_taylorfrancis_310_1080_10810730701807027.

16.   Chang, "Increasing Mental Health."

17.   Richard M. Perloff, *The Dynamics of Persuasion: Communication and Attitudes in the Twenty-First Century*, 7th ed (New York: Routledge Press, 2020).

18.   James C. McCroskey, "Goodwill: A Reexamination of the Construct and Its Measurement," *Communications Monographs* 66, no. 1 (1999): 90–103, https://uosc.primo.exlibrisgroup.com /permalink/01USC_INST/273cgt/cdi_crossref_primary_10_1080_03637759909376464.

19.   Perloff, *The Dynamics of Persuasion*.

20.   "What Are Nike Shoes Made Of?" Shoemakers Academy, accessed October 16, 2023, https:// shoemakersacademy.com/what-are-nike-shoes-made-of/.

21.   P. Smith, "Footwear Market Share of Nike and Adidas as of 2017, by Region," In Statista. N.p.: Statista, 2023, https://www-statista-com/statistics/895136/footwear-market -share-of-nike-and-adidas-by-region/.

22.   Pamela N. Danziger, "Nike Outranks Adidas, Under Armour and Lululemon Where It Counts Most: Consumer Perception," *Forbes*, May 23, 2019, https://www.forbes.com/sites /pamdanziger/2019/05/23/nike-outranks-adidas-under-armour-and-lululemon-where-it -counts-most-consumer-perception/?sh=76613ea02478.

23.   Cristina de balanzo, *Insights from the 2021 Creative Effectiveness Lions Winners* (London: WARC, 2021), https://www-warc-com/content/article/warc-exclusive/insights-from-the -2021-creative-effectiveness-lions-winners/138587.

24.   de balanzo, *Insights from the 2021 Creative Effectiveness Lions Winners*.

25.   Zoe McCready, "Emotion and Storytelling Top Creative Strategies in Effective 100," WARC, last modified May 2019, https://www-warc-com. /content/article/warc-curated -datapoints/emotion-and-storytelling-top-creative-strategies-in-effective-100/126426.

26.   Christina Brodzik, "Win Customers with Authentically Inclusive Marketing Initiatives," *Wall Street Journal*, April 18, 2022, https://deloitte.wsj.com/articles/win-customers-with -authentically-inclusive-marketing-initiatives-01650302320.

27.   Mark Hutcheon, Sid Maharaj, Keri Calagna, and Marcus Plattner, "Consumers Expect Brands to Address Climate Change," *Wall Street Journal*, April 20, 2021, https://deloitte .wsj.com/articles/consumers-expect-brands-to-address-climate-change-01618945334.

28.   D. Tighe, "Common Ways U.S. Consumers Will Change Their Behavior Based on a Company's Corporate Social Responsibility 2018," Statista, November 27, 2020, https://www. statista.com/statistics/818968/most-popular-ways-to-be-an-ethical-consumer-us/.

29.   Hutcheon et al., "Consumers Expect Brands."

30.   "Nike: Crazy Dreams," WARC, last modified 2021, https://www-warc-com/content/article /cannes/nike-crazy-dreams/136971.

31.   Saabira Chaudhuri, "Companies Say They Want to Save the Planet—But They Can't Agree How," *Wall Street Journal*, December 10, 2019, https://www.wsj.com/articles/companies -say-they-want-to-save-the-planetbut-they-cant-agree-how-11575973800.

32.   Larry Light, "Environmental Decency Makes Money," *Forbes*, October 19, 2020, https:// www.forbes.com/sites/larrylight/2020/10/19/environmental-decency-makes-money/?sh =45c849272979.

33. Stu Woo, "H&M Pays Price of Upsetting Beijing as China Sales Drop," *Wall Street Journal*, July 1, 2021, https://www.wsj.com/articles/h-m-pays-price-of-upsetting-beijing-as-china -sales-drop-11625136844.

34. WARC, "Nike: Crazy Dreams."

35. Jeff Beer, "Patagonia's Reversible Poem Ad Is a Check on Runaway Black Friday Cyber Monday Spending," *Fast Company*, November 30, 2020, https://www.fastcompany.com /90580854/patagonias-palindrome-poem-ad-is-a-check-on-runaway-black-friday-cyber -monday-spending.

36. Beer. "Patagonia's Reversible Poem Ad."

37. "About Us," IKEA, accessed May 20, 2022, https://about.ikea.com/en/about-us.

38. Derrick Bryson Taylor, "Ikea Will Buy Back Some Used Furniture," *New York Times*, October 14, 2020, https://www.nytimes.com/2020/10/14/business/ikea-buy-back-furniture.html.

39. Chaudhuri, "Companies Say."

40. "Sustainability—Caring for People and the Planet," IKEA, accessed May 20, 2022, https:// about.ikea.com/en/sustainability.

41. One Club for Creativity, "2022 One Show—Public Relations: Buy Back Friday," accessed February 5, 2023, https://www.oneclub.org/awards/theoneshow/-award/44522 /buy-back-friday.

42. One Club for Creativity, "2022 One Show—Public Relations."

43. Mary Ann T. Ferguson and Sora Kim, "Dimensions of Effective CSR Communication Based on Public Expectations," *Journal of Marketing Communications* 24, no. 6 (2018): 549–567, https://doi.org/10.1080/13527266.2015.1118143.

44. One Club for Creativity, "2022 One Show—Public Relations."

45. Ferguson and Kim, "Dimensions of Effective CSR Communication."

46. One Club for Creativity. "2022 One Show—Public Relations."

47. IKEA, "Sustainability—Caring for People and the Planet."

48. Jenny Rooney, "How Hyundai Pulled Off an Unexpected Reunion of U.S. Troops and Their Families in Super Bowl 2017," *Forbes*, February 5, 2017, https://www.forbes.com/sites /jenniferrooney/2017/02/05/how-hyundai-pulled-off-an-unexpected-reunion-of-u-s -troops-and-their-families-in-super-bowl-2017/?sh=36169df5e62c.

49. David Mesfin, email interview by author Greg Braun, July 31, 2022.

5. BEGINNING, MIDDLE, AND END (OR NOT)

1. Flash fiction by Robin Landa.

2. Hyun Seung Jin, Gayle Kerr, Jaebeom Suh, Hyoje Jay Kim, and Ben Sheehan, "The Power of Creative Advertising: Creative Ads Impair Recall and Attitudes Toward Other Ads," *International Journal of Advertising* 41, no. 8 (June 18, 2021): 1521–1540, DOI: 10.1080/02650487.2022.2045817.

3. Jin et al., "The Power of Creative Advertising."

4. Joerg Wolter, Vincent Barth, Eva Barthel, Julia Gröbel, Elena Linden, Yvonne Wolf, and Eva Walther, "Inside the Host's Mind: Psychological Principles of Viral Marketing," *International Journal of Internet Marketing and Advertising* 10, nos. 1/2 (2016): https://www .researchgate.net/publication/304066785_Inside_the_host's_mind_Psychological_principles _of_viral_marketing.

5.   Wes Phelan, email correspondence with the author, August 31, 2022.

6.   Yousuke Ozawa, email correspondence with the author, August 17, 2022.

7.   David Suarez, email correspondence with the author, September 6, 2022.

8.   "Work: Sign with Fingers Big and Small," VCCP London, accessed October 18, 2023, https://www.vccp.com/work/cadbury/sign-with-fingers-big-and-small.

9.   Cadbury, "Cadbury Dairy Milk Fingers: Sign with Fingers Big & Small," YouTube video, :30, accessed November 20, 2023. https://www.youtube.com/watch?v=5HV1hisoxNI. Also see VCCP London, "Sign with Fingers Big and Small."

10. Rebecca Stewart, "Cadbury Uses Its Chocolate Fingers to Encourage People to Take Up Sign Language," *Adweek*, August 31, 2022, https://www.adweek.com/brand-marketing/cadbury -uses-its-chocolate-fingers-to-encourage-people-to-take-up-sign-language/.

11. "Be Somewhere Else," Lush, accessed October 19, 2023, https://www.lushusa.com/social -departure.html.

12. Erin Evon, email correspondence with the author, October 7, 2022.

13. "Here Today, Here Tomorrow: Varieties of Medical Ephemera," U. S. National Library of Medicine, National Institutes of Health, last updated September 21, 2011, http://www .nlm.nih.gov/exhibition/ephemera/medshow.html.

14. John Berger, *Ways of Seeing* (New York: Penguin, 1990), 131.

15. Gatorade, "Gatorade/Serena Williams/Love Means Everything," YouTube vide, 1:49, https://www.youtube.com/watch?v=sLzYLs3aUT4. See also Tim Nudd, "Sports: Beyoncé Salutes Serena in This U.S. Open Ad for Gatorade: A Special VO for a Special Retirement Piece," *Muse by Clio*, August 29, 2022, https://musebycl.io/sports/beyonce-salutes-serena -us-open-ad-gatorade?utm_source=ActiveCampaign&utm_medium=email&utm_content =Beyonc%C3%A9+Salutes+Serena+in+This+U+S++Open+Ad+for+Gatorade&utm_campaign =Museletter+8%2F29%2F22.

16. Shannon Miller, "Gatorade and Beyoncé Celebrate Serena Williams' Enduring Legacy in Moving Short Film," *Adweek*, August 29, 2022, https://www.adweek.com/creativity /gatorade-beyonce-celebrate-serena-williams-legacy/?itm_source=related_articles&itm _medium=position2.

17. Phelan, email correspondence.

18. Phelan, email correspondence.

19. Terence A. Shimp and Elnora W. Stuart, "The Role of Disgust as an Emotional Mediator of Advertising Effects," *Journal of Advertising* 33, no. 1 (March 4, 2013): 43–53, https:// www.tandfonline.com/doi/abs/10.1080/00913367.2004.10639150; Minxia Zheng, "When and Why Negative Emotional Appeals Work in Advertising: A Review of Research," *Open Journal of Social Sciences* 8, no. 3 (March 2020): 7–16, https://www.scirp.org/journal /paperinformation.aspx?paperid=98722.

20. Matthias J. Gruber, Bernard D. Gelman, and Charan Ranganath, "States of Curiosity Modulate Hippocampus-Dependent Learning via the Dopaminergic Circuit," *Neuron* 84, no. 2 (2014): 486–496, https://www.sciencedirect.com/science/article/pii/S0896627314008046.

21. Adrian J. Duszkiewicz, Colin G. McNamara, Tomonori Takeuchi, and Lisa Genzel, "Novelty and Dopaminergic Modulation of Memory Persistence: A Tale of Two Systems," *Cell* 42, no. 2 (November 16, 2018): P102–P114, https://www.cell.com/trends/neurosciences /fulltext/S0166-2236(18)30273-X.

22. "Burger King: The Whopper Detour," Effie, accessed May 9, 2022, https://www.effie.org
     /case_database/case/US_2020_E-5696-571.

23. TED, "Andrew Stanton: The Clues to a Great Story," YouTube video, 19:16, https://www
     .youtube.com/watch?v=KxDwieKpawg.

24. Parker Herren, "Oscar Meyer Made a Hot Dog Popsicle," *AdAge*, August 26, 2022, https://
     adage.com/creativity/work/oscar-mayer-makes-hot-dog-popsicle-cold-dog-f/2427501.

25. "KFC Australia Boosts Quality Perceptions with 11-Course Tasting Menu," *Contagious*,
     August 23, 2022, https://www.contagious.com/news-and-views/campaign-of-the-week-kfc
     -creates-fine-dining-tasting-menue.

26. Keira Wingate, " 'SNL' Star Chloe Fineman Wears an Instacart Dress for 2022 MTV
     VMAs," *AdAge*, August 29, 2022, https://adage.com/creativity/work/snls-chloe-fineman
     -wears-instacart-dress-vmas/2427656.

27. Annabelle Timsit and Sofia Diogo Mateus, " 'Hello Literally Everyone': Twitter Flooded
     with Users During Facebook, Instagram Outage," *Washington Post*, October 5, 2021, https://
     www.washingtonpost.com/technology/2021/10/05/twitter-users-facebook-outage-instagram
     -whatsapp/.

28. Laurence Vincent, *Brand Real: How Smart Companies Live Their Brand Promise and Inspire
     Fierce Customer Loyalty* (New York: Amacon, 2012), 2.

29. Hershey's, "Heartwarming the World: School," iSpot.tv, :15, accessed November 20, 2023.
     https://www.ispot.tv/ad/bh2C/hersheys-heartwarming-the-world-school.

30. "Our Shared Goodness Promise," Hershey Company, accessed on September 3, 2022,
     https://www.thehersheycompany.com/content/dam/hershey-corporate/documents/pdf
     /shared-goodness-promise-infographic.pdf.

31. Audrey Kemp, "Best Ads for August: New Balance, Gatorade and Hershey's," *The Drum*,
     August 29, 2022, https://www.thedrum.com/news/2022/08/29/best-ads-august-new-balance
     -gatorade-and-hershey-s.

32. Hershey Company, "Our Shared Goodness Promise."

33. Caleb Miller, "BMW i7 M70 to Star in New Action-Packed Short Film at Cannes Film
     Festival," *Car and Driver*, May 15, 2023, https://www.caranddriver.com/news/a43892079
     /bmw-i7-m70-short-film-cannes/.

34. Charlie Allenby, "The Story Behind the Custom-Made Carbon Fiber Don't Look Down
     Bowl," Redbull, April 13, 2023, https://www.redbull.com/gb-en/bmx-bowl-dont-look-down.

35. "Work: State Street Global Advisors: Fearless Girl," McCann, accessed October 20, 2023,
     https://www.mccannny.com/work/fearless-girl.

36. Robin Landa, *Strategic Creativity: A Business Field Guide to Advertising, Branding, and Design*
     (New York: Routledge, 2022), 142.

37. "How to Build a Consistent Archteype-based Brand Strategy," Landor & Fitch, accessed
     October 20, 2023, https://landorandfitch.com/en/articles/thinking/how-to-build-a
     -consistent-archetype-based-brand-strategy.

38. Alexandra Jardine, "Blink Fitness Will Hypotize You Into Loving the Gym," *AdAge*, August
     17, 2022, https://adage.com/creativity/work/blink-hynpotizes-you-loving-gym/2426321.

39. Martin Guerrieria, "What are the Most Valuable Global Brands in 2022?" Kantar, June
     15, 2022, https://www.kantar.com/inspiration/brands/what-are-the-most-valuable-global
     -brands-in-2022.

40. "VMLY&R South Africa Wins a Pride of Lions at Cannes Lions 2022," VMLY&R, June 28, 2022, https://www.vmlyr.com/en-za/south-africa/news/vmlyr-south-africa-wins -pride-lions-cannes-lions-2022.

41. Vodacom via Alex White, email statement to the author, August 23, 2022.

42. Alexandra Jardine, "Tiger Beer Champions Korean Premiere League Soccer Star Son Heung Min," *AdAge*, August 19, 2022, https://adage.com/creativity/work/tiger-beer-champions -korean-soccer-star-son-heung-min/2426481.

43. Jardine, "Tiger Beer Champions."

44. Kim Shaw, "FCB India Wins India's First Fusion Pencil at One Show 2022 for 'The Nominate Me Selfie,'" *Campaign Brief Asia*, May 23, 2022, https://campaignbriefasia.com /2022/05/23/fcb-india-wins-indias-first-fusion-pencil-at-one-show-2022-for-the-nominate -me-selfie/.

45. Anne-Christine Diaz, "Google and Marie Kondo Clean Keegan Michael Key's Digital Life," *AdAge*, August 16, 2022, https://adage.com/creativity/work/google-campaign-marie -kondo-cleans-keegan-michael-keys-digital-life/2426241.

46. "Orchard Thieves and Rothco Launch Innovative Reversible Commercial," *Little Black Book*, last updated May 5, 2017, https://www.lbbonline.com/news/orchard-thieves-and -rothco-launch-innovative-reversible-commercial; The AdStasher, "Heineken's Orchard Thieves Cider Brand 'Start bold/End bold' New Film, YouTube video, 1:20, https://www .youtube.com/watch?v=E-zTa26Wakk

47. "Orchard Thieves and Rothco Launch Innovative Reversible Commercial."

48. *Little Black Book*, "Orchard Thieves and Rothco."

49. Alexandra Jardine, "This Cider Commercial Plays Out Either Forwards or Backwards," *AdAge*, May 8, 2017, https://adage.com/creativity/work/reversible-commercial/51723.

50. "90 Minutes of Air Conditioning: The Movie," Pereira Odell, accessed October 21, 2023, https://pereiraodell.com/client/midea/90-minutes-of-air-conditioning-the-movie.

51. "Superb Owl," RGA, accessed October 21, 2023, https://rga.com/work/reddit-superb-owl.

52. RGA, "Superb Owl."

53. Jeff Beer, "How Super Bowl Ad Teasers Manipulate You—in the Best Possible Way," *Fast Company*, February 5, 2023, https://www.fastcompany.com/90844618/super-bowl-teaser -ads-squarespace-doritos-michelob-avocados; Tiffany Hsu, "Reddit's 5-Second Ad Was an Unlikely Super Bowl Winner," *New York Times*, February 8, 2021. https://www.nytimes .com/2021/02/08/business/media/reddit-super-bowl-ad.html

54. Kevin Koller and Greg Braun in conversation, September 14, 2022.

55. Fred Schmalz, "For Brands, Perfection Is Out and Authenticity Is In," Kellogg Insight, May 3, 2022, https://insight.kellogg.northwestern.edu/article/for-brands-perfection-is-out -and-authenticity-is-in.

56. Assumpció Huertas, "How Live Videos and Stories in Social Media Influence Tourist Opinions and Behavior," *Information Technology & Tourism* 19, nos. 1–28 (2018): https:// doi.org/10.1007/s40558-018-0112-0.

57. "Brand Film Awards U.S.: Industry Sectors," MM+M, May 25, 2021, https://www.mmm -online.com/home/channel/mmm/brand-film-awards-u-s-industry-sectors/.

58. MM+M, "Brand Film Awards."

59. Luiz Sanches, interview with author Greg Braun, September 29, 2022.

6. THE NORTH STAR

1. Suncorp, "House no.2 on Resilience Rd.," YouTube video, 0:90. https://www.youtube .com/watch?v=yTTeX5fkRdI.

2. David Gianatasio, "Leo Burnett Designed a Home Able to Withstand Extreme Weather, *Muse by Clio*, May 4 2021, https://musebycl.io/makers/leo-burnett-designed-home-able -withstand-extreme-weather.

3. "How Leo Burnett Brought the House Down with Australia's Cannes Lions Grand Prix," Little Black Book, last updated July 7, 2022, https://www.lbbonline.com/news/how-leo -burnett-brought-the-house-down-with-australias-cannes-lions-grand-prix.

4. "One House to Save Many," D&AD, accessed October 22, 2023, https://www.dandad.org /awards/professional/2022/235897/one-house-to-save-many/.

5. Little Black Book, "How Leo Burnett Brought the House Down."

6. Tayla Foster, "Why Is Leo Burnett's 'One House To Save Many' Campaign so Good?" *AdNews*, July 8, 2022, https://www.adnews.com.au/news/why-is-leo-burnett-s-one-house -to-save-many-campaign-so-good.

7. Foster, "Why is Leo Burnett's 'One House To Save Many' Campaign so Good?"

8. "One House to Save Many/Suncorp," *Contagious*, accessed October 22, 2023, https://1725887 .fs1.hubspotusercontent-na1.net/hubfs/1725887/Grand%20Prix%20Winners%20 Report%202022%20V4.pdf?_hstc=62055283.07005472a2328b75db72b66ofcc28ae1 .1657210666404.1659204005531.1659285186725.5&__hssc=62055283.2.1659285186725& _hsfp=868227580.

9. Wes Phelan, email correspondence with the author, August 31, 2022.

10. Patrick J. Kiger, "Science: Why Is the North Star So Stellarly Important?" How Stuff Works, February 5, 2021, https://science.howstuffworks.com/north-star.htm.

11. Harsh Kapadia and Robin Landa on Google Chats, July 14, 2022.

12. Hanisha Besant, "The Journey of Brainstorming," *Journal of Transformative Innovation* 2, no. 1 (2016): https://www.regent.edu/journal/journal-of-transformative-innovation/the -history-of-brainstorming-alex-osborn/.

13. Margaret A. Boden, *Artificial Intelligence: Handbook of Perception and Cognition* (Cambridge, MA: Academic Press, 1996), 267–291.

14. Margaret A. Boden, "Précis of The Creative Mind: Myths and Mechanisms," *Behavioral and Brain Sciences* 17, no. 3 (September 1994): 519–531, DOI:10.1017/S0140525X0003569X.

15. Jules Henri Poincaré, *The Foundations of Science: Science and Hypothesis, the Value of Science, Science and Method*, trans. G. B. Halstead (New York: Science Press, 1921), 387.

16. J. Hadamard, *The Psychology of Invention in the Mathematical Field* (Princeton, NJ: Princeton University Press, 1945), 147.

17. Paul Thagard and Terrence C. Stewart, "The AHA! Experience: Creativity Through Emergent Binding in Neural Networks," *Cognitive Science* 35, no. 1 (January/February 2011): 1–33, https://onlinelibrary.wiley.com/doi/10.1111/j.1551-6709.2010.01142.x.

18. Hal Gregersen, "Innovation: Better Brainstorming," *Harvard Business Review*, March–April 2018, https://hbr.org/2018/03/better-brainstorming.

19. Robin Landa, *The New Art of Ideas: Unlock Your Creative Potential* (Oakland, CA: Berrett-Koehler, 2022).

20. "That's an Insight?!," Millennial Marketing, accessed October 22, 2023, https://millennial marketing.com/2009/10/thats-an-insight/.

21. James Swift, "Everything You Wanted to Know About Insights but Were Afraid to Ask," *Contagious*, February 19, 2020, https://www.contagious.com/news-and-views/Contagious-asks-strategists-for-insight-definitions.

22. Swift, "Everything You Wanted."

23. Swift, "Everything You Wanted."

24. Gareth Price, "Ask an Expert: How Do You Identify an Insight?" Brandwatch, September 15, 2016, https://www.brandwatch.com/blog/gareth-price-how-do-you-identify-an-insight/.

25. Robin Landa, *Strategic Creativity: A Business Field Guide to Advertising, Branding, and Design* (New York: Routledge, 2022).

26. "Malcolm Gladwell: Choice, Happiness and Spaghetti Sauce," filmed February 2004, TED video, 17:16, https://www.ted.com/talks/malcolm_gladwell_choice_happiness_and_spaghetti_sauce?language=en.

27. Thomas Wedell-Wedellsborg, "Are You Solving the Right Problem?" *Harvard Business Review*, January–February 2017, https://edisciplinas.usp.br/pluginfile.php/4603288/mod_resource/content/1/Are%20You%20Solving%20the%20Right%20Problems_.pdf.

28. Peter Frost, "Coors Light Unveils 'Made to Chill' Campaign," Beer & Beyond, July 29, 2019, https://www.molsoncoorsblog.com/news/coors-light-unveils-made-chill-campaign.

29. "Coors Light: Ads No Can See But Everyone Can Feel," Doyle Dane Bernbach, https://staging.ddb.com/creative/ads-that-no-one-can-see-but-everyone-can-feel/.

30. APA Dictionary of Psychology, s.v. "associative thinking," American Psychological Association, accessed October 22, 2023, https://dictionary.apa.org/associative-thinking.

31. Caroline Newman, "What Actually Happens When Your Mind Wanders? (This Professor Can Tell You)," *Chronicle of Higher Education*, accessed May 14, 2022, https://sponsored.chronicle.com/what-actually-happens-when-your-mind-wanders/index.html.

32. Clios, "Burger King Confusing Times," Clios video, 1:38, https://clios.com/awards/winner/film/burger-king/confusing-times-113168.

33. Newman, "What Actually Happens."

34. "Magnum Honors Master of Music Mozart with Epic Remixed Music Video," Little Black Book, August 2, 2022, https://www.lbbonline.com/news/magnum-honours-master-of-music-mozart-with-epic-remixed-music-video.

35. Little Black Book, "Magnum Honors Master of Music."

36. "Unveiling The 2020 Zeno Strength of Purpose Study," Zeno, June 17, 2020, https://www.zenogroup.com/insights/2020-zeno-strength-purpose.

37. Sarah Priestman, "Growing a Brand by Tracking the Ins and Outs of Experiential Marketing Trends," *AdWeek*, October 8, 2018, https://www.adweek.com/brand-marketing/growing-a-brand-by-tracking-the-ins-and-outs-of-experiential-marketing-trends/.

38. Khalem Charles, "What Is Purpose-Driven Marketing?" Ad Council, February 1, 2021, https://www.adcouncil.org/all-articles/what-is-purpose-driven-marketing.

39. Vainavi Mahendra, "Cannes Lions 2022: How 'Purpose' Grew Business of Unilever's Dove, and Lowe's," *Financial Express*, June 24, 2022, https://www.financialexpress.com/brandwagon/cannes-lions-2022-how-purpose-grew-business-of-unilevers-dove-and-lowes/2571558/.

40. Mahendra, "Cannes Lions 2022."

41. Audrey Kemp, "Coors Banquet Supports Firefighters During Peak Wildfire Season," *The Drum*, August 4, 2022, https://www.thedrum.com/news/2022/08/04/coors-banquet -supports-firefighters-during-peak-wildfire-season.

42. Ann-Christine Diaz, "Coors Banquet Extends Hand: Firefighters Midst Wildfire Season," *AdAge*, August 4, 2022, https://adage.com/creativity/work/coors-banquet-extends-hand -firefighters-midst-wildfire-season/2425411.

43. Craig Bagno, "Examining Brand Purpose over Six Years Cannes Lions Winners," *PRWeek*, June 19, 2022, https://www.prweek.com/article/1790292/examining-brand-purpose-six-years -cannes-lions-winners.

44. David Suarez, email correspondence with the authors, September 6, 2022.

45. Alexandra Jardine, "Condom Brand Hypnotizes Married Couple to Have First Date Feelings," *AdAge*, August 3, 2022, https://adage.com/creativity/work/skyn-condom-ad -hypnotizes-couple-first-date/2425271.

46. "Oreo: Doomsday Vault," The Community, accessed October 23, 2023, https://www .thecommunityagency.com/case-studies/oreo-doomsday-vault.

47. Daniel Victor and Eduardo Medina, "Missing Girl Is Rescued After Using Hand Signal from TikTok," *New York Times*, November 8, 2021, https://www.nytimes.com/2021/11/08 /us/tiktok-hand-signal-abduction.html#:~:text=But%20one%20person%20in%20a,the%20 Laurel%20County%20Sheriff's%20Office.

48. "The Canadian Women's Foundation," Juniper Part/TBWA, accessed October 23, 2023, https://www.juniperparktbwa.com/work/signal-for-help.

49. Anne-Christine Diaz, "EA Sports Wins Titanium Grand Prix for Campaign that Resurrected Soccer Hopeful Kiyan Prince," *AdAge*, June 24, 2022, https://adage.com/article /special-report-cannes-lions/titanium-lions-grand-prix-2022-kiyan-prince-ea-sports -long-live-prince/2421721.

50. Diaz, "EA Sports Wins."

51. Engine UK, "Long Live the Prince," Engine on LinkedIn, accessed October 23, 2023, https://www.linkedin.com/feed/update/urn:li:activity:6867469195043471360/.

52. "More Extra Than Guac: e.l.f. X Chipotle Brand Partnership," Movers+Shakers, accessed October 23, 2023, https://moversshakers.co/elf-chipotle-brand-partnership.

53. Movers+Shakers, "More Extra Than Guac."

54. Jeff Beer, "The 10 Most Innovative Companies in Advertising 2022," *Fast Company*, March 8, 2022, https://www.fastcompany.com/90715441/most-innovative-companies-advertising-2022.

55. "Area 23 for Woojer: Area 23 and Woojer Debut World's First Music Powered Air Clearance Vest for Cystic Fibrosis," IPG, May 4 2021, https://www.interpublic.com/case -study/area-23-and-woojer-debut-worlds-first-music-powered-airway-clearance-vest -for-cystic-fibrosis/.

56. IPG, "Area 23 for Woojer."

57. Aprajeeta Tripathi, "Mastercard and Its Multi-Sensory Marketing Game," ET Brand Equity, September 1, 2022, https://brandequity.economictimes.indiatimes.com/news /marketing/mastercard-and-its-multi-sensory-marketing-game/93904432?action =profile_completion&utm_source=Mailer&utm_medium=newsletter&utm_campaign =etbrandequity_news_2022-09-01&dt=2022-09-01&em=cmxhbmRhQGtlYW4uZWRu.

58. Tripathi, "Mastercard and Its Multi-Sensory Marketing Game."

59. "Behind the Work: Problem Solved: How DDB Tribal Aotearoa Created an Innovative Way to Persuade iPhone Users to Try Out Samsung," Little Black Book, May 26, 2021. https://www.lbbonline.com/news/problem-solved-how-ddb-tribal-aotearoa-created-an-innovative-way-to-persuade-iphone-users-to-try-out-samsung.

60. Doyle Dane Bernbach, "DDB Aotearoa/Samsung."

61. Brett Colliver, email correspondence with author Robin Landa, August 20, 2022.

62. "Contagious Grand Prix Insights," Contagious, July 26, 2022, https://www.contagious.com/news-and-views/download-the-2022-cannes-lions-grand-prix-winners-report.

63. Contagious, "Contagious Grand Prix Insights."

64. Contagious, "Contagious Grand Prix Insights."

65. Tim Nudd, "An A.I. combined Music and Nature to Make These Festival Posters," Muse by Clio, August 16, 2022, https://musebycl.io/music/ai-combined-music-and-nature-make-these-festival-posters.

66. Ivo Purvis, email correspondence with the author, September 27, 2022.

67. Diego Machado, Zoom conversation with the author, June 14, 2023.

69. Luciana Cani, email exchange with the author, August 23, 2022.

7. BRAND AS ACTIVIST: DIVERSITY, EQUITY, AND INCLUSION

1. "Alexa, What is Love? Creating a More Inclusive World One Voice at a Time," Amazon.com, https://www.amazon.com/adlp/lovehasnolabels?ref_=a2om_us_blg_lvnlbl_lp.

2. Amazon, "Alexa, What is Love?"

3. Amazon Staff, "Amazon and the Ad Council Unveil 'Love Has No Labels' Campaign," Amazon, February 1, 2022, https://www.aboutamazon.com/news/devices/amazon-and-the-ad-council-unveil-new-love-has-no-labels-campaign.

4. "Diversity & Inclusion," Ad Council, accessed July 2, 2022, https://www.adcouncil.org/campaign/diversity-inclusion.

5. Sebastian Parker, "The Next Opportunity: Let's Build in DEI as a Game-Changer for Trust in Advertising," Campaign US, October 12, 2021, https://www.campaignlive.com/article/next-opportunity-lets-build-dei-game-changer-trust-advertising/1730006.

6. Microsoft Advertising, The Psychology of Inclusion and the Effects in Advertising, Gen Z, (Redmond, WA: Microsoft, 2020), https://advertiseonbing-blob.azureedge.net/blob/bingads/media/insight/whitepapers/2020/07-july/inclusive-marketing/microsoft-advertising-whitepaper-the-psychology-of-inclusion-and-the-effects-in-advertising-gen-z-final.pdf?s_cid=en-us-gct-web-src_contributor-sub_oth-cam_hubspot.

7. Constantine von Hoffman, "By The Numbers: Diversity And Inclusion Are Good For Business," Detroit Regional Chamber, April 5, 2020, https://www.detroitchamber.com/by-the-numbers-diversity-and-inclusion-are-good-for-business/.

8. United States Census Bureau, "2020 Census Statistics Highlight Local Population Changes and Nation's Racial and Ethnic Diversity," August 12, 2021, https://www.census.gov/newsroom/press-releases/2021/population-changes-nations-diversity.html.

9. Jason Tomassini, "What We're Learning by Telling More Inclusive Stories," Muse by Clio, March 22, 2021, https://musebycl.io/diversity-inclusion/what-were-learning-telling-more-inclusive-stories.

10. Justin Jennings, *Finding Fairness: From Pleistocene Foragers to Contemporary Capitalists* (Gainesville: University Press of Florida, 2021), 3.

11. Shelley Zalis, "Inclusive Ads Are Affecting Consumer Behavior, According to New Research," Think with Google, November 2019, https://www.thinkwithgoogle.com/future -of-marketing/management-and-culture/diversity-and-inclusion/thought-leadership -marketing-diversity-inclusion/.

12. Sophie Gold, phone conversation with the author, September 2022.

13. Wes Phelan, messaging conversation with the author, August 30, 2022.

14. Ally Marotti, "Ulta Facing Boycott Threats Over Trans TikTok Star's Podcast Appearance," *AdAge*, October 18, 2022, https://adage.com/article/marketing-news-strategy/ulta -facing-boycott-threats-over-trans-tiktok-star-dylan-mulvaneys-podcast-appearance /2443531?.

15. "Ulta Beauty Launches Beauty&, Celebrating Beauty as a Force for Good," Ulta Beauty, August 30, 2022, https://www.ulta.com/investor/news-events/press-releases/detail/158/ulta -beauty-launches-beauty-celebrating-beauty-as-a-force.

16. Becky Sullivan, "Bud Light Sales Dip After Trans Promotion, but Such Boycotts Are Often Short-Lived," NPR, April 27, 2023, https://www.npr.org/2023/04/27/1172299478 /bud-light-sales-fall-trans-influencer-boycott.

17. Kimberle Crenshaw, "Demarginalizing the Intersection of Race and Sex: A Black Feminist Critique of Antidiscrimination Doctrine, Feminist Theory and Antiracist Politics," *Univesrity of Chicago Legal Forum* 1989, no. 1, article 8 (1989): https://chicagounbound .uchicago.edu/cgi/viewcontent.cgi?referer=&httpsredir=1&article=1052&context=uclf.

18. Will Chau, email with author, February 4, 2024.

19. Mor Regev, Christopher J. Honey, Erez Simony, and Uri Hasson, "Selective and Invariant Neural Responses to Spoken and Written Narratives," *Journal of Neuroscience* 33, no. 40 (October 2, 2013): https://doi.org/10.1523/JNEUROSCI.1580-13.2013.

20. Elena Renkin, "How Stories Connect and Persuade Us: Unleashing the Brain Power of Narrative," NPR, April 11, 2020, https://www.npr.org/sections/health-shots/2020/04/11 /815573198/how-stories-connect-and-persuade-us-unleashing-the-brain-power-of-narrative.

21. Marc Sestir and Melanie C. Green, "You Are Who You Watch: Identification and Transportation Effects on Temporary Self-Concept," *Social Influence* 5, no. 4 (July 8, 2010): 272–288.

22. Lynn Hunt, *Inventing Human Rights: A History* (New York: Norton, 2008), 112.

23. Robin Landa, "Interview with NiRey Reynolds," *Strategic Creativity* (New York: Routledge, 2022),161–63.

24. "Visibility of Disability: Portrayals of Disability in Advertising," Nielsen, August 19, 2021, https://www.nielsen.com/us/en/insights/article/2021/visibility-of-disability-portrayals -of-disability-in-advertising/.

25. Nielsen, "Visibility of Disability."

26. Stella Young, TEDxSydney, "I'm Not Your Inspiration, Thank You Very Much," TED, April 2014, 09:03, https://www.ted.com/talks/stella_young_i_m_not_your_inspiration _thank_you_very_much?language=en.

27. Ann-Christine Diaz, "An Apple 'Underdogs' Ad and Channel 4's 'Super.Human' Win 2022 Cannes Lions Film Grand Prix," *AdAge*, June 24, 2022, https://adage.com/article

/special-report-cannes-lions/cannes-lions-2022-film-grand-prix-apple-underdogs-channel
-4-superhuman/2421771.

28. "Inspiring Everyone to Move Your Way," Unilever, December 3, 2020, https://www.unilever
.com/news/news-search/2020/inspiring-everyone-to-move-your-way/.

29. "Championing Inclusion Through Our Brands," Unilever, accessed October 27, 2023,
https://www.unilever.com/planet-and-society/health-and-wellbeing/championing
-inclusion-through-our-brands/.

30. David Gianatasio, "PG 'Widens the Screen' to View the Black Experience Through a Fresh
Lens," *Muse by Clio*, April 5, 2021, https://musebycl.io/diversity-inclusion/pg-widens
-screen-view-black-experience-through-fresh-lens.

31. "Widen the Screen," PG, accessed November 30, 2023, https://us.pg.com/widen-the
-screen/

32. "Widen the Screen," PG, accessed October 31, 2023, https://us.pg.com/widen-the-screen/

33. Sophie Gold, phone conversation.

34. Ann Christine Diaz, "Super Bowl Director Diversity Once Again Fell Short in 2022,"
AdAge, February 24, 2022, https://adage.com/article/special-report-super-bowl/super-bowl
-director-diversity-once-again-fell-short-2022/2401811.

35. Tim Nudd, "Super Bowl Ads Get Another Failing Grade for Director Diversity," *AdAge*,
February 27, 2023, https://adage.com/article/special-report-super-bowl/super-bowl-ads
-get-another-failing-grade-director-diversity/2474436

36. Diaz, "Super Bowl Diversity."

37. Garett Sloane, "Google's 'Real Tone' Technology Wins Mobile Award at Cannes,"
AdAge, June 22, 2022, https://adage.com/article/special-report-cannes-lions/googles-real
-tone-technology-wins-mobile-award-cannes/2421321.

38. Sloan, "Google's 'Real Tone' Technology."

39. "Real Tone," Google, accessed October 27, 2023, https://store.google.com/intl/en/discover
/realtone/.

40. Owen Lee, LinkedIn message to the author, August 16, 2022.

41. "Dyslexic Thinking," FCB London, accessed July 4, 2022, https://www.fcbinferno.com
/work/case-studies/dyslexic-thinking/.

42. FCB London, "Case Study: Dyslexic Thinking +", accessed November 19, 2023, https://
www.fcbinferno.com/work/case-studies/dyslexic-thinking/.

43. FCB London, "Dyslexic Thinking."

44. Saabira Chaudhuri, "Does Your Mayo Need a Mission Statement?" *Wall Street Journal*,
May 20, 2022, https://www.wsj.com/articles/unilever-purpose-marketing-social-cause
-11653050052.

45. Ann-Christine Diaz, "Dove's Heartbreaking Ad Highlights Race-Based Hair Discrimination Against Girls," *AdAge*, January 26, 2022, https://adage.com/creativity/work/dove
-study-finds-girls-young-five-experience-race-based-hair-discrimination/2394941.

46. "Dove Launches New 'As Early as Five' Campaign to Highlight How Early Race-Based Hair
Discrimination Starts," *Marketing Communication News*, February 3, 2022, https://marcomm
news.com/dove-launches-new-as-early-as-five-campaign-to-highlight-how-early-race
-based-hair-discrimination-starts/#:~:text=and%20hit%20enter-,Dove%20Launches%20
New%20%E2%80%9CAs%20Early%20As%20Five%E2%80%9D%20Campaign%20To%20

Highlight,Race%2DBased%20Hair%20Discrimination%20Starts&text=Dove%20has%20
released%20a%20new,in%20schools%20and%20the%20workplace.

47. Dee Patel, "How to Avoid 'Rainbow Washing' During Pride Month," *Penn Today*, June 24, 2022, https://penntoday.upenn.edu/news/how-avoid-rainbow-washing-during-pride-month.

48. Jess Zafarris, "Marketing Morsels: Pride Projects, an Animal Anthem, S'more Songs and More," *Adweek*, June 10, 2022, https://www.adweek.com/commerce/marketing-morsels-pride-projects-an-animal-anthem-smore-songs-and-more/.

49. Christina Brodzik, Sarah Cuthill, Nathan Young, and Nikki Drake, "Authentically Inclusive Marketing," Deloitte Insights, October 19, 2021, https://www2.deloitte.com/us/en/insights/topics/marketing-and-sales-operations/global-marketing-trends/2022/diversity-and-inclusion-in-marketing.html.

50. "Indeed Presents Rising Voices," Tribeca, accessed October 27, 2023, https://tribecafilm.com/films/indeed-presents-rising-voices-2021.

51. Wilson Chapman, "Lena Waithe's Hillman Grad Productions and Indeed Announce Second Class of Rising Voices Initiative," *Variety*, February 24, 2022, https://variety.com/2022/film/news/lena-waithe-indeed-hillman-grad-productions-1235189033/.

52. "Indeed, Lena Waithe and Hillman Grad Productions Announce 10 Filmmakers for 'Rising Voices' Season Two Initiative Celebrating BIPOC Filmmakers," Indeed, February 24, 2022, https://www.indeed.com/press/releases/indeed-lena-waithe-and-hillman-grad-productions-announce-10-filmmakers-for-rising-voices-season-two-initiative-celebrating-bipoc-filmmakers?hl=en&co=US.

8. WHAT'S THE NEXT STORY? HOW TO TELL A STORY WITHOUT A PLAYBOOK

1. Tim Murphy, "Mad Men, George Lois, and Advertising's Creative Revolution," *Fast Company*, October 27, 2008, https://www.fastcompany.com/1061476/mad-men-george-lois-and-advertisings-creative-revolution.

2. "Truth in Advertising: DDB and VW Encourage the World to Think Small," 4A's (American Association of Advertising Agencies), accessed December 11, 2022, https://www.aaaa.org/timeline-event/vw-encourages-world-think-small/?cn-reloaded=1.

3. "The History of Cat Food and the Evolution of Cat Food Industry," CPC Cares (blog), September 22, 2020, https://www.cpccares.com/blog/the-history-of-cat-food/.

4. "Hope Reef," The One Club for Creativity, accessed December 10, 2022, https://www.oneclub.org/awards/theoneshow/-award/43920/hope-reef.

5. Johanna Reed, "The SHEBA Hope Reef Brings Hope to Coral Reefs Everywhere—You Can Help Too," *Forbes*, May 5, 2021, https://www.forbes.com/sites/johannaread/2021/05/05/the-sheba-hope-reef-brings-hope-to-coral-reefs-everywhere-you-can-help-too/?sh=2001c44735c8.

6. Reed, "The SHEBA Hope Reef Brings Hope."

7. The One Club for Creativity, "Hope Reef."

8. Reed, "The SHEBA Hope Reef Brings Hope."

9. The One Club for Creativity, "Hope Reef."

10. Reed, "The SHEBA Hope Reef Brings Hope."

11. The One Club for Creativity, "Hope Reef."

12. Joe Otterson, " 'Game of Thrones' Finale Sets New Series High with Staggering 19.3 Million Viewers," *Variety*, May 20, 2019, https://variety.com/2019/tv/ratings/game-of-thrones-series-finale-draws-19-3-million-viewers-sets-new-series-high-1203220928/.

13. Ryan Prior, "The Red Cross and HBO Are Partnering on a 'Game of Thrones'-Themed Blood Drive," CNN, February 20, 2019, https://www.cnn.com/2019/02/20/us/red-cross-hbo-game-throne-trnd.

14. Prior, "The Red Cross and HBO Are Partnering."

15. "For the Throne: Bleed," The One Club for Creativity, accessed December 11, 2022, https://www.oneclub.org/awards/theoneshow/-award/37383/for-the-throne-bleed.

16. The One Club for Creativity, "For the Throne: Bleed."

17. The One Club for Creativity, "For the Throne: Bleed."

18. Prior, "The Red Cross and HBO Are Partnering."

19. Prior, "The Red Cross and HBO Are Partnering."

20. The One Club for Creativity, "For the Throne: Bleed."

21. J. Robinson, personal communication with the author, January 9, 2023

22. "Manson," The One Club for Creativity, accessed December 19, 2022, https://www.oneclub.org/awards/theoneshow/-award/1617/manson.

23. The One Club for Creativity, "Manson."

24. The One Club for Creativity, "Manson."

25. Ellis Verdi, interview by the author, December 1, 2022.

26. The One Club for Creativity, "Manson."

27. Anthony Vagnoni, "Special Report: Advertising Age Best Awards," *Advertising Age*, May 28, 2001, s16.

28. Tim Arango, "Derek Chauvin Is Sentenced to 22 and a Half Years for Murder of George Floyd," *New York Times*, June 25, 2021, https://www.nytimes.com/2021/06/25/us/derek-chauvin-22-and-a-half-years-george-floyd.html.

29. Kurt Wilberding and Georgia Wells, "Facebook's Timeline: 15 Years In," *Wall Street Journal*, February 4, 2019, https://www.wsj.com/articles/facebooks-timeline-15-years-in-11549276201; Seth Stevenson, "Instagram's Kevin Systrom on the Platform He Built for One Billion Users," *WSJ Magazine*, September 25, 2018, https://www.wsj.com/articles/instagrams-kevin-systrom-on-the-platform-he-built-for-one-billion-users-1537886795; Meghan Bobrowsky, Salvador Rodriguez, Sarah E. Needleman, and Georgia Wells, "TikTok's Stratospheric Rise: An Oral History," *Wall Street Journal*, November 5, 2022, https://www.wsj.com/articles/tiktoks-stratospheric-rise-an-oral-history-11667599696.

30. Christina Merritt, "Why Leaning into the Edge of Purpose Unlocks Opportunities for Growth," *Ad Age*, December 8, 2022, https://adage.com/article/marketing-news-strategy/shaping-purposeful-possibilities-key-unlocking-growth/2456831.

31. Richard Branson, *Screw Business as Usual* (New York: Penguin, 2017), 1.

INDEX